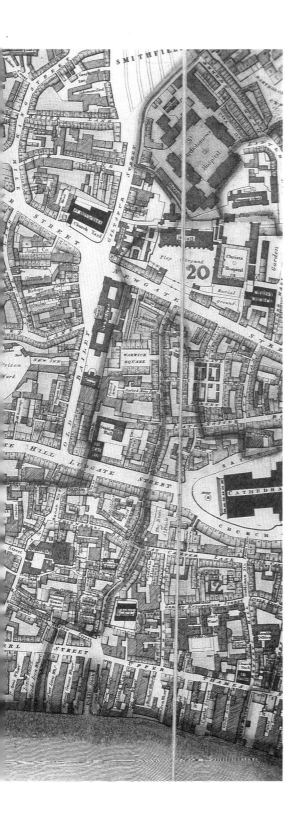

The Temple and Environs 1845 (Wyld's Plan of the City)

The Inner Temple with the Temple church, for some reason, was heavily outlined in this map; the Middle Temple is shown immediately to the west of Middle Temple Lane which led down from Temple Bar to Temple Stairs on the Thames, before the Victoria Embankment was formed in 1870.

From Fleet Street, Chancery Lane runs northwards, with Lincoln's Inn to the west. New Square was the site of Fikettesfield, the Knights' martial ground. At the junction of the Lane and Holborn and towards Staple Inn to the east was the site of the Old Temple, the Knights' first home, 1128-61.

North of the Strand the maze of alleyways was swept away when the Royal Courts of Justice were built on the the site in 1882. This included the demolition of New Boswell Court, where the Choir School shared by the Temple and Lincoln's Inn choristers stood, 1854-75. They next attended the Stationers' Company School in Bolt Court, north of Fleet Street, from 1875-97 and afterwards the City of London School on the Victoria Embankment, the site of the City Gas Works shown here. More recently the CLS moved to a new site on the Embankment due south of St Paul's Cathedral.

St Dunstan-in-the-West in Fleet Street, between Chancery Lane and Fetter Lane, was the home of the Temple Sunday services during the last War. On either side stood the Knights' forges in medieval times. The Fleet river now flows underground beneath New Bridge Street at Blackfriars and into the Thames.

the
TEMPLE CHURCH
in London

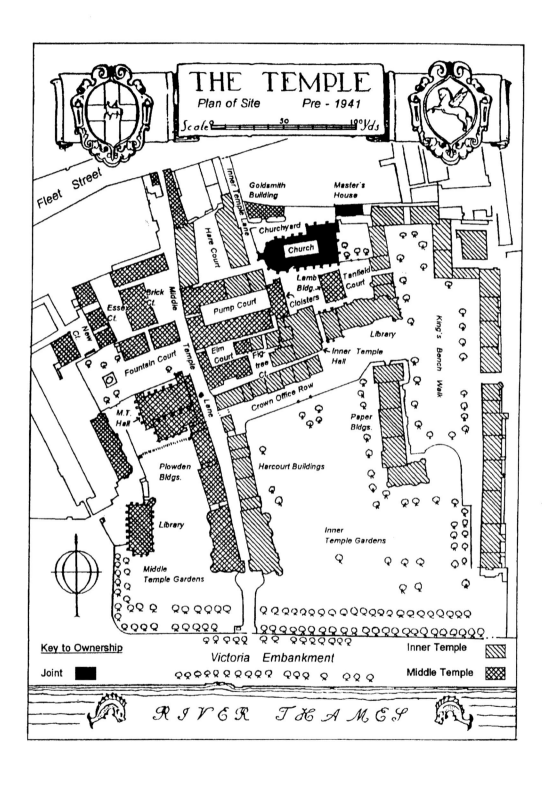

THE TEMPLE

Plan of Site   Pre - 1941

Scale   50   100 Yds

Fleet Street

Goldsmith Building

Master's House

Inner Temple Lane

Hare Court

Churchyard

Church

Brick Ct.

Middle

Esse Ct.

New Ct.

Pump Court

Lamb Bldg.

Tanfield Court

Cloisters

Library

Elm Court

Fig-tree Ct.

Inner Temple Hall

Fountain Court

King's Bench Walk

Temple Lane

M.T. Hall

Crown Office Row

Paper Bldgs.

Plowden Bldgs.

Harcourt Buildings

Library

Inner Temple Gardens

Middle Temple Gardens

Key to Ownership

Joint

Victoria Embankment

Inner Temple

Middle Temple

RIVER THAMES

the
TEMPLE CHURCH
in London

David Lewer
and Robert Dark

HISTORICAL PUBLICATIONS

DEDICATION

to the grateful memory of Walter H. Godfrey
and his son W. Emil Godfrey, architects,
who resurrected the Temple church in London
after its grievous wartime damage in 1941.

The Illustrations

We would like to thank the undermentioned for permission to reproduce the
following illustrations:

Arthur Bernard: *114, 115*
British Library: *28-30, 39*
British Museum *34, 35, 56, 60, 85, 86, 87, 88, 89, 90*
Carden & Godfrey, architects: *112, 118*
Cassell & Co: *1*
Guildhall Library, London *32, 40*
Inner Temple Collection: *77, 81*
Middle Temple Library: *26, 46, 50, 55, 82, 83, 84, 116*
Sydney W. Newbery: *122*
Phoenix House: *12, 18*
Pitkin Pictorials: *13*
Chris Rutter: *124*
St John's Gate Museum, the Order of St John: *5*
Society of Antiquaries: *21, 22, 23*

First published 1997
by Historical Publications Ltd, 32 Ellington Street, London N7 8PL
(Tel: 0171-607 1628)

ISBN 0 948667 48 6
Typeset in Palatino by Historical Publications Ltd; reproduction by G & J Graphics,
London EC2; printed by Edelvives in Zaragoza, Spain

Contents

FOREWORD by the Very Reverend Robert Milburn *6*
PREFACE *8*
ACKNOWLEDGEMENTS *8*
1   THE KNIGHTS TEMPLARS *9*
2   THE ROUND *18*
3   THE CHANCEL *39*
4   SUPPRESSION *49*
5   THE LAWYERS *54*
6   THE STUARTS *62*
7   THE GEORGIANS *80*
8   THE EARLY VICTORIANS *94*
9   THE SURPLICED CHOIR *106*
10 THE LATER VICTORIANS *112*
11 THE DIRECTOR OF THE CHOIR *129*
12 THE TWENTIETH CENTURY *133*
13 DESTRUCTION *145*
14 RESURGENCE *152*
15 THE END OF AN ERA *163*
16 THE MUSIC RESTORED *173*
    APPENDICES *177*
    SELECTED BIBLIOGRAPHY *185*
    SUBSCRIBERS *186*
    INDEX *188*

Foreword

by the Very Reverend Robert Milburn
formerly Master of the Temple

Sandwiched between the City of London and the City of Westminster lies an area as rich in history as anywhere in the Kingdom. Many buildings have their notable story to tell but none can, for variety of interest and fortunes, surpass the Temple Church. The story goes back as far as the twelfth century, when the Knights Templar, a military Order established at Jerusalem for the protection of pilgrims to the Holy Land, moved their English headquarters down what is now Chancery Lane to an agreeable site close to the river Thames. Encouraged by the patronage of successive Popes, a deputation, including the Patriarch of Jerusalem, arrived in England and offered King Henry II the crown of the Latin Kingdom of Jerusalem. Henry prudently declined this honour, but the Patriarch, Heraclius, was prevailed upon to consecrate the Round church which the Templars, mindful of Constantine's Church of the Holy Sepulchre, had constructed in circular form. The style was that now known as Transitional Norman, where the solidity of the round arch combines happily enough with the first essays in the pointed manner (1185 AD).

Style in art is a subtle compound, the product of countless minds feeling after truth as it is displayed to them through the shimmer of the elusive and ever-changing spirit of the age. For as T.S. Eliot has it,

> For last year's words belong to last year's language
> And next year's words await another voice.

Certainly the next major development was in marked contrast with the robust manner of the Norman style even in its later forms. Only some fifty-five years after the construction of the Round church a new chancel was added more spacious than the nave, which had become encumbered by tomb-effigies of knightly patrons of the Order. The style adopted for the chancel was that which had ousted the Norman, the so-called Early English, lofty and graceful, with shafts of Purbeck marble 'lightly dancing', as used to be said, around the central column.

But, behind all this charm and splendour, lay menacing clouds of disaster. Becoming less mindful of the needs of pilgrims and more concerned with the administration of large estates, the Templars incurred the envy of the Pope and the King of France, Edward II of England being a less baleful opponent but ready to play his part in suppressing the Order. Opportunity was thus given, after a somewhat half-hearted reappearance by the Hospitallers, for two companies of lawyers to establish themselves in the Temple and to continue, after the upheaval of the Reformation, a state of affairs confirmed by King James I when he granted to the two Inns the freehold of their property on condition that they maintained the fabric of the church and provided for the Master. The story at this point might be described as complicated, but is told with the ease and scholarship which characterises the present work throughout.

The Great Fire of London stopped just short of the church though creating havoc elsewhere in the Temple. Sir Christopher Wren was invited to plan alterations which were in later times judged to be unsuccessful and, apart from the graceful reredos, have not survived. The writing of our two architect-historians continues with a careful study of the work of renewal that was carried out by a succession of nineteenth-century architects, some concerned primarily to restore to the original state, others ready to preserve anything that remained of beauty and interest.

Guardianship of the fabric was matched by concern for the quality of the worship offered in the church, as witnessed by the establishment in 1842 of the first surpliced choir in London after those of St Paul's and Westminster Abbey.

The study concludes with a detailed account of the triumphant restoration after the calamity of May 1941, by Walter Godfrey, his son and a group of dedicated craftsmen. The historian Burkhardt may perhaps be allowed to add a coda: 'It is a lofty necessity of the human spirit that an irresistible impulse forces us to the investigation of men and things, and that we must hold this enquiry to be our proper end and work.'

Preface

During my chorister days at the Temple church before the war, I grew to love the building as well as the music and wanted to find out more about its history. Encouraged by the late Captain Alfred Dewar, noted historian at the Admiralty, a member of the congregation and a supporter of the Temple Choir, it led me during my architectural training to think of writing a book about the church since that by T.H. Baylis QC had been published at the turn of the century.

The war put all this aside, and with the disastrous fire in 1941 we wondered whether the church would ever rise again. Thankfully, in 1946 Walter Godfrey, an eminent architect and antiquary, partner with Andrew Carden in the firm Carden & Godfrey, was appointed to restore the church and to enhance its former glory. He was in this assisted by his son, Emil Godfrey.

The work was finished when the Round Church was re-dedicated by the Archbishop of Canterbury in November 1958. Afterwards, Emil supervised the maintenance of the church until his untimely death in 1982. He had discussed with me the proposal for a book about the church as a memorial to his father, but once again it was put aside.

In 1994 the present senior partner of Carden & Godfrey, Ian Stewart, lent me his copy of a recent impressive thesis on the Temple church, written and illustrated by Robert Dark, an architect who wished to gain a further qualification in building conservation. Our meeting and a suggestion for a joint book met with enthusiasm, and *The Temple Church in London* is the result.

In 1961 I wrote *A Spiritual Song: the Story of the Temple Choir and a History of Divine Service in the Temple Church, London*, a book which I was asked to write as a memorial to the late Alfred Capel Dixon, fifty years a Temple chorister. Much of my earlier research on the church's architecture was omitted in favour of the detailed account of the establishment of the Choir, but in this new book I have been able to use the notes which I had discarded. The subject of Robert Dark's thesis dealt largely with the successive restorations of the church by Wren, the Victorian architects and the Godfreys. It was felt that a comprehensive story of the Temple church should include the important establishment of the Choir since 1842, and the achievements of the successive organists and choirmasters until the death of Sir George Thalben-Ball in 1987.

Insofar as quotations have been freely made from numerous books and records, we would echo John Playford's words in the preface to his *Brief Introduction to the Skill of Musick* (printed at his 'Shop in the Inner Temple, neer the Church dore, 1658'): 'The work as it is, I must confess, is not all my own, some part thereof was Collected out of other men's Works, which I hope will the more Commend it.'

David Lewer

Acknowledgements

Acknowledgement is gratefully made to Ian Stewart and Neil Macfadyen of Carden & Godfrey; Millicent Godfrey; the Under Treasurer of the Middle Temple; the Sub Treasurer of the Inner Temple; the Librarians and staff of the Middle and Inner Temple Libraries; the Archivists of the two Societies; the Master of the Temple; the Verger, John Holderness; the British Museum Print Room; the British Library; the Victoria & Albert Museum; the Museum of London; the Guildhall Library; the Society of Antiquaries; English Heritage; Robert Milburn former Master of the Temple, Deborah Stene and Jane Fawcett for commenting on the text; Jo Allerton for doing much of the typing; Geremy Butler the photographer; L. Joan Crump; W. J. Haysom & Son.

Acknowledgement is gratefully made for permission to quote passages from Jane Fawcett's *The Future of the Past*, Edith Simon's *The Piebald Standard*, and Eileen Gooder's *Temple Balsall*.

Finally to John Richardson of Historical Publications and all the subscribers to the book who have made everything possible.

CHAPTER ONE

The Knights Templars

The celebration of the seven hundredth anniversary of the consecration of the Round church in London took place on 10 February 1885. The Reader of the Temple church, Alfred Ainger, remarked in the course of his evening sermon that the story of the Knights Templars[1] had taught us that no institution can survive its purpose. Towards their end, the Templars were divorced from the Spirit and so the Order was doomed to dissolution. He went on to say:

> 'The Templars have bequeathed us, as legacy, this lesson which we must not forget in the hour when we would fain recall the days of their grandeur and fresh enthusiasm: there is no promise of continuance for any institute, any party, any church, any creed, out of which the Spirit shall have departed... after 700 years the truth remains unchanged for all who pass to worship through the nobly beautiful building that, as on this day, was consecrated.'

Two years after the consecration of the Transitional Round church in 1185, Jerusalem, the Holy City, was captured by Saladin, the great sultan of Islam. When the pure Gothic chancel extension to the Nave was consecrated in 1240, in the presence of Henry III, there were less than eighty remaining years before the Knights of the Temple were no more. But their demise remained a tantalising mystery for centuries to come.

The Crusades make an astonishing chapter in the history of the western world. In 1099 Jerusalem had fallen from the Infidel into the hands of the Christian armies under Godfrey de Bouillon. In the new century the concept of the New Jerusalem, a spiritual paradise on earth, gathered momentum and the second Crusade was launched. Pilgrims from far and wide flocked to the Holy City by land and sea, despite great hardship and difficulty. People of every age and condition, men, women and children, knights and vassals, were caught up in the new movement for various reasons, spiritual, economic or purely for the love of adventure. Warfare was, as ever, an attraction for the young and strong.

The Order of the Temple was founded in January 1119[2] by two French knights, Hugh de Payens from Champagne and Godfrey de Saint Omer from Picardy. With a handful of companions they took upon themselves the task of protecting pilgrims on their way to Jerusalem. As 'fighting-monks', they bound themselves to live under the Augustinian rule and embraced the vows of chastity, individual poverty and obedience. They were known as 'the poor fellow-soldiers of Christ and the Temple of Solomon' – *Pauperes commilitones Christi templique Salomonis.*

Little is known of Hugh de Payens except that he was a widower before he left for the Holy Land[3]. It is evident that he possessed a natural ability for organisation, coupled with great resource, energy and the gift of confidence. At first without either wealth or many followers, the Order grew rapidly under his leadership. Baldwin II, King of Jerusalem, gave the Templars their headquarters (*ill. 1*) in part of the Royal Palace on Mount Moriah where Solomon had built his Temple and where stood the great mosque, the Dome of the Rock. In 1141 it was

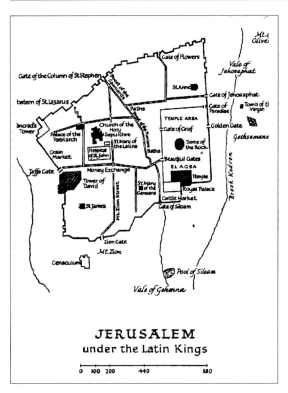

1. Jerusalem under the Latin Kings.

consecrated as the Church of the *Templum Domini*.[4] To the west was the Church of the Holy Sepulchre, where Christ was believed to have been buried, the most sacred spot in the Christian world, and nearby the palace of the Patriarch of Jerusalem. To the south was the Hospital of St John, a hospice for pilgrims founded by merchants from Amalfi before the first Crusade. By now a need had arisen to form an ambulance corps and to care for the sick and wounded in the armies. From this hospice developed the Order of Knights Hospitallers who also became 'fighting-monks.' At first they co-operated with the Templars but later became bitter rivals. This contributed in part to the eventual fall of Jerusalem and the loss of the Holy Land.

The less famous Teutonic Knights, set up by German merchants, were established later in 1198. They wore white mantles with a black cross, the Hospitallers black mantles with a white cross and the Templars white mantles with a red

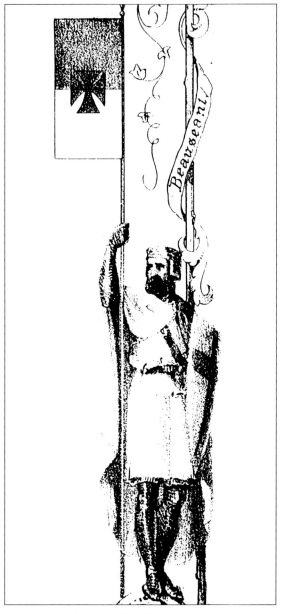

2. A Knight Templar and Banner.

cross - hence their popular name of the Red Cross Knights. The Templars' first banner was the *Beauséant*[5] the piebald standard, (*ill. 2*) with the upper part black, signifying death to their enemies, and the lower white, meaning love to their friends and Christians. On the banner were the words '*Non nobis Domine, non nobis, sed nomini*

3. *Seals of the Knights Templars, Agnus Dei and Two knights on one horse.*

tuo da gloriam' - 'Not unto us, O Lord, not unto us, but unto Thy Name give the glory.' When the Saracens heard the cry of *Beauséant* or saw the standard of the Order unfurled, they fled in terror for their lives, (or so the chroniclers relate). The Templars later adopted the *Agnus Dei* with its nimbus and banner, which became the emblem of the Honourable Society of the Middle Temple in London. According to Matthew Paris, a thirteenth-century monk of St Albans, a Templar seal depicting two knights on one horse indicated their lack of horses and poor beginning. Stow, the sixteenth-century historian, and others preferred the explanation that it was an emblem of charity showing a knight taking up a wounded Christian soldier to carry him out of danger. (*Ill. 3.*) Edward Richardson said:

'The Knights were men of honourable family; they wore long beards, and their general costume consisted of a hauberk or tunic of ringed mail reaching to the knee, with sleeves and gloves; chausses covering the legs and feet of the same kind of mail; a light sleeveless surcoat over the hauberk, girded about the waist with a belt; a guige, or transverse belt, passing round the body, over the right shoulder, and under the left arm, by which a long or kite-shaped shield was supported; a sword-belt obliquely round the loins, with a long heavy sword attached; and single-pointed or goad-shaped spurs: over all a long white mantle fastened under the chin and reaching to the feet, with a red cloth eight-pointed cross, now known as the Maltese, sewn on the front of the left shoulder: on the head was worn a linen coif, and above that a bowl-shaped skull-cap of red cloth turned up all round. When completely armed, the coif and cap were exchanged for a hood of mail covering the neck and head, and over that one of the variously formed helmets or caps of mail or steel then in use. The parts of their dress peculiar to the Order were, the mantle with its cross, the coif and cloth cap[6].' (*ills 2 & 10*)

In 1130 the Crusaders began to make plans for the rebuilding of the ancient church of the Holy Sepulchre, which had been rebuilt earlier by the Byzantines in the mid-eleventh century with a rotunda to enclose the Sepulchre, the Tomb of Christ[7]. During the 1140s an extensive chancel, crossing and ambulatory (or aisled walkway) were added to the rotunda, with a magnificent south main entrance. The reconstructed church was dedicated on 15 July 1149, fifty years after the crusaders' conquest of Jerusalem. It incorporated a mixture of western and oriental styles and motifs, and decoration continued for several years. The bell-tower was added in 1153 (*ill. 4*).

The architectural historian George Jeffery[8] wrote that the 'The remarkable conical roof of timber covered with lead as at first designed by the Byzantine Patriarch Thomas seems to have been repeatedly restored and repaired.' The roof was probably destroyed in 1245 in the Tartar invasion. He added that in 1621 George Sandys mentioned that this Round was 'covered with a Cupola sustained with rafters of cedar, each of one piece, being open in the midst like the Pantheon at Rome.' Pococke, writing of the Rotunda of the Holy Sepulchre in his *'Description of the East'* (1745), stated: 'The roof was of cypress, and the King of Spain giving a new one, what remained of the old roof was preserved as relics, and they make beads of it to this day.'

The building was destroyed by fire in 1808. Jeffery continued:

'It consumed the cupola of wood covered with lead of the Rotunda, but the Sepulchre,

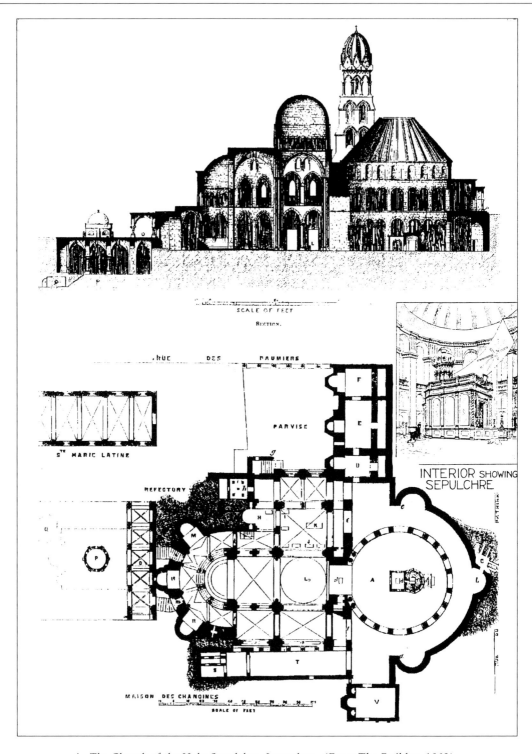

4. The Church of the Holy Sepulchre, Jerusalem. (From The Builder, 1863)

though crushed without, was uninjured within. The marble columns supporting the great roof was calcined and the walls injured... in the old illustrations of the church before the fire, the covering of the rotunda is invariably shown as a straight-lined conical roof. The straight beams of the original construction show as a ceiling within the church.'

John Britton[9] recorded that the circular part of the church was of Roman architecture and that its roof, which was mostly of cedar, gradually diminished from its base upwards and terminated in a round aperture. This shape he considered rather singular, differing from the usual form and construction of domes. The description by Jeffery of the fire in the Holy Sepulchre of 1808 reminds us of the disastrous conflagration of 1941 in the Temple church in London.

After a decade spent in establishing the Order, Hugh de Payens left for France during the peaceful winter season to attend the Council of Troyes on 14 January 1129 and to secure official approval of his Brotherhood. Pope Honorius II gave his final sanction which was achieved with the blessing of the saintly Abbot Bernard of Clairvaux who drew up the Rule for the Order.

There were 72 articles laid down to be followed by the Knights in their duties and routine. All meals were to be taken in the hall or refectory. Talking was discouraged, signs were to be used where possible. Eating was to be moderate with meat three times a week and dishes of pulse and beans on other days. Wine was allowed 'in equal proportions and of equal strength.' During meals there were to be sacred readings. For sleeping, a sack, a mattress and a covering were to be sufficient. He must sleep in a linen shirt, drawers and hose, and with a small girdle round his waist. He must attend divine service punctually. Daytime clothes consisted of white for celibate knights and black or brown for others. Hair and beards were to be kept trim. Each knight was permitted three horses. Absolute obedience to the Master of the Order was required.[10]

Initiatory trials and proofs of the aspirant knight first took place. After preliminary questions had been put to him and satisfactory answers received, he kneeled before the Master who told him something of his duties. Following further interrogation, the habit of a white mantle with a red cross was placed upon him. He listened to a discourse by the Master: he was not to swear, nor to kiss a woman, even his mother or sister, and was never to assist in any baptismal ceremony. When he heard of the Master's death he must repeat immediately two hundred *pater nosters* for the repose of his soul.

During the rest of the year following the Council of Troyes, Hugh de Payens travelled far and wide from Flanders to Spain to further his Order. In France he made over his estate to the Temple and met King Henry I of England in his dukedom of Normandy. Henry bestowed many riches upon him. Hugh crossed the Channel with this royal recommendation and, in England and Scotland, the nobles vied in showering gifts and lands upon the Templars.

Preceptories, as their houses were known, were established throughout Europe where recruits would be admitted and regulated before leaving for the Holy Land. The urgent need was for more soldiers and consequently for money and property for their support. However, these Templar knights henceforth owned nothing personally, as all was given to the Order itself. Nevertheless, everywhere men of all classes clamoured to help by making any sort of offering, cash or legacies, for apparel, horses or armour.

The organisation of the Order was impressive. The possessions in the East were divided into three provinces, Palestine, Antioch and Tripoli. The Templars built several strong castles which defied Saladin, while the Hospitallers built others including the famous Krak des Chevaliers. Europe was divided into nine provinces, these being Sicily, Italy, Portugal, Castile and Leon, Aragon, Germany and Hungary, Greece, France with the Netherlands, and Britain.

Matthew Paris stated in his *History* that by 1244 the Templars had in Christendom 9000 manors and the Hospitallers double that number. But it seems that the total number of Knights in Europe was never more than two thousand, and those engaged in a single battle in the Holy Land rarely exceeded four hundred. The Society consisted of several classes, knights, sergeants, priests, and serving brethren, all bound together by their vow of obedience to the head of the Order, the Grand Master at Jerusalem. Bailiffs and other officials controlled the estates and the agricultural labourers.

The preceptories in Europe, sometimes fortified, varied in size with some lying in remote places. But each had at least a chapel and sometimes, as in Paris and London, built on a circular plan like the church of the Holy Sepulchre in Jerusalem. The twelfth-century chapel at Petronell near Vienna is a good example (*ill. 5*).

Jerusalem was the centre of the network, but Paris was next in importance. Situated on the Right Bank, a spacious *enclos* of nearly thirty acres was surrounded by stone walls 25ft high (*ill. 7*). Within were extensive buildings which included the grim and massive Donjon Tower, or keep, the famous *Tour du Temple*, and the renowned church dedicated to the Blessed Virgin, *Sainte Marie du Temple*. The circular nave, built after the plan of the Holy Sepulchre, was called *la rotonde du Temple*. It probably had a small eastern apse and was built soon after the

Templars first came to Paris. In the thirteenth century a magnificent two-storey western porch was added. A new aisle-less Gothic Chancel, more than a hundred feet long and ending in an apse, was also built (*ill. 6*).

The rotunda, 60ft in diameter internally, was built with very thick walls, notionally divided by twelve attached shafts with comparable external buttresses. It was said that the windows were originally unglazed. Six massive pillars[11] formed the circular aisle and central cupola, supported by a stone 'umbrella' vault (*ill. 9*).

6. *Plan of the Church of the Temple in Paris.*

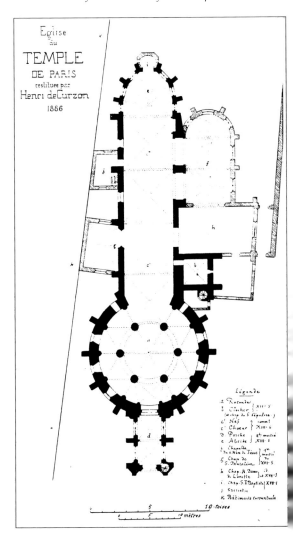

5. *The Round Church, Petronell, Austria.*

7. Enclos du Temple in Paris, 1450. (From Paris à travers les âges, Hoffbauer)

'Viollet-le-Duc noted that the proportions of the Romanesque rotonde were those of an equilateral triangle imposed upon another inverted and, without adducing any evidence, gave them a Masonic significance[12].' When one observes the Round Church in London, it will be seen that there the aisle vault plan was more subtle, avoiding the problem of east and west pillars.

Hoffbauer[13] gives a good view of the church of *Sainte Marie du Temple* from the south-west *(d'apres* I. Sylvestre, 1650) *(ill. 8).* It shows the aisle and clerestory roofs of the rotunda without parapets and with corbelled eaves, *'une rotonde qui... semblait avoir été primitivement surmontée d'un dôme et devait ressembler en petit a la chapelle du Sainte-Sepulcre de Jerusalem.'*

Surrounding three sides of the church were cloisters. Senior knights had a cell within, while the serving brothers lived in a dormitory. The Prior (or Grand Master of France) at first had a simple room, but as wealth increased he eventually lived in a palace within the *enclos.* There

was a chapter-house, infirmary, refectory, kitchens, cellars, stores, extensive gardens and a cemetery.

In the fourteenth century *le Temple* was given to the Knights Hospitallers after the demise of the Templars, and the church was still standing until 1650. By then alley-ways, houses and shops formed a bustling *faubourg.* Not a vestige remains of the Paris Temple, destroyed at the hands of Napoleon, except for the name of the *Rue du Temple*[14]. The London Temple precinct survives as the private property of the Inner and Middle Temple, two of the four Inns of Court. Little is known of the plan in the time of the Templars. The only building erected by them and still standing is the Temple church, apart from two small vaulted butteries attached to the modern Inner Temple Hall A possible plan is shown at *ill. 21.*

Hugh de Payens returned to Palestine as Grand Master of the Order. He died in 1136 before he could address the problems arising from the contradiction between their vows of poverty and

8. View of the church of S. Marie from the Cloisters. (From Les Templiers by Ollivier)

their accumulating wealth with the privileges that came in its wake. The jealousy, the quarrels, the fighting were flaws which eventually widened and brought down the great edifice.

By his Bull of 1139, *Omne datum optimum*, Pope Innocent II made the Order of the Temple responsible only to the Holy See and exempt from all jurisdiction, lay or ecclesiastical. He also extended the membership, which had at first been restricted to knights, by admitting priests:

> '... And so that nothing shall be wanting for the welfare of your souls, you shall have your own clerks and chaplains, to keep in your House and under its jurisdiction, without reference to the Diocesan Bishop, by direct authority of the Holy Church of Rome.'

But they were not placed on an equal footing with the lay brethren to whom were reserved all the powers of government:

> 'These chaplains shall undergo a novitiate of one year, and should they turn out troublesome or simply useless to the House, you shall be at liberty to send them away and appoint better priests. And these chaplains shall not meddle in the government of the Order ... It shall be their duty to obey you, my dear son Robert, as their master and prelate.'[15]

'In the church at large', comments Williamson[16]

> 'authority lay with the priest, only he could bind and loose, could pronounce the dread sentence of ex-communication and grant deliverance from it by absolution ... In the fra-

9. S. Marie du Temple, showing Rotunda. From 'Le Maison du Temple de Paris', by Henri de Curzon, 1888

ternity of these military monks the position was different. For here the priest was subservient to the layman, being bound by decisions and regulations of the Chapter in which he had no voice other than that of a consultant, if and when called into Council. It was this peculiar feature of the Order, coupled with the secrecy of their Chapters, which later led to the charge preferred against them that the Grand Master and Preceptors, when reconciling an offending brother after penance, presumed though laymen to pronounce in Chapter sentence of absolution from sin.'

10. A Hospitaller and a Templar. (From Fairholt's 'Costume in England' (1860)

NOTES TO CHAPTER ONE

[1] Some writers prefer the title 'The Knights Templar' as being more correct. The majority used the plural.

[2] Barber, M., *The New Knighthood – a History of the Order of the Temple* (1994). He corrects the date from 1118, usually stated, and also uses the Knight's name as 'Hugh of Payns', no doubt more correctly; but it seems awkward and most writers quote 'Hugh de Payens'.

[3] Simon, Edith, *The Piebald Standard* (1959).

[4] Folda, J., 'Art in the Latin East, 1098-1291' in *Oxford Illustrated History of the Crusaders* (1995).

[5] Baylis, T.H., *The Temple Church* (3rd end, 1900). *Beauséant* derived from Bausan, in Old French: balzan – a black horse with white stockings. The Scottish word 'baws'nt' meant 'piebald'.

[6] Richardson, E., *The Monumental Effigies of the Temple Church* (1843). Though he states that the Knights wore long beards, they were told to keep them short.

[7] Forey, A., 'The Military Orders, 1120-1312' in *Oxford Illustrated History of the Crusaders* (1995).

[8] Jeffery, G., 'The Church of the Holy Sepulchre, Jerusalem', in *RIBA Journal*, 3rd S., Vol. xvii, 18-20.

[9] Britton, J., *The Architectural Antiquities of Great Britain* (1835).

[10] Williamson, J.Bruce, *The Temple, London* (1924).

[11] de Curzon, H., *La Maison du Temple de Paris* (1888). La Rotonde: '*Six grosses colonnes appareillées, munie de bases et de chapiteaux, supportent cinq grandes arcades en tiers-point, de section plane, et non doublées... Quicherat appelait one 'voute en ombrelle.*' This, he said, was similar to the London rotunda.

[12] Ryan, F., *The House of the Temple* (1930).

[13] Hoffbauer, M., *Paris à travers les âges, 1875-82*, Vol. 2, The Temple.

[14] The last traces of the walls survived until 1820. In 1848 Napoleon III set out a grand square on the site of the Temple, designed by M. Alphand.

[15] Simon, *op. cit.*, 47. Robert de Craon had succeeded Hugh de Payens as Grand Master on the latter's death in 1136. *Omne datum optimum* was re-issued and its provisions extended by Pope Alexander III in 1162.

[16] Williamson, *op. cit.* 13.

CHAPTER TWO

The Round

The settlements of the Templars in England had followed the visit of Hugh de Payens in 1129. Before long they were setting up preceptories in their newly acquired properties. By 1150 six or seven had been established, the earliest in London followed by Shipley (Sussex), Cressing (Essex), Temple Cowley (Oxfordshire), Temple Guiting (Gloucestershire) and Temple Disley (Cheshire). By the end of the thirteenth century there were hundreds of preceptories in Europe, particularly in France, Spain and Portugal. In England there were more than thirty, nine or ten in Ireland and two or three in Scotland. The Templars appear prominently in Sir Walter Scott's novel *Ivanhoe*, in which the imagined preceptory of Templestowe figures.[1]

The first establishment and headquarters in London, known as the Military Temple and later as the Old Temple, was in the parish of St Andrew, Holborn 'beyond the Barres' of the City, as Stow relates,[2] and lay between the north end of the later Chancery Lane and Staple Inn. Within the boundary ditch there was a garden, orchard and several buildings erected for the accommodation of the knights, squires, chaplains and their servants. At an early date an imposing round church was begun, inspired by the Holy Sepulchre in Jerusalem, and was built in Caen stone from Normandy. Stow recorded that

'It hath of late years belonged to the Earles of Southampton and therefore called Southampton house. Mayster Roper hath of late builded there, by meanes whereof part of the ruines of the Old Temple were seene to remaine

builded of Cane stone, round in forme as the New Temple by Temple barre... A great part of this olde Temple was pulled downe but of late in the yeare 1595.'

Stow's statement was confirmed in 1875 during excavations for the building of the London and County Bank in High Holborn. A plan [3] made at the time showed

'that there was then discovered the concrete foundation, 5½ft broad, of a circular wall of 20ft internal diameter, and upon it the base of six round pillars each 2ft 9ins across and resting on a square plinth. These evidently belonged to the nave of the Old Temple and gave for it an approximate span of 22½ft, and a probable total diameter of 45ft for the round part of the church. Unfortunately no note seems to have been made of any possible remains of the presbytery.'

Probably these discoveries were destroyed at this time, for when a new building took the place of the former bank a century later, the extensive excavation in the basement disappointingly revealed no vestige of the Templars' first home.[4]

It seems that the Knights occupied their first church for some two decades only. It must have taken many years to build, which suggests that the consecration took place not earlier than 1135. The design of this round church may have been similar to that of St Sepulchre, Cambridge, thought to be of the early twelfth century and which had a diameter of 41ft with the central columns 'short and massy' in Norman style. No doubt both had a narrow chancel or presbytery attached to the round nave as there was at the Hospitallers' church in Clerkenwell.

The Knights Hospitallers had continued to rival the Templars and they too had spread across Europe. It was Brother Gerard who in 1113 founded the Order at the Hospital of St John of Jerusalem. Gerard died in 1120 and his successor, Raymond du Puy, the first Grand Master of the Order, guided their destinies for forty years.[5] By then the brethren had become 'fighting-monks' like the Templars, but they continued to care for the sick. In a similar way the modern St John's Ambulance Brigade in England has its roots.

Long before the death of du Puy the Hospitallers had become firmly established in England. The headquarters of the Order was made in Clerkenwell, only half a mile from the Old Temple. The Priory was built on part of the land given c.1100 by Jordan de Bricet and his heiress wife, Muriel de Munteni, in order to found the Nunnery of St Mary. Following a dispute concerning the original ten acres, Prior Walter in 1148 confirmed the ownership of half the area for the Knights, yet it was well before this that the Priory had been largely built. Clerkenwell Road crosses the former precincts (ill. 11) and little remains today except St John's Gate (rebuilt in 1504), the crypt of St John's Church and the outline of the Hospitallers' original round church, shown by stones set in a circle 65ft in diameter in the roadway of St John's Square.[6] Adjacent is the Grand Priory Church, reconstructed after severe war damage and used for services and investitures for the Order of St John.

The date of the Hospitallers' church, again built after the plan of the Holy Sepulchre in Jerusalem, is uncertain, although J.H. Round made out a strong case for its consecration being in 1140.[7] Apart from the circle in the roadway, nothing remains of the Round except a small portion of the wall of the nave at the entrance to the surviving crypt which was limited to the area under the chancel. This was a small extension to the large round nave, 15ft wide and 40ft long, possibly terminating with an apse. There may have been a double flight of steps in the nave, one rising to the sanctuary and the other

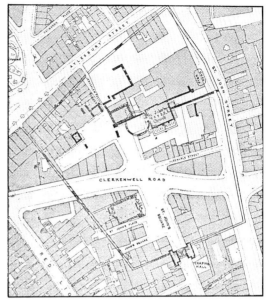

11. Plan of the precincts of the Priory of St John's at Clerkenwell, by H.W. Fincham.

12. Plan of the crypt at St John's, Clerkenwell. From W.H. Godfrey, 'A History of Architecture in and around London' (1962).

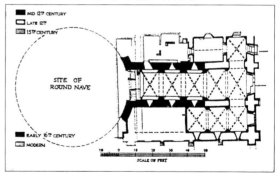

descending to the crypt. Some fifty years later the sanctuary was enlarged into an aisled chancel. Similarly the crypt was extended and was dedicated in 1185, the same year as the New Temple Round.

An interesting question arises in regard to these two Romanesque round churches, built by the Templars and the Hospitallers at about the same time. The Old Temple round church was not more than 45ft in diameter, whereas that at Clerkenwell measured 65ft. It is suggested, therefore, that the Old Temple Round was the earlier as it is unlikely that the Templars would be setting out a church so much smaller than that of their rivals. In his plan, (*ill. 12*) of the Clerkenwell church, Walter Godfrey shows only a circular outline of the Round, but Daniel Roth[8] indicated an arcade of eight columns, as against six in the Old Temple, but there appears to be no proof of this. The crypt at Clerkenwell retains interesting stone vaulted arches showing the development of piers and ribs from *c*.1130 to *c*.1180. At the Old Temple there were no remains of the probable chancel nor any indication of a similar crypt at Clerkenwell.

In Europe, plans for round churches modelled on the form of the Church of the Holy Sepulchre at Jerusalem received a remarkable impetus as a result of the early Crusades. These were not confined to the military orders. But the form is unusual in England, and Clapham[9] lists only fifteen, though there may have been others with remains still undiscovered. Of the above, seven were Templar, two Hospitaller, three parish churches and three private chapels. Of these round churches only five survive to any extent, these being the New Temple in London, Little Maplestead (Hospitaller), Cambridge and Northampton (parish churches), and the ruined chapel in Ludlow Castle.

Of the seven Templar round churches, the Old Temple has already been described and details of the New Temple will be given later. Temple Bruer (meaning 'on the heath') in Lincolnshire was described in *Archaeologia*.[10] It was thought that it was founded late in the reign of Henry II. The preceptory was visited in 1538/9 by John Leland who noted that:

> 'There be great and vaste Buildings, but rude at this Place, and the Este end of the Temple is made *opere circulari de more...*'

A mention in 1306 of a licence to the Templars to 'make and crenellate a certain great and strong gate' points to an enclosure by a walled precinct. The round church was approximately 50ft in diameter with eight inner cylindrical columns and a presbytery no more than 12ft wide and 27ft long with an apse and crypt below. Later the presbytery was extended beyond the apse to make a square end. An adjoining tower of an earlier date survives. Temple Bruer was investigated by the Rev. G. Oliver in 1837, and was excavated in 1908 by St John Hope and others with the help of eight labourers. From the remaining evidence he judged that the round nave probably carried a triforium (or high-level arcaded passage) and clerestory and perhaps a belfry stage above. There was a western doorway and the remains of a 'magnificent porch', as mentioned earlier by Dr Oliver.

The other Templar round churches in Clapham's list were at Garway (Hereford), Bristol, Dover and Aslackby (Lincs.). Hope visited the latter in 1903 but found nothing but stone fragments. The remains of a thirteenth-century Templars' round church on the western heights of Dover were uncovered early in the nineteenth century. This consisted of a circular nave, 35ft in diameter, with a square-ended presbytery about 22ft long and 13ft wide. Hope suggested that there was an internal arcade to the nave with six columns, but Clapham considered that it was of the smaller type with no inner arcade. Similar buildings included the destroyed twelfth-century parish church of West Thurrock (Essex),[11] and the private chapels in Ludlow Castle and Woodstock Palace.

The Ludlow Castle chapel of St Mary Magdalene is about 28ft in internal diameter and the walls 'built of thin courses of well-laid rubble.'[12] Externally there is a string course about third-way up, the wall below being partly plastered. A fine Norman entrance doorway appears to have been further enriched from its original design. The nave probably had a conical roof with eaves but this was later taken off and the walls raised with a battlemented parapet. A floor was inserted to make a two-storey apartment, probably the upper floor being for the benefit of the gentry. The chancel has gone, but Hope made some excavations which showed that it was 12ft square with a semi-octagonal apse beyond.

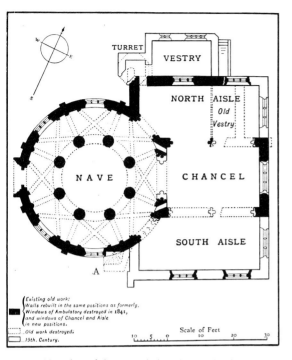

13. Plan of the Round church, Cambridge.

14. The Round Church, Cambridge, as restored by Salvin, 1841.

'The chapel of St Giles' Hospital at Hereford was also of this type and was peculiar in that it appears to have had a small eastern apse springing directly from the round nave in a manner similar to that of the little ruined chapel in the Orkney Isles.'[13]

Temple as a forename occurs in many place names indicating Templars' settlements such as Temple Combe (Somerset), Temple Ewell (Kent) and Temple Newsam (Yorks.). Temple Balsall (Warwick), an important Templar preceptory, had only a small oblong chapel and was typical of other centres.[14] However, the thirteenth century preceptory seal from Ferriby North (Yorks.), which shows a round church with conical roof, may indicate such a building there.

The church of St John of Jerusalem, Little Maplestead, was built in the early fourteenth century by the Knights Hospitallers and was the last of the round churches in England.[15] It is small, the round being only 26ft in diameter internally with six clustered columns forming an arcade. The apsidal chancel forms a total length

of 60ft from the fine Transitional west doorway. Britton remarked that the village was nearly deserted and that the church was suffering gradual decay. However, the building was heavily restored in 1851.

The Church of St Sepulchre, Cambridge, (ills. 13 & 14) was 'restored' extensively by the architect Salvin in 1841.[16] According to Baylis it was built by the Knight Pain Peveril and consecrated in 1101. The exterior was almost entirely rebuilt but the handsome west doorway survives, though much restored. Internally the Round, 41ft in diameter, retains the eight heavy Norman columns supporting the drum and triforium with its interesting double arches above each arcade. The aisle vaulting is decorated with diagonal zigzag ribs. The fifteenth century bell tower and clerestory were removed and replaced with an 'authentic' conical roof, as was to be repeated at the Temple church in London by St Aubyn twenty years later. The aisled chancel was built in 1313 and probably replaced a small aisle-less presbytery.

Although the over-restoration of the church in 1841 is to be deplored, it is interesting to read Britton's comments[17] made a few years before:

'Much of the original design and pristine character of this building have been altered and injured by the injudicious operations of the carpenter, whitewasher and bricklayers, whose performances are commonly, though

15. The Church of the Holy Sepulchre, Northampton, before restoration.

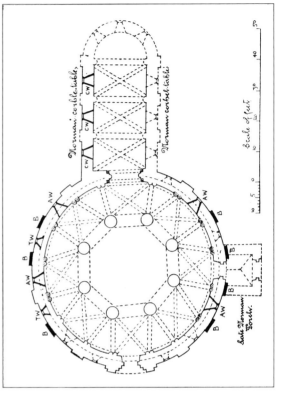

16. Probable form of the original church of the Holy Sepulchre, Northampton.

really ironically, called "beautifying". The masonry of the ancient circular wall, and also of the columns and arches, evince considerable skill, as the stones are all squared and chiselled with mathematical accuracy to suit their respective situations. As the columns and wall are circular, and each faced with small wrought stones, it was necessary to form two of the sides and the exterior surface by geometrical rules: the first being regulated by the lines of the radius and the latter by the diameter of the circle. In examining this building, we are struck with its ponderous and durable appearance, as if it was intended for a castellated building and calculated to defy the warfare of time and of man.'

The Church of the Holy Sepulchre, Northampton (*ills 15 & 16*), was founded about 1100 and probably completed by 1115.[18] The round

nave is 55ft in diameter with eight sturdy circular Norman columns. At the close of the fourteenth century the upper part of the circular nave was taken down and pointed arches were constructed upon the Norman columns. Clapham thought that this was the result of the vaulted aisle forcing the circular wall outwards. The original narrow aisle-less chancel was approximately 50ft long but was replaced eventually with a new quadruple nave and eastern sanctuary, the Round remaining as a vestibule and baptistry.

The wealth of the Templars and their numbers increased rapidly, and eventually their London headquarters became inadequate. At some time between 1155 and 1162 they sold the property to their neighbour, Robert de Chesney, Bishop of Lincoln,[19] for the sum of 100 marks and moved to a new site on the banks of the Thames. Dugdale wrote in the seventeenth century:[20]

'About the beginning of King Henry the Second's reign, the Knights Templars, leaving their House in Holburne ... did for then more conveniently, set up another habitation for themselves over against the end of a Street hereafter called New Street, but now Chancery Lane, which had therefore the name of the New Temple.'

FitzStephen [21] stated that from the City walls to the King's palace at Westminster there were houses, gardens and orchards alongside the Thames, and it is known that there were buildings already there, perhaps some being suitable for immediate occupation.

It is not known how the Knights came to possess their new domain, whether by purchase or gift, but the land was part of the honour of Leicester which was held from the King by the service or office of Steward of England. The Beaumont family held the Earldom of Leicester and in 1185 they were receiving the rent of one pound of cummin from the Templars. It seems that the Bishop of Ely had had a town house or 'hostilage' here since the Conquest, and it was suggested that this became the quarters of the Master of the Temple. In modern times this is the site of Farrar's Building to the south-west of the Round church.[22] At a later date the establishment of the White Friars lay to the east of their holding and the Bishop of Exeter's house on the west, in the Outer Temple. In the absence of any evidence of sale, the present boundaries of the Temple (*frontispiece*) indicate the approximate extent of their new acquisition.[23]

To the south was the river, in those days wider and some way north of the present Embankment. To the north of their property was the new road out of Ludgate and over the River Fleet which continued by the Strand, west of Temple Bar. Chancery Lane was then known as 'Newstrete of the Templars,' with Fikettescroft, a martial exercise field to the east, now the site of New Square, Lincoln's Inn, and two forges near St Dunstan's church to the west, all in their possession.[24]

The Knights soon began to build a new and larger church which was to be a fine jewel set among splendid halls, cloisters and walks. But this would take time. Henry II granted the advowson of the church of St Clement Danes in the Strand to the Templars, who probably used that building while the new Round Church was being erected.[25]

The Round was built at a time when exciting innovations, following the introduction of the pointed arch, were transforming the hitherto heavy Romanesque style into a new heavenward-aspiring architecture which came to be known as Gothic. The Temple Round is one of the most important examples of this Transitional style and it presents some striking features (*ill. 17*). It will be seen that the clerestory and aisle windows are semi-circular headed, as is the great West doorway, but the six arches of the main arcade cut, as it were, into the round drum are pointed and are necessarily twisted in form, being of double curvature when viewed on plan and section. The triforium (*ill. 17*) arcading is

17. The Round Church as seen in 1838 (but without monuments). Illustrated by R.W. Billings.

18. Above are 3 of 7 Norman capitals and heads in the arcade. From a Nash engraving of 1818. Below are Norman capitals in the triforium. From W.H. Godfrey's 'A History of Architecture in and around London' (1962).

truly Transitional, a series of interlaced semi-circles resulting in pointed arches which are supported on small shafts of Purbeck marble with carved capitals. The main piers and the columns in the aisle are also in this marble with caps carved similarly in Norman style. They have considerable variation with unusual design, perhaps with eastern influence. It seems that the central drum, unlike the aisle, was never vaulted in stone, although springers remained and the Paris *rotonde* was certainly so.

Britton[26] asserted that the semi-circular, intersecting and pointed arches here were all constructed at one time:

> 'It was, however, at that period when the pointed-arch system was in its infancy, and therefore too weak to effect a complete conquest over its veteran rival.'

But it should not be forgotten that it took many years to complete the Round and its appended chancel. So the question arises: if the Round was designed at one time in its entirety, were the details changed as it grew in the light of new thinking and the knowledge of new ideas and construction, as in France? Probably at first the new Round was to repeat the form of the old one

in Holborn, for the ground plan was similar, with six main concentric pillars within an outer circular wall. However, the internal diameter between the walls was to be approximately 60ft compared with 45ft at the Old Temple, and the building would be on a much grander scale.

Having said that the various arches exhibited in the Round church were all constructed at the same time, Britton goes on to suggest that the exterior wall with the great West doorway is what remains of the original building of 1185, but that the six clustered columns within, with the incumbent arches, were later. Although the windows of both the aisle and clerestory

> '... have semi-circular tops, the height and shape of the opening, with the three-quarter columns at the angles, and the groining above, are all of the pointed style.'

The possibility that the clerestory windows were originally pointed arises from an early drawing of the interior of the church made by William Emmett in *c.*1682 (*ill. 56*), though it must be admitted that his drawings were highly stylised. Certainly the windows are clearly detailed in Nash's engraving of 1818 and without doubt were rounded. Reverting to the question of the date of the main arcade in the Round, it seems highly unlikely that it could have been rebuilt only fifty years after its first foundation, as Britton appears to suggest.

We may consider first the building of the outer circular wall with its buttresses. It is known that the Old Temple was constructed with Caen stone and this was again used in the new Round, at least for the interior. The Templars may even have re-used the stone from Holborn as there was no sign of the outer wall at the Old Temple church when remains of the arcade foundations were discovered in 1875. Before 1860 the north side of the Round was closed-packed with old buildings until cleared away at that time. The outer wall of the Round was then revealed, possibly never previously refaced. A photograph of 1861 and drawings by Wykeham Archer[27] show the walling in detail, (*ills 88, 97 & 98*) consisting of coursed Kentish rag, whereas today the present finish is seen to be un-coursed work. Clearly the subsequent restoration by St Aubyn was more extensive than he implied at the time.[28]

The earliest drawing of the exterior of the church[29] in any detail, but again stylised by Emmett, shows the south front and indicates ashlar walling which is certainly not original. In any case, the chancel was masked by buildings up against it until 1826. On the north side of the Round, Wykeham Archer illustrated the decrepit ancient buttresses (*ills 86 & 88*) including some top stones below the eaves, evidently the remains of the two buttresses removed when the medieval porch was added. There were also plain stone corbels at the eaves supporting a parapet.

The most puzzling aspect of the Round is the shape of the original roofs. Billings, in his *Architectural Illustrations and Account of the Temple Church, London* of 1838, said that the hip-roof over the aisle is a modern addition. From his careful examination of the way the groining underneath is flattened and plastered externally, it was most probably covered in lead and formed a circular walkway. To support this view he pointed out the weathering of parts of this area, especially the doorway opening at this level from the staircase tower. The four steps from this doorway were also very worn, indicative of much use which would not have been the case if they had only led to a roof space. He also felt that the squat proportions of the windows to the clerestory suggested that they had been partially blocked to allow support to the rafters of a later roof. This view is supported by an entry in the Inner Temple Records of 27 June 1563 which states: '...to go as well about the roundel of the steeple...'

The original shape to the clerestory roof is even more difficult to determine. Cottingham recorded in his survey of the condition of the church of 1840 (*see Appendix Four*) the roof at that time was a shallow timber cone shape, and was obviously of some antiquity. It rested on six stone springing mouldings which were indicative of an original intention of having a groined stone roof. There is no way of determining whether this roof was ever built. If so, it would

have put great outward pressure on the clerestory walls where the supporting thin pilasters would not in time have been able to resist. Sydney Smirke in his *Account of the Recent Restoration of the Temple Church* of 1845 pointed out that even with the ancient timber roof the top of the Round measured an extra foot in diameter, as a result of the lateral pressure. If a roof of stone or timber followed the springing of the mouldings, Billings and Cottingham both say that it would have been of a horse-shoe shape. Billings calculated that it would have been six feet higher than the ceiling that was currently there. Historical descriptions vary. Strype's Stow says: 'You enter first into a large Circular Tower, which on the top terminates in something like a Dome...' The ITR of 1563 says: '...also unto the leads of the same church in every part thereof, and up into the steeple by means whereof the lead there hath been perished, broken and taken away.'[30]

Building of the inner circle with its six clustered Purbeck marble piers surely followed the completion of the outer wall. It may have taken at least ten years to complete the whole church and, as the consecration took place in 1185, it is reasonable to suggest that the marble columns were being erected by 1180 and that the stone had been ordered well before then.

Purbeck marble was known by the Romans who used it for decorative work, especially for memorial inscriptions. It was then forgotten until its revival in medieval times when it was at first used for tombs and effigies, those dating from the early twelfth century being sculptured in low relief. Soon it was realised that the use of white Caen stone with dark Purbeck marble made an impressive contrast. Moreover the marble, when not affected by the weather, was hard and strong and could support a tower or stone vault.

It has been said that the earliest use of detached Purbeck shafts was at Canterbury Cathedral in the new choir, built by the Frenchman William of Sens and completed by William the Englishman in 1184. However, the powerful and wealthy Templars were building their new Round church in London in the 1170s, and the six main piers in the nave provide perhaps the earliest

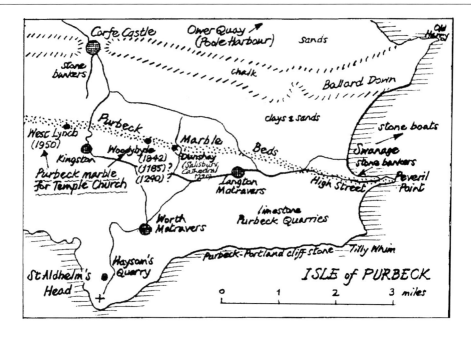

19. Map of the Isle of Purbeck showing the location of the marble beds. (David Lewer)

example of Purbeck marble used structurally on a large scale (*ill. 72*). This 'marble', which is not metamorphic, consists of freshwater limestone and tiny fossilised snails (*viviparus*) and takes a high polish when worked. In Dorset a narrow band outcropping from the Upper Purbeck beds (*ill. 19*) runs from Swanage through Corfe Castle parish to Worbarrow Bay and was quarried in vast quantities from the twelfth to the fifteenth centuries. Its heyday was in the thirteenth century, when many cathedrals and churches were built or rebuilt in the 'Early English' style, as at Salisbury and Lincoln. The provenance of the original marble used in the Round church is uncertain, as it was replaced in the restoration of 1842.[31] However, the near contemporary shafts at Canterbury show, in the texture of the stone, a similarity to the marble recovered from Peveril Point, including a large block from the seashore seen when alterations were recently made to the Swanage lifeboat slipway.[32] The original marble was probably shipped from Swanage and arrived in the Thames at Temple stairs, though it is uncertain whether it was worked in Purbeck or on site in the New Temple, as was done so

in part at Westminster Abbey fifty years later.

The six main piers in the Round each consist of four linked columns, the two larger built as drums laid on bed, the two smaller built as vertical shafts in two sections,[33] all linked together half way also by Purbeck marble bands. The bases and carved Transitional caps are fashioned as one, though built with large blocks. On each cap stands an attached shaft rising through the triforium to the clerestory. Each of the six triforium bays consists of seven small Purbeck marble shafts with decorated caps supporting freestone semi-circles resulting in pointed arches.

The aisle wall is divided into twelve bays by attached Purbeck marble shafts from whose caps spring the ribs which support the stone vaults. The arrangement of the aisle vaults and the disposition of the main piers is worthy of study. The six clustered piers are not placed in line with the external buttresses, as they were at the Paris *rotonde*, but result in six quadripartite vaults and alternate six triangular ones, thus avoiding a west doorway and a possible central pier at the entrance to a chancel (*see back endpapers*).[34] The circular aisle wall contains eight round-headed

26

windows. Below them on either side the wall is decorated with arcading, each bay having six pointed arches. The small stone shafts dividing them show a wealth of differing caps with Transitional designs. Their bases are similarly varied. Between and above each arch is a grotesque head. The appearance of these heads range from the regal or legal to saracenic or bestial. It was said that on the south side the heads showed heavenly aspects but on the north side they were in purgatory; but in any case the heads were renewed in the 1820s and their likeness to the originals is in some doubt. *Illustration 70* shows some of these heads before they were replaced.

Edward Clarkson in Billings' 1838 publication of *Illustrations and Account of the Temple Church, London* sets out his views on the mystical significance of the six free-standing four-faced columns. Together with the twelve columns of the aisle walls, within which are seven minor columns, the 42 columns of the triforium arranged in groups of seven, he concluded that this was no accident but had direct links with sacred numbers that can be traced back to Egyptian masonry, Jewish cabalists, Pythagorians, Gnostics, the Romans and the Druids.

Perhaps the most striking achievement is the great Norman West doorway (*ill. 20*), truly magnificent in its design. It has seven orders with alternate high relief and plain mouldings, with decorated shafts and capitals.[35] The vaulted square porch was added a little later to the entrance to the Round, as there was evidence of the remains of the two original buttresses then removed. It undoubtedly helped to preserve the west doorway and probably preceded the new chancel of 1240. It is thought that it was the remaining bay of a west cloister extending southwards to connect with the Knights' hall,[36] though it is not quite in line with the present cloisters. Remains of the porch are seen in Wykeham Archer's watercolour painting before their drastic restoration in 1861 (*ill. 88*).

Above the great West doorway is a beautiful Norman wheel window dating from the later porch and composed of Caen stone 7ft 6ins in diameter. The eight spokes of the wheel are formed by Romanesque columns grooved on either side to receive glass and possibly coloured.

Addison wrote that:

> 'The centre of the wheel consists of two stones, and the top and bottom of the caps and bases of the spokes form portions of concentric circles, so that the whole would stand alone without any lateral support.'[37]

Wykeham Archer made an accurate and delightful watercolour drawing of this window when revealed in 1861, following demolition of the chambers formerly built over the porch (*ill. 90*).

As in the other similar round churches, an aisle-less chancel led out from a single eastern bay of the Round nave and was 20ft wide and some 50ft long. It was discovered during the 1842 restoration of the church and again uncovered after the last war, when excavations began as a preliminary to the restoration of the chancel following the fire.

The four western-most Purbeck pillars in the present chancel stand upon the wide foundation walls of the earlier building. During excavation work by Walter Godfrey in 1953 a substantial stone wall across the central aisle was revealed, faced on the east side but indistinct on the west. Godfrey was disappointed not to find the re-

20. The West doorway of the Temple church. Drawing by J.T. Smith, 1808.

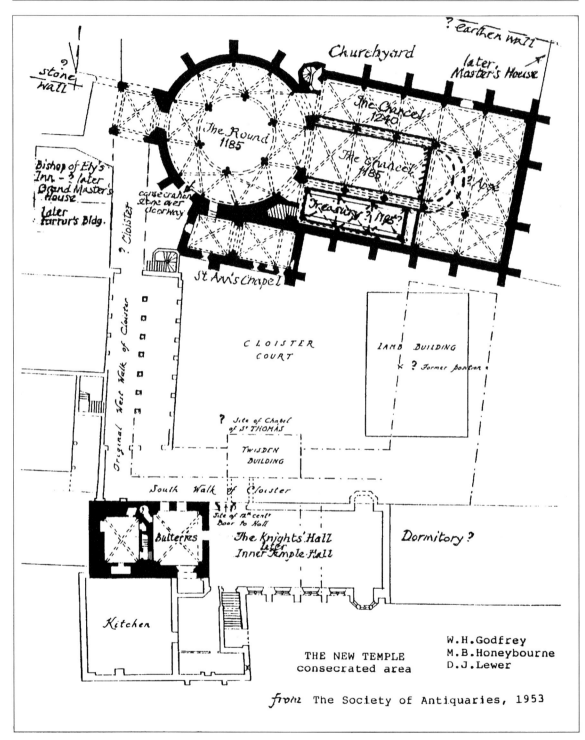

21. Plan of the consecrated part of the New Temple, London, including the church, cloisters, knights' hall and butteries.

mains of an apse and, though shown as conjectural in his plan of 1953 for the Society of Antiquaries (*ill. 21*), there was certainly no sign of one at the time of close observation on site. As previously described, it is known that there were apsidal ends to the churches in Paris, Northampton, Temple Bruer, Little Maplestead and probably at Clerkenwell. Other churches, as at Dover and perhaps Cambridge, had no such apsidal ends.

A further exciting discovery was made in 1953 when digging below the church floor against the south wall of the chancel for proposed heating ducts. Less than a foot below the floor level in the south-west corner, there came to light a stone capital carved with foliage in Transitional style and its shaft and cap below in situ (*ill. 22*). Further east were two more equally spaced shafts, though their caps were missing. Deep excavation followed and, after the removal of rubble, coffins, bones and skulls, it was realised that here had been an 'undercroft' attached to or alongside the original chancel (*ill. 21*). There were indications of a stone stair down to this lower level, perhaps this being the only entrance, although it may

have been the base of a belfry[38] tower as at the Templars' church in Paris and at the Holy Sepulchre in Jerusalem. There was also evidence of three blocked windows in the south wall now below courtyard level, together with a double piscina (a basin for washing the sacred vessels) and two stone lockers, still retaining their hinges (*ill. 23*). A stone bench runs the length of the basement building along both north and south walls but the floor between gave no evidence of paving. The east wall, in line with the continued central wall in the chancel, did not indicate any recess such as an altar though the proximity of the piscinas suggests that the building was a chapel.

As there were originally eight attached shafts in this building, it is clear that they formed three compartments which evidently were vaulted, but whether the chancel itself was also vaulted is doubtful. Its roof was probably quite low since the eastern segment of the main wall of the Round still retains the external curve above the later chancel arch.

The purpose of this building south of the original chancel is uncertain, but Walter Godfrey conjectured that it might have been the Templars' treasury.[39] It is known that King John deposited much treasure in the New Temple into their keep-

22. Building under the south aisle. Capital of angle shaft and cap. From 'Recent Discoveries at the Temple, 1953', by W.H. Godfrey in Archaeologia, Vol. XCX.

23. Building under the south aisle. Lockers and double piscina. (Source as for ill. 22)

ing, and that he resided here for a week in January 1214. Six months later at Runnymede he conceded to the Barons' demand, and the name of the Master of the Temple in England, Aymeric de St Maur, was included in the list of magnates in the preamble of the Great Charter.[40] There is also much evidence that the Templars acted as bankers on a wide scale, and it is quite possible that this building was indeed a treasury stronghold.

One other point of interest may be considered regarding the building of the Round. Access to the triforium and roofs is from a circular staircase at the base of the present bell tower (*ill. 32*). The doorway is in the north-west corner of the Early English chancel but the arch over it, though restored, is semi-circular with a drip-mould finish. The stone ceiling over the vestibule within has an interesting vault of Norman appearance, and it would seem that the tower and stair were built at the same time as the Round. It has been established that there was no north aisle to the original chancel and therefore the staircase door was probably entered from the open air. There might have been a north door from the chancel only a few feet away, and leading to the tower.

Half way up the stair is the notorious Penitential Cell in the thickness of the wall, four and a half feet long and two and a half wide, making it impossible for a man to lie down. Addison wrote:

'In this miserable cell were confined the refractory and disobedient brethren of the Temple, and those who were enjoined severed penance with solitary confinement. Its dark secrets have long since been buried in the silence of the tomb.'

Herein died Walter le Bacheler, Grand Preceptor of Ireland. His dead body was taken out at dawn and was buried by Brother John de Stoke and Brother Ralph de Barton in the middle of the court between the church and the hall.

The belfry tower has been repaired, altered and rebuilt over the centuries. Whether it was in the same place from the beginning is uncertain, but in 1192 the ringing of the bells was suspended in deference to the obnoxious Geoffrey, Archbishop of York, who was lodging in the Temple.[41] A curious representation of the tower is evident in both of the earliest drawings of the Temple. The first (*ill. 52*) is a 1671 bird's-eye view from the south, showing an octagonal castellated tower which appears to be as high or higher than the Round, with a connecting bridge. The second (*ill. 60*) is William Emmett's stylised south view of the church of *c.*1682 showing a similar tower with connecting walk-way to the clerestory roof. On the north side of the medieval church was a tower known as the 'Bastelle'[42] which could hardly have been this same building. However, though there was little evidence of walls or battlements surrounding the Temple precincts, the Paris Temple certainly had walls and a ditch with a great tower flanked by four smaller ones.

When the building of the church in the New Temple was approaching its completion, the Holy Land was in peril and there seemed to be no successful leader to oppose Saladin. King Baldwin IV sent the Grand Masters of the Temple and the Hospital and also Heraclius, Patriarch of Jerusalem, on a mission to engage the help of Henry II in launching another Crusade. The elderly Master of the Temple, Arnold de Torroge, died in Italy on the way. In due course the others arrived in London where Heraclius consecrated both the Round Church in the Temple and the Hospitallers' enlarged church in Clerkenwell.

The consecration of the Temple church took place on 10 February 1185 and it undoubtedly must have been a glorious and memorable occasion. No account of it comes down to us, but the King was in London at this time when:

'He summoned a great Council to meet him in the Hospitallers' House at Clerkenwell, and the high esteem in which he held the Knights of the Temple there can be little doubt that Henry II himself was present with the chief nobles of his Court.[43]

A painting made by Maud Tindal Atkinson (*ill. 24*) in 1912, conjecturing the scene at the Consecration, used to hang in the Round church. Although a fine work, it gave the impression of the building as restored in Victorian times, but

24. *The consecration of the Round church, 1185, as depicted by Maud Tindal Atkinson.*

nevertheless the painting caught something of the twelfth century splendour. The indication of an altar against the assumed east wall of the Round was in error, as it is known that originally there was an extended chancel forming the sanctuary, as described previously.

The ancient Latin inscription recording the dedication of the Round was engraved within the tympanum of the round arch above a small south-west door 'leading into the cloisters' (Addison) or 'next the cloisters' (Williamson). *Master Worsley's Book* (1734) records:

> 'This Church is a plain but neat and beautiful Gothic structure, erected about the year 1185, as appears by an ancient inscription on stone, which stood over one of the doors till being taken down in the year 1695, in order to repair that part of the Church, it was by some accident broken in pieces. The inscription was in the form and character following:

25. Round church Dedication inscription, 1185, originally over the small south-west door.

The Rev. H.G. Woods, Master of the Temple, rendered the above inscription as follows:

> 'On the 10th of February in the year from the Incarnation of our Lord 1185, this Church was consecrated in honour of the Blessed Mary by the Lord Heraclius, by the grace of God Patriarch of the Church of the Holy Resurrection, who to whose yearly visiting it granted an Indulgence of sixty days off the penance enjoined upon them.'

Mrs Esdaile[44] relates the fate of the original inscription stone, having examined the four editions of Burton's *Leicestershire* in which there is a description of the Temple church. The first edition (1656) stated: 'Over the door of the Temple Church was this inscription in ancient characters, remaining legible till April 1656, when the cloister was new white and this defaced.' The second edition (1661) says '... till April 1656, since which time the latter part of it defaced.' The third edition (1670) repeats this statement, but the fourth (1674) says '... till April 1656, but soon after defaced... which inscription was again by order restored in May 1671, and within a few days defaced.' Mrs Esdaile continues,

> 'It is clear that during the Commonwealth some Puritan or other noticed the allusion to the virgin, and to the Indulgence offered to pilgrims, and promptly erased the latter part of the inscription. It was restored in the less controversial days of 1671, but a second time as promptly defaced; no wonder that, when it was destroyed by accident in 1695, it was, as we are told, difficult to read.'

A final puzzle: Why was the original inscription placed over the small south-west door and not over the principal doorway? The former was situated in the second bay south from the West door and one wonders why there should have been a second doorway so near the principal entrance, although possibly it was more convenient and privy to the Knights, the main door being used for processions or other ceremonies.

King Henry resisted the Patriarch's offer of the crown of Jerusalem and also his plea for a new Crusade to the Holy Land. He had already sent a large amount of money to the Orders in trust for the intended English Crusade, but he told Heraclius, whom he accompanied to Dover, that his own sons would rise against him in his absence. The Patriarch retorted: 'No wonder, for of the Devil they come and to the Devil they shall go!' and re-embarked for Palestine in disgust, only to experience the fall of Jerusalem two years later.

To have the Patriarch's name for ever over the door of the Round church is perhaps unfortunate. Fuller says that he was 'for his handsomenesse' made Patriarch of Jerusalem and he caused great scandal by his conduct. Edith Simon says that:

'Heraclius was good-looking and little else, unless one counts his amatory prowess. For he owed his position to the favour of the King's mother, and was famous for his harem, headed by the beautiful wife of an Italian merchant, whom men dubbed Madame la Patriarchesse. The appointment of Heraclius made a mockery of the holy office to which he had been elevated'[45]

It had been thought that the magnificent Purbeck marble effigy of a bishop (*ill. 26*), which is set in a recess in the south wall of the present chancel, represented the Patriarch, but now it seems unlikely. Mrs Esdaile made a strong case for Heraclius having been buried in the church, but this was in error as there is not the slightest evidence that his body was brought back to London.[46] In the Holy City he 'lived viciously and died obscurely', possibly in the terrible Siege of Acre in 1191. Henry died in 1189. 'To the last he maintained cordial relations with the Order, and the first bequest in his will (dated Waltham 1182) was a legacy of 5000 marks in silver to the Knights of the Temple.'[47]

Regarding the effigies (*ill. 27*) these are of later date than the consecration of the Round and, since laid there, have been repositioned more than once. They were fully described, with photographs, in the RCHM Vol. IV, *The City* (1929), but no attempt was made to attribute them or to explain the cross-legged effigies. This may or may not indicate that they had been on a crusade. This appears to be unique in Britain. The fact that none have beards suggests they were not Knight Templars but only associates. The single effigy in the south aisle was bought from Yorkshire by Sargeant Belwood in about 1682. The effigy, thought to be of Roche Abbey stone, represents a young warrior, bareheaded with long curly hair, and displays an armoured shield of the Ros family.

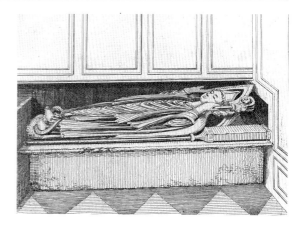

26. *The monument of a bishop under the south-east window in the Temple church. From J.T. Smith's 'Antiquities of London' (1792).*

In the centre of the round on the south side, three of the effigies represent William Marshal, Earl of Pembroke, and his sons Gilbert and William the younger. These are said to be made in Sussex marble and Reigate stone. The fourth effigy, in chain mail, is in Purbeck marble and unattributed. Three of the four effigies on the north side are in Purbeck marble and are also unattributed. The last, in Sussex marble with a cylindrical flat-topped helmet, was traditionally thought to represent Geoffrey de Mandeville, Earl of Essex, but was proved to be otherwise.[48]

Geoffrey de Mandeville[49] ravaged East Anglia. He was struck by a chance arrow in August 1144 and was dying by the wayside. A passing Knight of the Temple threw over him the garb of the Order that he might at least die with the red cross upon his heart,[50] as it was doubtful if anyone but the Pope could absolve so great a sinner. His unshriven body was carried to the Old Temple where the corpse was enclosed in a lead coffin, which was either left hanging on a tree or thrown into a pit outside the consecrated ground. Twenty years later, owing to the persistence of the Prior of Walden (the priory being a foundation of the Earl), absolution was given by Pope Alexander III on behalf of his son. The Prior hastened to London to claim his patron's remains but the Templars, warned of this approach, removed the coffin and buried it in the

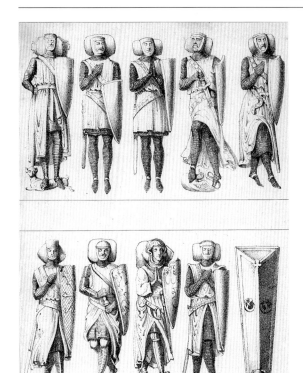

*27. Monumental effigies in the Round church.
From Addison, 'The Temple Church' (1843).*

newly consecrated churchyard in the New Temple. A grant dated 6 April 1163 to Ramsey Abbey in connection with the matter confirms the approximate time of moving the coffin from the Old Temple.

William the Marshal, Earl of Pembroke,[51] was chief regent during the minority of Henry III.

'Stephen Langton, Archbishop of Canterbury, spoke about him with dignity and authority, as one great man may speak to another.......He died in May 1219.....During his illness and approaching death, he called for his faithful companion Jean d'Erlée of Early near Reading. Then he brought out the silken cloths which his lord had asked for. The Marshal gave orders for them to be unfolded so that their full beauty and exquisite work could be seen. Then calling his son and his knights he said: "See here, my lords. I brought

these wrappings back from the Holy Land thirty years ago and have kept them for the use to which they will now be put. I wish them to be wrapped around me when I am placed in the ground. I have kept them for this purpose." Then his son reminded him that they did not yet know where he wished to be buried. Said William, "When I was overseas (outre-mer) I asked permission for my body to lie in the Temple when I died." Then he turned to Jean d'Erlée and told him in a firm voice to take the cloths and see that his body and bier were enveloped in them, adding with his usual prudence, "If it is snowing and the weather is bad, buy some grey woollen material and place it over the silk so that the wraps do not get wet or soiled. Then let them be given to the House of the Brethren for them to dispose of as they like." He sent for Brother Aymeric de St Maur, Master of the Temple, who reached London, but on his arrival he was stricken down by a mortal illness and died almost at once. He had requested to be buried alongside the Marshal "for I loved his company during his life down here.... and wish to lie beside him now; and may God grant that we remain companions in Heaven."'

The news was kept from the Marshal, who was duly buried with his robes. The Archbishop and many knights were present and watch was kept with suitable pomp. Bread and money was distributed to 100 poor people.

A curious story is given by Williamson[512]concerning the dispute between the Irish Bishop of Ferns and the Marshal. The Bishop claimed two manors in his See of which the Earl had taken possession. Restitution having been demanded and refused, he pronounced ex-communication against his adversary which the Earl treated with contempt, considering that the Bishop's claim had no foundation. After the Earl's death, the Bishop appealed to King Henry and journeyed to London where they met in the Round. The bishop addressed the Marshal's tomb, as one living person to another, demanding that if those possessions were not restored to his church he would not absolve him and that 'entangled in your sins you may remain in hell for ever.' The King objected to his behaviour and reproached the vindictive Prelate, at which they departed without the expected absolution. The Bishop then appealed to the late Earl's son, without result. In an outburst he predicted that the Earl of Pembroke's name would be blotted out in a single generation. He then departed sorrowfully. Nor did the events which followed belie the prediction. All five sons died childless and in the prime of life, mostly either by poison, or in warfare or by tournament or by wounds. The great inheritance passed to Matilda, the eldest of five daughters. Her husband, Roger Bigod, Earl of Norfolk, became hereditary Marshal of England.

At a later date, when it was necessary to re-inter the bodies buried in the Round, it was found that the covering of the old Earl was still intact, but nevertheless the body *'putridum et prout videre potuit detestabile.'*

In 1843 Edward Richardson[53] published a report of his restoration of the monumental effigies. He recorded that after removing the various coatings that had built up over the centuries he discovered the remains of rich original colours and gilding. He described in some detail what he found on each effigy. This colouring no longer exists but to give some idea of how the effigies were originally coloured his description of the colouring found on the effigy of the Earl of Pembroke is given below:

'Traces of delicate flesh colour remained on the face. The embattled tower had some red left on it; the mouldings some light green. In the two longitudinal recesses on the sides of the cushion fragments of blue or violet glass remained. Traces of gilding appeared on the ring-mail throughout, excepting those rings which passed over the narrow bands at the coif and wrists, which, with the band at the coif, appeared to have been blue. The buckles, spurs, and squirrel had also been gilt. There were some traces of the surcoat which had upon it considerable remains of crimson lake;

the under side, of light blue. There remained on the edges of the belts some red, and some orange on the plinth near the feet.'

At a meeting on 9 January 1845 at the Society of Antiquaries, Edward Richardson exhibited a series of drawings of several coffins discovered during excavations in the Round of the Temple church. These were being carried out in order to strengthen the foundations of the piers, which had become decayed by time and to address the problem resulting from interring corpses under the pavement of the building. The coffins were found on 18 March 1841, and casts were taken of the elegant ornaments with which some of the coffin lids were decorated. Richardson exhibited a ground plan (*ill. 28*) showing the arrangement and position of the various interments. It was his view that these took place in the early thirteenth century. Coffins both of stone and lead were found, the former being deposited a little beneath the ancient pavement, whilst those which were formed of lead lay about a foot or fifteen inches deeper. The stone coffins had been broken open at some previous time but the leaden ones appeared to have been left uninjured, although surrounded by numerous coffins of later date which were wedged in above and around them. As according to early fashion, the breadth was found to be greater at the head than at the feet and one of the leaden coffins was shaped to the general form of the head and shoulders. Ornamental bands disposed lengthwise and transversely appeared upon them, which seemed to represent the cross embroidered upon the pall. The dimensions were in length from six feet six inches to six feet ten inches. Of the skeletons inside one was six feet four inches and another six feet two inches. It is thought that most of the knights were tall, if only because they were ideally suitable for battle. Two of these leaden coffins were enclosed in small graves formed with masonry, and an interment was found on the north side in a grave formed in the solid rubble foundation. The bones and fragments of coarse cloth which remained were temporarily stored, but they soon fell to dust. Eight inter-

28. *Plan of the Round showing positions of the monumental effigies and ancient coffins found in 1841. From ''The Ancient Stone and Leaden Coffins etc ... lately discovered in the Temple Church' by Edward Richardson (1845).*

29. A stone coffin discovered in the Round, 1841. (Source as for ill. 28)

ments were found arranged in a line from north to south a little eastward of the centre of the Round church, and several other coffins were also brought to light in and adjacent to the porch. On examination it was disappointing not to find any relation between the coffins and the effigies. The remains of the bishop, whose effigy is placed at the south-eastern angle of the church, were found wrapped in a sheet of lead, placed within a cist of Purbeck marble, as described by Mr Jekyll in 1811. The elegant bands of trailing or foliated design which ornamented the leaden coffins were formed during the operation of casting the sheets of metal, and appeared to be of the style prevalent during the reign of Henry III (*ill. 30*). The stone coffins were possibly from an earlier date (*ill. 29*).

30. A lead coffin discovered in the Round, 1841. (Source as for ill. 28)

NOTES TO CHAPTER TWO

1   Lees, B.A., ed., *Records of the Templars in England in the twelfth century* (1935) (Map); Barber, M.C., *The New Knighthood, A History of the Order of the Temple* (1994) (Map); Gooder, E., *Temple Balsall, The Warwickshire Preceptory of the Templars* (1995) lists Templar preceptories in the British Isles, 144.

2   Stow, John, *Survey of London* (1598).

3   'A Plan made by Mr Zephanian King, kindly lent to me by Mr Walter Spiers'. A paper read by W.H. St John Hope, 21 May 1908, in *Archaeologia*, Vol. LXI. See also William Kent, *An Encylopaedia of London*, 640 (1937).

4   Baylis, T.H., *The Temple Church* (2nd edn, 1895). He wrote that some of the foundations were still visible, but he was probably referring to the 1875 discoveries. St John Hope (*op. cit.*) said that 'part of the foundations of the great church at Clerkenwell was uncovered in 1900 and may still be seen'.

5   King, E.J., *The Knights of St John in England* (1924).

6   King (*op. cit.*), *Plan of the Precincts of the Priory of St John, Clerkenwell*, by H.W. Fincham.

7   Round, J.H., 'The foundation of the Priories of St Mary and of St John, Clerkenwell' in *Archaeologia*, Vol. LVI, 223 (1899).

8   Godfrey, W.H., *A History of Architecture in and around London*, 27 (1962); Roth, Daniel, 'Norman Survivals in London' in *RIBA Journal*, 872 (1935).

9   Clapham, A.W., *English Romanesque Architecture after the Conquest* (1934).

10   Hope (*op. cit.*), 'The Round Church at Temple Bruer, Lincolnshire', 177 (1908).

11   Clapham (*op. cit.*), 'The Church of St Clement, West Thurrock', in *Trans. of the Essex Arch. Soc.* Vol. XIII 53-60 (1913).

12   Hope (*op. cit.*), 'St Mary Magdelene, Ludlow Castle', Vol. LXI, 273. Illustrated in Baylis (*op. cit.*) 118.

13   Plans of proposed new parish church and remains of a round church, Orphir, Orkney (1899-1901).

14   Gooder (*op. cit.*), 71.

15   Britton, J., *Architectural Antiquities of Great Britain*, Vol. I, 52 (1835); Dickinson, P., *The Round Church at Little Maplestead, History and Description* (1967, 4th edn).

16   Britton (*op. cit.*), *St Sepulchre, Cambridge*, 43; Ruston, M., *Holy Sepulchre Church, Cambridge* (Pitkin Pictorial).

17   Britton (*op. cit.*) 45.

18   Britton (*op. cit.*) 45, *St Sepulchre, Northampton*; Sarjeantson, R.M., *Church of the Holy Sepulchre, Northampton* (n.d.).

19   Lees (*op. cit.*), Lincoln Cathedral charters yielded an early transcript of the deeds of sale to the Bishop of Lincoln of the Old Temple in Holborn; Williams, J.B., *The Temple, London*, 8n2 (1924, 2nd edn): 'The King's confirmation of the sale to the Bishop is undated but was witnessed by Thomas Becket as Chancellor. He held that office from 1155 till August 1162. The Sale included '*domos que fuerunt fratrum templi in London. In parrochia Sancti Andree de holeburn cum capella et gardiniis et omnibus earum pertinentiis*' (Cotton MS). The See of Lincoln held the Old Temple till the reign of Edward VI, when it passed to John Dudley, Earl of Warwick and later Duke of Northumberland, who sold it to L.C. Wriothesley, Earl of Southampton.

20   Dugdale, W., *Origines Jurisdiciales*, 144 (1680, 3rd edn).

21   Stow (*op. cit.*).

22   Godfrey, W.H., 'Recent Discoveries at the Temple' in *Archaeologia*, Vol. XCV (1953). Plan by M.B. Honeybourne at 138.

23   Williamson, J. Bruce, *The History of the Temple, London* (1924, 3rd edn) 9.

24   Williamson (*op. cit.*), 10 n1, n2, n3.

25   Williamson (*op. cit.*), 8 n5

26   Britton (*op. cit.*) 49.

27   Archer, J. Wykeham, watercolour painter, etcher, engraver and antiquary. Commissioned by Mr W. Twopenny, a Temple Bencher, to make many pictures of old London. See Portfolio IX, BM Print Room for illustrations of the Temple done 1860-61.

28   *The Ecclesiologist*, June 1863: the northern half of the aisle walls 'has merely repointed the original rubble of the remaining ... in concert with our committee.'

29   William Emmett fecit (*c.*1682).

30   Stow (*op. cit.*).

31   Frederick Pollock, Treasurer of the Middle Temple in 1839, 'carted away' the Round Church marble which was replaced for the restoration of 1842. The marble replaced for the restoration of 1954-58 was buried in the basement of bombed Lamb Building which was not rebuilt and is now paved over.

32   Observations by Treleven Haysom of St Aldhelm's Head Quarry, Dorset, where much of the Purbeck marble was fashioned for the post-war restoration.

33   In the post-war restoration of the Round, all the columns of the main piers were rebuilt in marble drums.

34   Compare the vaulting plan of the Paris *rotonde*, as Ryan (*op. cit.*) fp36, with that of the Temple Round, London, as Godfrey (*op. cit.*) fp140. Viollet-le-duc shows a central pier at the entrance to the chancel while de Curzon does not.

35   'The Great Western Entrance to the Temple Church', drawn by F. Nash, engraved by J. Basiere for the Society of Antiquaries (1818).

36   Godfrey (*op. cit.*) 138, from a plan by M.B. Honeybourne (1951).

37   Addison, C., *The Temple Church* 47 (1843).

38   Godfrey (*op. cit.*).

39   Godfrey (*op. cit.*), and Williamson (*op. cit.*) 30

40   Williamson (*op. cit.*) 19.

41   Baylis (*op. cit*) 4.

42   *Master Worsley's Book*, ed. Ingpen, A.R., (1910).

43   Williamson (*op. cit.*) 11.

44   Esdaile, Mrs Arundell, *Temple Church Monuments* 6 (1933).

45   Simon, Edith, *The Piebald Standard* 119 (1959).

46   Some authorities asserted that the effigy was that of Silvester de Everdon, Bishop of Carlisle, killed in 1255 by falling from a horse while in London.

47   Williamson (*op. cit.*) 18.

48   Nichols, J.G., 'The Effigy attributed to Geoffrey de Mandeville and the Other Effigies in the Temple Church', in *Herald and Genealogist* (1866).

49   Round, J.H., *Geoffrey de Mandeville - A Study of Anarchy* (1892).

50   But the red cross is said not to have been assumed by the Order until the time of Pope Eugene (1145).

51   Crosland, Jessie, *William the Marshal, the Last Great Feudal Baron* (1962).

52   Williamson (*op. cit.*) 23.

53   Richardson, Edward, *The Monumental Effigies of the Temple Church, with an Account of their Restoration in the Year 1842* (1843).

CHAPTER THREE

The Chancel

The Holy Land was in disarray. Jerusalem had fallen and was no longer the headquarters of the Order. The Knights had retreated to Rhodes but Paris and London became more and more important, not least in the realms of politics and banking. During the thirteenth century the wealth of the Order increased enormously and attention was being paid more to the prosperity of their possessions in Europe than in sustaining Palestine. Enthusiasm for the Crusades was waning fast.

The Hospitallers had increased the size of their church in Clerkenwell in 1185. It was high time for the Templars to outshine their rivals when it came to providing more space and splendour for the brethren and their entourage.

Who designed their new handsome chancel? We do not know, but the skilled architect was no doubt in touch with other master-masons who, in the new century, were building or rebuilding many cathedrals and monasteries, both in England and on the Continent, in the new Gothic style. There was constant exchange of trade, finance and ideas between the Temples in London and Paris.

The concept of the new building was again unusual (*ill. 31*). This was for an aisled chancel where the side aisles would be at the same height as the lofty central one, thus forming a 'hall church'. This type was very suitable for the gathering of the Knights and was a special feature of German Gothic, more especially in the north of that country. St Elizabeth, Marburg, is typical, but the nave there is half again higher than the Temple vault. The only English cathedral built in part in a 'hall' manner may be seen

in the Bristol choir. The large church of St Mary, Warwick, was similarly rebuilt as a 'hall'[1] but not until 1694. However, there were some smaller English churches with aisles of equal height as in the enlarged chancel of St Sepulchre, Cambridge but this was not stone vaulted.

The new Temple chancel was to be the same width as the diameter of the Round, about 60ft, and 90ft long (*ill. 32*). There would be five bays, all stone vaulted, supported by eight free-standing piers and substantial external buttresses to take the thrusts of the vaults. The walls between would be pierced with triplets of lancet windows, giving abundant light to the interior (*ill. 33*).

On the south side of the Round there stood a two-storey building, later known as St Ann's Chapel, sadly demolished in 1826. Before dis-

31. The chancel, cross-section looking east. From R.W. Billings, 'Account of the Temple Church' (1838)

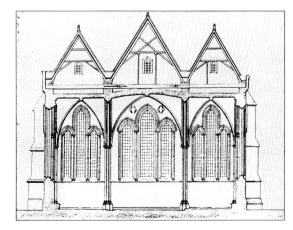

39

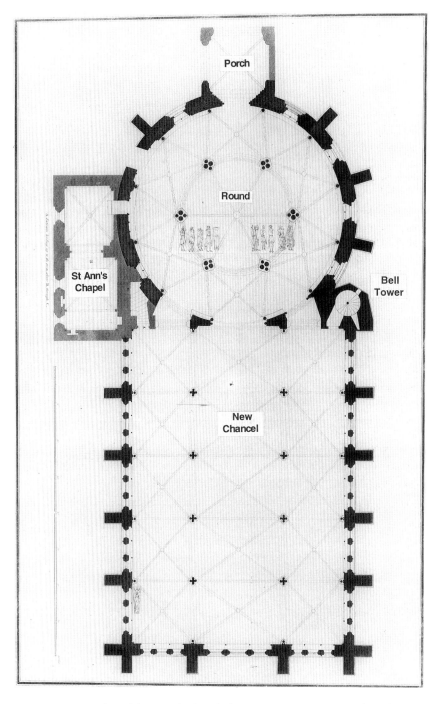

Porch

Round

St Ann's
Chapel

Bell
Tower

New
Chancel

32. Plan of the Temple church, from Vestusta Monumenta (1835).
Drawn by F. Nash, 1818.

*33. The chancel, triple lancets and vault.
Drawn by R.W. Billings, 1838.*

noticed was the crypt: the latter has a doorway at the West end, and is lighted by elegant single lancet windows, with slender pillars on the South and East sides; and the walls of the entire edifice, which are as substantial as those of the Norman Church, have double buttresses at the angles, and one at the division of the room on the South side, rising to the parapet, which terminated at the level of the triple windows of the Church, the height from the pavement being about thirty feet.

The upper or principal room was evidently built for a Chapel. It had elegant triple windows at the altar end; composed of arches richly moulded, and slender pillars of Purbeck marble detached from the walls, but these have been sadly mutilated for the accommodation of sash windows. In the East and South walls are trefoil piscinas, and in the North wall is a similar recess, with a closet underneath. The pillars supporting the groins of the roof are slender, and very short; having circular capitals and bases, exhibiting a great variety of beautifully carved mouldings.

The front or South wall appears to have been excessively mutilated at the time this ancient building was converted into private dwellings, but the groins and vaulting were not at all dilapidated; the style of the ribs correspond with those underneath, but they are more slenderly formed, and rise to a point considerably higher; but their intersections are without carved bases. The most Eastern of the three divisions is the widest, but the groins spring from the four corners, which is not the case with the undercroft, where the groined spaces are equally proportioned. Among the rubbish which was dispersed on the pavement beneath the ruins, several carved stones were to be seen, one of which deserves notice: it was a well-sculptured Norman capital, resembling those of the windows in the side aisles of the Round church.'

cussing its age, it is as well to give verbatim the contemporary and valuable account of the remains of the chapel as given in the *Gentleman's Magazine* in 1824, when all the buildings on the south side of the church were being removed:

'By the style of its architecture we may suggest its date to be coeval with that of the inner Church. In the wall of the round church is a small doorway leading to a double apartment forty feet long and fifteen feet wide, groined with cross ribs only, in the plain and elegant manner common to the period. This room is now occupied by books and papers, and it will not, it is hoped, share the fate of the superstructure, which is now more than half demolished, and to which the room just

A fine watercolour drawing by John Buckler (*ill. 81*) of 1826[2] depicts the remains of the chapel, which closely resembles the description in the

Magazine. It shows the west end pointed doorway having several orders to the arch. A few steps within led down to the basement in which five steps on the north side led up to the small door into the Round. An indication of this later blocked doorway, before its disappearance, may be observed in the 1809 illustration by Pugin & Rowlandson (*ill. 80*). Another view of the chapel from the east is a drawing (*ill. 34*) by an unknown amateur[3] taken at the time of the demolition of the buildings which masked it. John Britton in 1807 also described the chapel as having an arched ceiling with large ribs, and in the east end four square niches, probably piscinas. The lower part of the basement below the present court is still accessible from the modern south porch.

As to the date of the chapel, it has been suggested as *c.*1220. Godfrey in 1953[4] said he had no reason to quarrel with this date and therefore he thought that the chapel was constructed to replace the earlier 'treasury' before this was abandoned. This seems reasonable, except there is a puzzle. In the upper storey there was a north doorway, visible in Buckler's painting, which led to a staircase of fourteen steps descending into

the new chancel of 1240. By 1842 it had been blocked up. The plan in *Vetusta Monumenta*, drawn in 1818 (*ill. 32*), shows the staircase marked 'A' leading up to the room 'B' through 'C' (the upper doorway). There is no other stair descending into the basement. Moreover, the vaulted ceiling shows three divisions in the upper chapel depicted by Buckler as against the unrelated two

35. Remains of the basement of St Ann's Chapel, 1862, by J. Wykeham Archer. (Source as ill. 34)

34. Demolition of the remains of St Ann's Chapel and north end of the cloisters, 1826, by an unknown artist. (Crace Collection, British Museum)

equal divisions below shown in the plan. The basement pillars which still exist and are seen in Wykeham Archer's drawing *(ill. 35)* appear to be earlier in design than those in the building above shown by Buckler. The conclusion is that the basement was built earlier than the upper chapel, the latter being coeval with the chancel of 1240 or even later.

It is possible that the old 'treasury' was being used as a workshop for the construction of the new chancel, as the plastered south wall still shows geometrical circles and lines, perhaps as guides in setting out the new vaulting.

William Clarkson's essay on Masonic influences in the Temple church was included in R.W. Billings *The Temple Church* in 1838. He wrote of St Ann's Chapel:

> 'We infer therefore that it was in these chambers that the novice was prepared for his acceptance as a brother by the Master... and that it was here also and, as we suspect, in subterranean galleries connected with these chambers, that the initiatory trials, and proof of the aspirant were undergone and applied.'

No trace of these supposed underground vaults, apart from the 'treasury' building, supports Clarkson's theories. But the upper storey of St Ann's Chapel appears to have had access only by the narrow staircase of fourteen steps from the new chancel, indicating that it was a private place, and perhaps Clarkson's ideas took place here.

St Ann's Chapel was also said to have been a resort for barren women where they prayed to be 'joyful mothers of children' (Psalm 113).[5] However, the dedication must have been later as St Ann, mother of the Virgin, was not venerated until the fourteenth century. There is in fact slender evidence for the dedication to St Ann, and there is only one entry in the Registers with this reference, being a burial in 1664 'in the Round Walk near St Ann's Chapel door.' Addison relates that it was in this chapel that the papal legate and the English bishops frequently had conferences respecting the affairs of the English clergy. Here in 1282, Almeric de Montforte, the Pope's chaplain, who had been imprisoned by Edward I, was set at liberty at the instance of the Roman pontiff in the presence of the Archbishop of Canterbury and bishops of London, Lincoln, Bath, Worcester, Norwich and Oxford.[6]

The reconstruction of the greatly enlarged chancel probably began about 1220 following demolition of the original building. Intense activity was taking place in the Isle of Purbeck at this time, and Purbeck marble was all the rage. The building of the new Salisbury cathedral had begun, using this material for the main pillars as used in Lincoln cathedral and in the rebuilding of Westminster Abbey. The marble used for the main pillars of the Temple Round had proved to be excellent, and now orders for the stone were made for building the new chancel. Again, it was shipped up the Channel and probably delivered at Temple Stairs.

The foundations were deep and substantial, as observed in the opening made through the south wall below the new porch (1953). The walls were built of stone rubble and probably finished externally with Kentish ragstone and plastered similarly to the Round. The stone buttresses were particularly solid. The marble pillars stood partly on the foundations of the former building, but two on the south side oversailed the former treasury by six inches. The eight main pillars were surprisingly slender, being built up in successive drums; the section shows a central circle with four smaller ones forming a single piece of stone. The bases were tall and substantially wider, and the caps simply moulded without decoration. The finish to the walls internally was in Caen stone. Supports against the walls, in line with the buttresses, consisted of attached shafts, two in Caen stone and one forward of the others in marble. On the north and south sides a stone bench, as in the Round, was no doubt appreciated by the weaker brethren, for there would have been few fixed stalls if any *(ill. 33)*.

It is not known whether there were any other doors, apart from the entrance to the triforium stair, but the present vestry door in the northeast corner may mark an original entry. Indeed, in an Inventory of 1307 made at the suppression of the Order, the valuable contents in the building were considerable so the vestry itself was probably large and attached to the chancel. Godfrey suggested that it was also the 'treasury'.

At the base of the window openings a continuous sill of Purbeck marble continued right round the building, and the window arches were supported by slender marble shafts standing forward of the stone mullions. On the north and south towards the altars there were cusped niches, and on the south side a handsome double marble piscina (*ill. 36*). The present height of these openings indicates original rising steps forming a higher pavement level in the eastern bay. It is known from the Inventory that there were also

36. The chancel, south side. The Purbeck marble piscina damaged by fire in 1941 with the columns restored. (Photo by Robert Dark)

two side altars to St John and St Nicholas.[7]

There are also two double recesses in the east wall of the chancel behind the present altar and screen (*ill. 107*). When these were investigated in the late 1920s by the Council for the Care of Churches (C.C.C.) and the Ministry of Works it was discovered that their original depth was 2ft. There were smaller rebates at the front of these which could have housed the tenons and framework of wooden doors. Bolt holes were also found showing that the doors swung towards the middle. The conclusion was that these recesses were aumbries used to store sacred vessels and were part of the thirteenth-century chancel. The experts' view was that the original altar was some way forward of the existing one, probably between the first two central free-standing columns, and that it had a wooden altar screen immediately behind it. The space between this and the eastern wall of the chancel could have been a sacristy, closed off with doors similar to the arrangement at Westminster Abbey.

The erection of the stone vaults must have been a delicate task. This would have been carried out with templates and the use of temporary timber arches while the intersecting stone ribs were constructed; the infill spandrels between were of chalk which was a useful material as it was light in weight and could be carved easily. Two thick walls (*ill. 37*) were built above the springers over the main pillars, each running the full length from east to west, on which were constructed the steep roofs. Addison commented in 1843:

> 'The three great slanting timber roofs present to the beholder a vast mass of woodwork composed of oak and chestnut beautifully put together and framed in three compartments with coupled rafters. It was found in a very sound and perfect state.... We cannot but be struck with surprise and admiration at the skill and talents of the ancient builders, when we reflect that the vast mass of timber and stone rests upon the eight slender marble columns below.'

The covering of the roofs was probably in lead,

*37. The chancel, vaulting from above, after the fire of 1941 and before the erection of the temporary roof.
(Photo by David Lewer)*

with lead gutters and out-shots from the parapets and valleys. Each stone gable was crowned with a cross.

There remained the marriage of the chancel with the Round, not an easy matter. The original central opening between the two was enlarged and the bay in the Round on either side was partly opened to connect with the chancel side aisles. This is clearly visible in the Round today which shows the aisle arcades on either side severed, each leaving only one and a half wall arches. Addison was again overwhelmed when he saw the effect of the removal of the screen in 1843.

'The entrance from the Round to the oblong portion of the Temple Church is formed by three lofty pointed arches which open upon the Choir. The mouldings of these arches possess great beauty and elegance, and the central arch, which forms the grand entrance to the choir, is supported upon magnificent Purbeck marble columns. The lofty and deeply-recessed arches, with their rich mould-

ings, marble columns and capitals and graceful decorations tastefully harmonise with the other portions of the sacred edifice, and show with what consummate skill and correct taste [!] the square church was engrafted upon the circular, so as to combine the whole into one splendid building.'

38. Corbel head at the junction of the Round and chancel, south side. (Drawn by David Lewer)

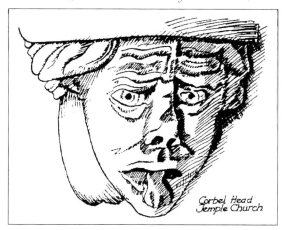

Corbel Head
Temple Church

45

As this was the last stonework to be completed in forming the junction of the two parts of the church, it can be seen that there is more decoration in detail, particularly in the undercut foliage carved at the responds to the side arches and the angel heads on either side. On the south side is a corbel head of a seraph (*ill. 91*), reputedly original, and still bearing traces of colour. High up on either side there are two menacing male heads, also probably original (*ill. 38*).

Finally there would have been the decoration. In 1840 on the removal of the whitewash, it was discovered that the vaulted ceilings had been highly coloured. These were recorded by Richardson[8] in 1845. The ceiling of the vaulting in the chancel was decorated with 'colours and metallic plating in, straight-sided oblongs with semi-circular heads'. Other coloured blocks were found when the closed up openings of the triforium were unblocked. The inner faces of the stonework used to fill up these openings had rich bands of colour, metallic plating and gilding. Colours included yellow, red, blue and lake. Also white, dark grey and metallic plating like silver. None of them had figural subjects. Perhaps the walls were decorated too or covered with tapestry. The floor, certainly in the chancel, was paved with medieval coloured tiles. Some of these were found during restoration work in the 1840s in the chancel between the two south-eastern columns under old pewing. None were found in the Round. A large number were plain, but others were patterned – the designs on some of these are shown in *ill. 39*. They varied in thickness from three-quarters of an inch to one inch and a quarter. and in overall size. From their designs and finish it was clear that they were manufactured at different periods, the earliest probably coeval with the date of the new chancel. These early tiles were of coarse red clay with designs filled in with a very thin layer of white or pipe clay. The transparent vitrification of the

39. Original encaustic floor tiles in the chancel. From E. Richardson, ''The Ancient Stone and Leaden Coffins, Encaustic Tiles etc., ... in the Temple Church (1845).

lead glaze changing the surface to a rich chocolate or deep red, and the white pattern to a bright orange. The glazing itself was of a green colouring as the result of some admixture. Amongst the earliest tiles illustrated were those of a knight and a grotesque bird or possibly a griffon. These tiles are similar to those in the chapter house at Westminster Abbey. Some of the unearthed tiles were believed to have been loose in the triforium before the fire of 1941. Two original tiles are in the Museum of London (one of a knight and one of a dragon) and one in the British Museum (of a grotesque bird).

The many windows were without doubt glazed and possibly were coloured too, seeing that the new chancel was to be the last word in the Templars' achievement. But there have been no discoveries of the remains of original stained glass. If there was indeed a multiplicity of it in these thirteen triple windows, the effect of the whole must have been sumptuous (*ill. 40*).

The grand consecration of the chancel took place on Ascension Day, 24 May 1240. Matthew Paris, who was probably present, gave the following account of the ceremony:

'About the same time [1240] was consecrated the noble church of the New Temple at London, an edifice worthy to be seen, in the presence of the King and much of the nobility of the kingdom who... after the solemnities of the consecration had been completed, royally feasted at a most magnificent banquet, prepared at the expense of the Hospitallers.'[9]

So the two Orders were not always at loggerheads!

It was during the reign of Henry III that the Templars reached the height of their power and privileges in England. Henry was now twenty and married to his young wife, Alianore of Provence. The Master of the Temple, Robert de Sanford, had had the honour, with the Bishops of Ely and Hereford, of conveying the bride to England at the close of 1235.[10] Shortly after this, Henry had chosen the Temple church as his future place of burial, and later his Queen made the same election. Probably for this reason, Henry, in 1237, endowed a perpetual payment to the Master and Brethren of the Temple of £8

40. The Temple church, long section, from Vetusta Monumenta (1835). Drawn by F. Nash, 1818.

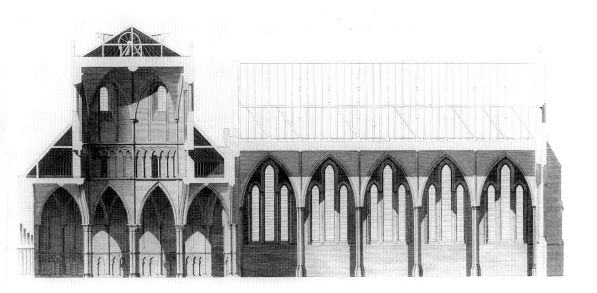

sterling per annum and three chaplains to celebrate there three daily masses 'one for us, one for all Christian People and one for the faithful departed.'[11] Unfortunately for the fame of the Temple church, Henry later changed his mind, preferring to be buried in the more splendid church he was erecting over the shrine of the Confessor at Westminster, which was consecrated in 1245. However, William Plantagenet, their fifth son who died in infancy, is believed to have been buried in the Temple church in about 1256, possibly at the feet of the unknown bishop whose fine Purbeck marble effigy lies on the south side of the chancel. But according to Weever, the marble coffin-lid, now on the north aisle of the Round, may have been the tomb of the young prince.

Another example of Henry's favour of the Temple is a royal presentation of plate for the church. There was an order to his Treasurer, dated 6 December 1239, to purchase and deliver to the Master of the Temple a silver gilt ciborium.[12]

The extended chancel in 1240 resulted in the removal of the High Altar eastwards, and it seems that there was some re-interment. The position of the effigies, still remaining in the Round, has changed several times and it is not known where they originally stood over their respective tombs.

The New Temple was indeed an important centre. When visits were paid there by the Archbishops of Cologne and Embrun in 1235 and 1243 respectively, the Knights received royal gifts of four hogsheads of wine on each occasion for the refreshment of the honoured visitors.[13]

In 1260 Simon de Montfort, and other barons in revolt against the King's misgovernment, assembled the Parliament in the New Temple to remedy the matter. It was during this dispute in 1263 that Prince Edward, with the royal treasury starved of funds, took the law into his own hands. With a band of supporters he went to the Temple and tricked his way into the Treasury on the pretext of wishing to see his mother's, the Queen's, jewels which were deposited there. Once inside he and his accomplices forced open various chests containing money deposited by others and stole £1,000. In 1270 he left the country to join a Crusade and on the King's death in 1272

another national council was held at the Temple to make provision for government until Edward I would return. He was on his way to Sicily when he received the letter sent from the New Temple informing him of the death of his father and his own succession to the throne.[14] Even at the close of his reign in 1307, despite the approaching suppression of the Templars, the Master of the Temple was still regularly summoned to Parliament or other Councils, and gifts continued to be showered on the Order.

Sir George Buc, writing of the Templars in the reign of James I, described their

'goodly large and magnificent house they had reared for themselves by the bank of the Thames and in this their house those Templars lived and continued in great honour and opulency for the space of one hundred years. For they had many fair Lordships and castles and goodly lands and seignories belonging unto them and their Order in many parts of England, and the Master of this Order was a Baron of the Kingdom.'[15]

NOTES TO CHAPTER THREE

[1] See illustrations of 'hall' churches in Sir Banister Fletcher, *A History of Architecture*, 346, 353, 530. St Mary, Warwick (1694), a strange swan-song of Perpendicular Gothic.

[2] John Buckler, watercolour painting of the chapel of St Ann before its demolition, 1826. The original drawing was presented to the two Societies of the Temple by the Revd W.H. Draper, MA., Master of the Temple 1920-30.

[3] The Cloisters and demolition of St Ann's Chapel and adjacent buildings *c*.1826. Artist unknown. (BM Crace Coll. P.XIX, no. 68).

[4] Godfrey, W.H., 'Recent Discoveries at the Temple', Society of Antiquaries, 1953. Details of building under south aisle, decoration on North Wall.

[5] Anecdotes and Traditions published by the Camden Society, No. Clxxxi, 110 (Addison 81).

[6] *Acta fuerunt haec in capella juxta ecclesiam, apud Novum Templum London ex parte Australi ipsius ecclesiae sita, coram reverendis patribus domino archiepiscopo et episcopis...* etc. 1282 (Addison 81).

[7] Contents of these two side altars given in Baylis, T.H. *The Temple Church and Chapel of St Ann* etc 1900), App. F, 143.

[8] Richardson E., *(op. cit.)*.

[9-14] Williamson, J.B., The History of the Temple, London (1924, 3rd edn)

[15] Williamson *(op. cit)* 43.

CHAPTER FOUR

Suppression

The blow fell suddenly on 12 October 1307. Without warning the Knights of the Temple were doomed.

The story of the final phase in the history of the Order is vividly told by Campbell, Simon, Gooder and Barber.[1] The unscrupulous and ambitious Philip IV of France (Philip le Bel) was determined to rid Christendom of the Templars as an excuse to lay his hands on their vast property. Yet, says Fuller,[2]

> 'We may believe King Philip would never have took away their lives if he might have took their lands without putting them to death: but the mischief was he could not get the honey unless he burnt the bees.'

That night every Templar in France was arrested, including the Grand Master Jacques de Molay. Yet there was no struggle. This is indeed a mystery and many books have been written on the subject. The case against Philip is well and fairly stated by Campbell and the other writers. With great cunning the King amassed information from all quarters, much of it false and fabricated by himself yet with kernels of truth, witnessing to the disreputable conduct of a few members of the Order. This he placed before the Pope, Clement V, who had recently won the tiara with his support and who dared not resist the King's will.

The French Templars were thrown into prison and their property seized against the coming trials. Then began a long period of inquisition. Charges of worshipping idols, including a cat, denying Christ, spitting upon the Cross at initiation, and extreme corruption were proclaimed against them. Hundreds confessed under torture and many died under interrogation or at the stake.

In England the Templars were treated much less severely and the new king, Edward II, clearly did not believe in their guilt. One of the accusations made against the Templars was that of sodomy but homosexuality was tolerated in the Middle Ages, and there was 'No stigma of effeminacy attached to practices which numbered many adherents among doughty Crusaders and distinguished princes such as (probably) Coeur de Lion and Edward II.'[3] Nevertheless, under pressure from Philip through the Pope, the King yielded and issued writs to the Sheriffs to arrest the Templars and seize their property. One might imagine the consternation and even panic when the news broke.

Of the Brothers living in the New Temple, the headquarters of the Order in Britain, were Sir William de la More, Grand Master, Sir Michael de Baskevile, Preceptor, John de Stoke, Treasurer, and twelve other brethren. There is a hint that William may have had prior warning from the King of events to come, for on 15 December he had granted William licence to empower two attorneys, Michael de Baskevile and Peter de Oteringham, another Brother at the New Temple, to act for the Master 'in divers matters touching that Order.'[4]

The Master was arrested at Temple Ewell near Dover with a French knight, the Preceptor of Auvergne, who may have come to warn him of the danger. Also with them were the Preceptor of Ewell, Ralph de Barton being the Templars' chaplain, Thomas de Ludham, a young man who had only been received eleven days before and Robert de Sautre of the New Temple, together with two clerks, five esquires and four of the Master's domestic servants. They were taken to Canterbury Castle where they remained for six weeks.

> 'All the Templars were allowed to take their beds and essential gear into custody; the beds were in fact just a sack to put straw in, and the bedding one linen sheet, a light woollen blanket and a large heavy blanket. But William de la More was also allowed to take the contents of his wardrobe which contained comparatively luxurious items, such as supertunics of fur and a gold bracelet.'

The Brothers were treated with more leniency than in France, as Edward was still hoping that no savage treatment would be necessary. The Master was set free so that he could prepare the defence of the Order.

> 'Michael de Baskevile was allowed his gear and one of his two horses, obviously so that he could move about as the Master's attorney. Most of the preceptors had two valuable palfreys and in all other cases these were confiscated and sold off.'[5]

Meanwhile in London, Edward had seized the New Temple for the Crown, though it was uncertain whether it would be restored to the accused owners after the outcome of the trial. Therefore during January to November 1308, the royal officers were instructed to make comprehensive inventories of the Knights' possessions there, and this was done by the Sheriffs of London. Baylis made a full translation of the rolls[6] (ill. 41). It includes particulars of all the rents and tenements formerly owned by the Knights and their property. It gives some idea of the New Temple precinct at that time, mentioning, among other items, the granary containing rye, oats and hay, five horses, thirty pigs and little pigs and fruit from the garden. Lists are given separately under the other buildings: cellar, storehouse, kitchen, stable, brewery, dormitory, Knights'

41. Portion of the Temple roll Inventory, 1307-8. (Exchequer Accounts, no. 24, Templars' Rolls no. 3, M3.)

chambers and the church itself. Extensive details of the contents are given in Appendix Three. Payments include the shoeing of horses, repairing of door locks and raising the timber of a derelict mill from the Fleet river. The wages of the Brothers, who were now held elsewhere, is given. Other expenditure includes the wages of six chaplains celebrating divine service, four clerks serving the above chaplains, a rent collector, four servants of the Brothers, a gardener, a groom and a porter.

In the Inventory, regarding the appearance of the church, the altars to St John and St Nicholas can be assumed to be in the side aisles to the high altar. We are left with the Great Church, the Choir and the Church of the Blessed Mary. The latter must be the Round church, though an altar is mentioned. Perhaps this altar was free-standing in the centre or at the junction of the two parts of the building. The Great Church would then be the oblong chancel, as here was the high altar and also 'two pairs of organs.' The organ would be quite small and no doubt portable.[7] The Choir was probably an enclosed area within the chancel where the choir chanted the Services (ill. 42). It was surely impressive, with the presence of 28 choir copes and four little copes for the choristers and with 22 banners and a variety of coloured vestments. One can imagine the scene a procession with plainsong chanting and the fragrance of incense (ill. 43).

In the Inventories there was no mention of St Ann's Chapel nor of the chapel of St Thomas

42. The Initial Letter from the Templars' Breviary 1233 with music which refers to Thomas à Becket of Canterbury. From M. Melville, 'La Vie des Templiers, Paris' (1951).

Becket, said to be at the south end of the cloisters 'by the Hall door' (*ill. 21*). Indeed, there is no mention of the two Halls themselves. One of these in the vicinity of the present Middle Temple Lane and Pump Court. The other was on the site of the later Inner Temple Hall. The consecrated ground extended from the north churchyard southwards to this Hall, including the church, chapels and cloisters. The Inventory mentions a few crossbows and swords but no spears, battle-axes or armour. The New Temple had by now become more of a bank than a fortress. The Treasury is not mentioned but no doubt any gold or money had already been removed by the King's order. In fact the Temple was heavily in debt, especially to the French Crown.[8]

The daily routine and ritual had now come to a sudden halt and the church may have been shut, at least for the time being. But only the Knights had been arrested and the chaplains, sergeants, servants and domestics were still in need of their wages. Subsistence for the Brothers, as well as for the others, was paid out of the revenues of the preceptories. In view of the long delay until the final trial and sentences, it would seem that the buildings and gardens were being maintained, pending the result of the trial.

Except behind the scenes, little happened for a year until at last on Tuesday 31 October 1309,

43. A knight's funeral procession. From Addison, 'The Temple Church' (1843).

the trial began in London in the chapter house of Holy Trinity[9] before two papal Inquisitors, the Pope's chaplain and the Bishop of London. A few Templars had escaped leaving 38 Brothers present including William de la More. Eighty-seven questions were put to the prisoners and all the charges were denied. Next they were examined individually and the matter dragged on into 1310. The Inquisitors had an idea that Sir Walter le Bacheler had been murdered in the penitential cell at the New Temple. They asked the prisoner John de Stoke, the treasurer:

'How was he buried, had he confessed and received the sacraments, of what sickness had he died? Was he buried in his habit? Why was he buried outside the cemetery?'

51

*44. The burial of Sir Walter le Bacheler who died in the
penitential cell above the staircase.
From Addison, 'The Temple Church' (1843).*

John de Stoke said that he himself and Brother Ralph Burton, Keeper (*custos*) of the New Temple chapel, now in the Tower, carried the body to be buried at dawn. He believed that Sir Walter was in the cell for eight weeks (*ill. 44*). It may have been, he said, that goods had been stolen from the House and whoever was responsible was thereby excommunicated unless he had confessed. This conflicted with an alleged receiving of the sacraments by Sir Walter.

By November 1310 over forty Brothers had been interrogated individually, some more than once, but still without result. Hilbert Blanke, the French Knight, was particularly strong in his defence and never confessed to the charges. Outside witnesses were now sought. Some of the parish priests who were jealous of the Templars' privileges, and others who disliked their haughty arrogance (the French have the expression 'as proud as a Templar'), were quick to make ac-

cusations even if based only on hearsay. A Franciscan witness swore before the Inquisitors that he had heard that a boy had been murdered by the Templars because he had crept by stealth into the Hall to witness proceedings of the assembled brethren at which a member was received. But there were still no confessions. Torture was illegal in England but Edward acquiesced only on Papal order, and torturers had to be imported from France. Some of the prisoners were removed from the Tower and chained separately in four of the City Gates, Newgate, Aldgate, Cripplegate and Ludgate, where they were put on bread and water and shown the instruments of torture.

In the summer of 1311 three Brothers confessed, one of whom was John de Stoke from the New Temple. He said that he had once been questioned by the Grand Master of the Order, Jacques de Molay, and in fear of death denied the Crucifix. He said that sworn obedience to the Order was the custom and he added that homosexual relations were allowed and were not considered a sin amongst Brothers.

Yet, despite all the confessions of corruption, it was the question of the absolution of sins by laymen – the Masters of the Temple – which led to the ultimate downfall of the Knights.

> 'The Brothers admitted, though often in vague and muddled manner, that they thought the Master could so absolve them, and the Master himself freely acknowledged that this could happen; but all were convinced that this was a privilege granted to the Order by the Pope. As far as the Inquisitors were concerned, however, they had convicted themselves out of their own mouths.'[10]

The Inquisitors had at last obtained the evidence to justify the attack upon the Order and were satisfied. Far from being punished for the grave sins to which they had admitted, they were, after public confession, pardoned and reconciled to the Church. After three years imprisonment and with the alternative of freedom or death under torture, it is little wonder that most of the other Templars yielded. After appearing on the steps of St Paul's and other churches to make the prescribed form of confession, they were mostly placed in monasteries of other Orders to do penance, whence many found their way back into the world. But Sir William de la More and the Preceptor of Auvergne stoutly maintained their innocence and their case was referred to the Papal Council at Vienne. However, the Master died shortly after, broken in health, in the Tower of London. The Preceptor was ordered to be bound with double fetters of iron and shut in the vilest dungeon, there to be further interrogated. On this ominous note, observes Campbell, the career of the Order in England ends.

In France it had been a different matter. In Paris 54 Brethren were burnt at the stake under one decree alone. Hundreds confessed under torture and Philip 'the Fair' had nearly won the day. The Order of Knights of the Temple was finally suppressed at the Council of Vienne in 1312, with the Archbishop of York being present. On 18 March 1314 the Grand Master of the Order, Jacques de Molay, who after six years was still a prisoner in Paris, was brought out with three other great dignitaries of the Order onto a scaffold erected in front of Notre Dame, in order to renew their confessions before the eyes of the world. Two of them did so, but the Grand Master said that he was guilty of one thing only, that being his previous confession to the accusations brought against him. Geoffrey de Charnay, Preceptor of Normandy, nobly followed his example. The King was furious and at dusk Jacques de Molay and his brave companion were taken to an island in the Seine and slowly burned to death over small fires of charcoal.

But this was not quite the end of the story. According to tradition, the Grand Master, as he died, summoned the Pope to appear before the Last Tribunal within forty days, and the King likewise within twelve months. Both died at the predicted times, Clement V 'of a foul disease' on 20 April 1314, and Philip the Fair 'of a mysterious malady' at Fontainebleau on 29 November. An even more extraordinary legend grew that de Molay had appointed a Grand Master to succeed him and that the Temple has indeed continued until the present day in unbroken line. Campbell mentions that:

> 'There is an organisation which calls itself the Temple, but the Order founded in Jerusalem died with de Molay. Some historians have claimed the Freemasons as the true successors of the Templars, but their arguments are more ingenious than convincing.'

Campbell concluded:

> 'Had the Temple survived, it might have had a splendid destiny. A strong papal army might perhaps have protected the spiritual power from many misfortunes, might have become a potent instrument for peace. This organisation of soldier monks, powerful in every country in Christendom, free from the dictation of the princes, might have developed into an international police force and saved the world from great tragedies. But it might also have developed into an instrument of oppression in the hands of the Church. The might-have-beens of history are dangerous.'

The guilt or innocence of the Templars must probably for ever remain a mystery. Whatever the truth of the matter, the Spirit had departed and in that way they had passed into history. But fortunately in London their glorious church remained.

NOTES TO CHAPTER FOUR

[1] Campbell, G.A., *The Knights Templars* (1937); Simon, Edith, *The Piebald Standard* (1959); Gooder, Eileen, *Temple Balsall* (1995); Barber, Malcolm, *The New Knighthood* (1994).
[2] Fuller, Thomas, *Historie of the Holy Warre* (1647).
[3] Simon (*op. cit.*) 228, but under the Rule of the Temple, sodomy entitled the loss of the house (expulsion from the Order) and imprisonment in chains – see Curzon (ed.) *La Regle du Temple* (1886).
[4] Gooder (*op. cit.*) 88.
[5] Gooder (*op. cit.*) 89
[6] Baylis, T.H., *The Temple Church etc.* (1895, 2nd edn) Appendix F
[7] See Scholes, Percy, *Oxford Companion to Music* under 'Organ' with illustrations of early organs.
[8] Williamson, J. B., *The History of The Temple, London* (1924, 3rd edn).
[9] Holy Trinity was in the Abbey of the Minories near the Tower of London where the captives from the New Temple had been sent.
[10] Gooder (*op. cit.*) 128.

CHAPTER FIVE

The Lawyers

On suppression of the Knights Templars, their property was granted by the Pope to the Knights Hospitallers who had escaped the fate of their rivals. However, this was nominal as, in England as well as in France, it was mostly seized by the Crown. Edward II first granted the New Temple to Aymer de Valence, Earl of Pembroke, but then he acknowledged the claim of the Earl of Lancaster. Six years later, Lancaster was executed for treason and Aymer de Valence regained the ownership. He died in 1324 and the King then granted the Temple to his favourite, Hugh le Despencer the younger, despite Parliament having decreed that all the Templars' former property was to be assigned to the Prior and Brethren of the Hospital of St John of Jerusalem in England. Hugh le Despencer was executed in 1326 and the King seized the Temple once more. In 1332 William de Langeford, clerk or chaplain to the Prior of St John, leased the Temple from the King but was found to be in unlawful possession of the consecrated places annexed to the church. Following a complaint from the Prior and an Inquisition in 1337, he was successful in acquiring these places too. The King finally delivered the whole of the manor to the Prior and Brethren but not until the Prior had paid £100 towards the expenses for Edward's war with France. Langeford was given life possession for his good service to the Order in negotiating with the King. He died in 1368.[1]

In 1326 Roger Blom, sometime 'nuncius' (messenger) of the Temple, built thirteen houses on the north part of the cemetery consecrated to the church near the highway, and let them, using the income to maintain lights and other ornaments of the church. From the reports of the 1337 Inquisition, it seems that there were also eight shops in the custody of Langeford, seven being in Fleet Street and one outside Temple Bar. The New Temple also included two Halls, one adjoining the Chapel of St Thomas à Becket, with rooms above, and the other with four rooms and stabling. There was also a room at the outside of the Great Gate, in the custody of Langeford. This suggests that no other buildings besides the shops had been built.

It is about this time that the Lawyers first make their appearance on the scene. The origin of the Societies of the Inner and Middle Temples is shrouded in mystery. This is not helped by the loss of records during the revolt of 1381 (see below). Williamson sums up the matter thus:

> 'All that can safely be said is that seventy years after the suppression of the Order of the Temple by Pope Clement V, Apprentices of the Law were settled in the New Temple and in possession of records which were unhappily destroyed. But when these apprentices first came there, on what terms they came, and from whence they came, no man knows.'

Neither is it known whether the lawyers came to the Temple in two bodies or whether they subsequently split into two societies. They came as tenants of the Order of St John, and there were already two halls in existence, probably the separate refectories of the Templar priests and knights. It is in the use of these halls by the lawyers that we may possibly find the origin of

45. *The crests of the Inner and Middle Temples. The Inner Temple's Pegasus was adopted in 1563. It was suggested that the horse with two wings was developed from the two knights on one horse. The Holy Lamb and Flag on the Cross, the Middle Temple crest, derived from the Templars' seals, one of which consisted of the Cross with the words 'Sigillum Templi'.*

the Inner and Middle Temples, 'the two learned and honourable Societies of this House.' Each developed its own crest (*ill. 45*). The names 'Inner' and 'Middle' seem to refer to their topographical position in relation to the City of London, the property of the Inner Temple being further east than the Middle and thus nearer to the City (see front endpaper). The two Inns have always denied the jurisdiction of the Lord Mayor. In the seventeenth century he was attacked by the students on two occasions, in 1668 and again in 1678, when he attempted to enter the Temple with his sword up. The Temple may be considered an extra-parochial liberty of the City of London, belonging to it geographically but not politically or administratively.[2]

There was also an area known as the Outer Temple, west of the Middle, which had been seized by the Bishop of Exeter and added to the grounds of his house. This later passed to Robert Devereux, Earl of Essex, and is now the site of Essex Street and Devereux Court.

The Hospitallers had reduced the number of chaplains from more than a dozen to eight. In a clerical subsidy roll of 1377 Brother John Bartylby was referred to as 'Master of the Temple', and this seems to be the first appearance of the term 'Master' as applied to the principal priest of the church. He had only four chaplains.

Williamson says:

'As the ancient ritual still continued, the internal appearance of the church may have been much the same as in the days of the Knights Templars, though probably the services were conducted in a humbler fashion than formerly, and lacked the imposing splendour with which the devotion of so rich an Order must have invested them.'[3]

Master Worsley observed:

'Perhaps their first landlords the Knights Hospitallers of St John of Jerusalem, when they left the House to the Students of the Law, left the Church unoccupied, so that they were compelled to devise some means of subsistence for a Clergyman to celebrate divine service, which they did by this method and assigned him a lodging in a Court then near to the South East angle of the Church, which contained part of Lamb Building and part of the Court now called Tanfield Court; and from which it acquired the name of Parson's Court.'[4]

In 1381 the Temple was 'illumined by the baleful fires of insurrection.' It was sacked by Wat Tyler and his mob in the course of the Peasants' Revolt as it was the home of the hated lawyers. All their records, which were kept in the church, were thrown out and burnt.[5] The lawyers were regarded as the oppressors of the people and 'it was marvellous to see how even the most aged and infirm of them scrambled off with the agility of rats and evil spirits.' As well as the damage caused in the Temple church the rebels destroyed the two ancient forges situated on either side of St Dunstan's church in Fleet Street. They had been established by the Templars and were still maintained by the Hospitallers. The Priory of the Hospitallers at Clerkenwell suffered even greater damage when it was set on fire and burned for seven days.

The Prior Robert Hales and the Archbishop of Canterbury were both beheaded.

Notwithstanding the destruction in the Temple, the students of the law were soon back and during the fifteenth century the two Societies were steadily building up their separate but similar traditions. The Temple church became by usage the lawyers' chapel, although until the Reformation the Hospitallers continued to be responsible for maintaining the priests. The lawyers only contributed on eighteen offering days, so that each Fellow paid 18d per annum. Early Masters of the Temple, whose names are recorded, were Sir John Burford who succeeded John Bartylby about 1380, Hugh de Lichfield, William Langham who died in 1437 and was buried in the church, and William May *c*.1448 (*for later Masters see Appendix Two*).

As well as offering legal education, the Temple also became a sort of university for noblemen's sons. Sir John Fortescue, writing in 1468 about the Inns of Court,[6] says 'There they learn to sing and exercise themselves in all kind of harmony', but it is unlikely that these pleasures had any connection with the church, and there are no details of the services which continued during the fifteenth century in the Temple church. A reference to the singing there does appear in a MS, dated not later than 1540. It describes the Middle Temple as follows:

> 'The manner of Divine Service in the Church, and their charges thereto. Item, that they have every day three Masses said; one after the other: and the first Masse doth begin in the mornying at seaven of the Clock, or thereabouts. The Festivall days they have Mattens and Masse solemnly sung; and during the Matyns singing, they have three Masses said.'[7]

The oldest surviving records of the two Inns date from the early years of the sixteenth century. Life as it was then lived in the Temple becomes more clear. An entry (in Latin) in the Inner Temple Records in 1519 reads:

> 'Order for a roll to be made containing the names of the members of the Society, in order that from them may be raised 70s for new organs in the church,[8] for the part of the Inner Temple.'

The mention of a new organ (or organs, as the instrument continued to be described) implies

that it would replace an old organ, and it is probable that there had been such an instrument in the church ever since the days of the Templars. The fact that the two Societies, rather than the Hospitallers, were to raise the money for the organ suggests that the church was now very much the concern of the lawyers, even though it did not as yet belong to them. But it was not long before possession was brought much nearer.

In 1540 the long-delayed blow fell upon the Knights Hospitallers. Their Order was dissolved by Henry VIII for maintaining 'the usurped power of the Pope within this realm,' and their possessions were transferred to the Crown. Yet the Reformation seems to have caused a minimum of upheaval in the Temple itself. The church building was unmolested. The Master, William Ermestede, and his two chaplains who now composed the total establishment of priests, were, under the Act of Parliament, to continue to enjoy their stipends and houses 'without lett or interrupcon, doing their dueties and services there as they have accustomed to doo.' After the demise of the Order of St John, churchwardens were at first appointed annually, one for each Society. The first of these was Master Robert Keilway, appointed in 1542.[9]

The two Societies held the Temple on lease from the Crown, at the same rental (£10 per annum) as before. Fuller quaintly remarks,

> 'the new Templars, defending one Christian from another as the old ones did Christians from Pagans.'

Ermestede weathered the ecclesiastical storms of twenty years with remarkable tenacity. Appointed by the Hospitallers, he had accepted the position secured to him by Henry VIII, accepted the new Book of Common Prayer (1549) under Edward VI but was content to revert to Rome in 1553 under Queen Mary. In her reign the Prior of St John was re-established and regained possession of the Temple for a brief period – with little effect on the two Societies.

The Latin ritual was restored in 1553 and orders were soon made concerning the church services. In April 1554 the Treasurer of the Inner

Temple was required to 'provyde boks for the syngyng in the Choir jointly with the Midel Yn', and in November 1557 both Inns record orders for the assessment of members to provide for the wages of the singing men:

'in the Middle Temple 12d from every Bencher and 4d from other members of the House; and in the Inner Temple 20d from Knights, 12d from Benchers, and 4d at least from every fellow under the Bench, every term.'

On 20 June 1557 orders were made, requiring all fellows of the Inner Temple in commons to come to the church from time to time and hear

'... devyne servyce, Mass Matens and Evensonge &c, as heretofore hath bene used, and to keep eighteen offering daies in the yeare accordyng to the auncyent laudable custome of this House.'[10]

With the accession of Elizabeth and the restoration of the Prayer Book and English liturgy in 1559, the Order of St John finally disappeared, though William Ermestede remained Master of the Temple, turning his final ecclesiastical somersault before his death in the first year of Elizabeth's reign. No provision had been made under the Act of 1540 for Ermestede's successors, and when Richard Alvey M.A. was appointed Master on 13 February 1560, the office was filled by letters patent from the Crown. This practice has continued to the present day. Dugdale wrote that to the Temple church

'there did antiently several Priests belong who had a Hall and lodgings assigned to them, as appears by some testimonials of H7 [Henry VII] time. But since the dissolution of the Hospitallers (temp.H.8) there hath been a Divine, by name of a *Master* or *Custos,* constituted by a King's Letters Patents, who administered the Sacraments, and performed other Divine service therein, without any Institution of Induction, as in other Churches, by the Bishop.'[11]

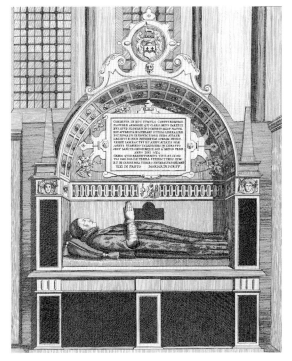

46. *Plowden's monument in the north-east corner of the chancel. Banished to the Triforium in 1842, but returned to the Round in 1933. From J.T. Smith, 'Antiquities of London' (1791).*

Dr Alvey was a distinguished scholar and

'a man of a strict life, of great learning and of so venerable behaviour as to gain such a degree of love and reverence from all men that he was generally known as Father Alvie.'[12]

The lawyers appear to have undertaken responsibility for all repairs in the Temple, but little was spent on the church. They did however complete the splendid Middle Temple Hall in 1572 when they were still nominally only tenants of the property. Sir Edmund Plowden, who saw the project through, was thought highly of by Elizabeth but he never attained the Chancellorship because of his adherence to the old religion, in spite of her persuasions. Plowden in his day was considered the Middle Temple's most illustrious son. A Member of Parliament, Treasurer of the Inn, he devoted himself to law once Elizabeth succeeded to the throne. His unique reputation is based on his law reports entitled *Commentaries*, which he put together at first for his own learning, but was persuaded to publish them. Written in Low French, they were published in 1571 and 1578 and were of such repute that they continued to be reprinted up until 1816. He died in 1584 and was buried in the church, where his monument (*ill. 46*) can still be seen.

Plowden was not the only member of the Temple who remained faithful to Rome. For a long time there was great concern about the return of 'Popery' and there are many orders in the records concerning compulsory attendance at church and at Holy Communion, which were conditions of membership of the Inns. In 1569

'it was thought fit to purge the Inns of Court, called the Two Temples, of sundry Papists that here harboured themselves. Many of them came not to common prayer nor communion, though sometimes to the sermons in the Temple Church. Among these was Paget, Under-treasurer of the Inner Temple; and Shaftow, who did business for the Earl of Northumberland, the traitor. These and others were brought before the Archbishop and other Commissioners in the Starchamber; and some of them were, by the said commissioners committed to the Fleet.'[13]

Among the questions put to 'G.H.' during his interrogation were:

'First, Whether you have commonly frequented the Temple Church at service time, as others of the house do? Item, Whether you have received the Communion in the Temple Church, accustomably, as others of the house do? Item, Whether you said of late time that the marriage of Priests was unlawful, and their children bastards? Item, You being requested to go to a sermon at Paul's Cross, whether said you, "That you would not hear one knave of them all," and, "That Mr Alvey, the Master of the Temple, stood in the pulpit like a crow-keeper?"'

There was at this time daily service in the Temple church at seven o'clock in the morning

(or half-past six in term time), with the church serving as a college chapel for the two Societies.[14]

Overseers were appointed under a Middle Temple order of 27 January 1583 to note absentees and to report offenders against 'good and decent order' during divine service. Mr Alvey was to admonish offenders and, privately if they did not reform, their names were to be disclosed to the Benchers for suitable punishment. A butler was to be appointed by each Society

'to keep the choir door that no woman come into the said choir, and to keep out of the said choir all other strangers except noblemen and knights.'[15]

Some time before his death Canon Alvey became very ill and Walter Travers was appointed Divinity Lecturer or Preacher, an appointment confirmed in 1580-1. A condition was that

'he also do preach two other days weekly besides the Sunday, and the Sunday at his own pleasure, and that he do preach in his gown or some other decent apparel and not in a cloak.'[16]

Towards the end of 1584 Dr Alvey died, and Walton wrote[17] that Dr Sandys, Archbishop of York, being at dinner with the Benchers,

'met with a great condolement for the death of Father Alvie, and with a high commendation of his saint-like life, and of his great merit towards God and man; and as they bewailed his death, so they wished for a like pattern of virtue and learning to succeed him.'

His successor was the famous and 'judicious' Richard Hooker (*ill. 47*), who for six years was Master of the Temple. This was 'a place', says Walton, 'which he accepted rather than desired.' Alvey had been a staunch protestant and in the reign of Queen Mary had been deprived of all his preferments,[18] and exiled at Frankfort until after the accession of Elizabeth. Walter Travers was an extreme protestant, and Alvey had expressed a death-bed hope that Travers would succeed him as Master. However, Travers was passed over in favour of his relation by marriage,

47. The bust of Richard Hooker by Alfred Gatley, formerly on the north-west wall of the chancel, lost in the fire of 1941.

Hooker, who received his letters patent on 17 March 1585 which appointed him *Magister sive custos Domus et Ecclesiae Novi Templi.* His differences in the pulpit with Travers, who was disposed to 'out-Calvin Calvin' in the afternoon sermons, are well known. Hooker denied that everything could be settled by reference to Biblical texts and rose to a noble eloquence in his defence of church music.[19] Thomas Cartwright was the leading Calvinist, and Hooker refuted his opposition to the choral service, made in 1570. Hooker wrote:

'Touching musical harmony whether by instrument or voice, such is the force thereof, and so pleasing effects it hath in that very part of man which is most divine, that some have been thereby induced to think that the soul itself by nature is or hath in it harmony. A thing which delighteth all ages and beseemeth all states; a thing as seasonable in grief as in joy... sovereign against melancholy and despair, forcible to draw forth tears of devotion if the mind be such as can yield them, able both to move and to moderate all affections... It carrieth as it were into ecstasies, filling the mind with a heavenly joy and for the time in a manner severing it from the body.'

It is doubtful whether Hooker was influenced by the music in the Temple and, in the absence of any further references until the nineteenth century, it seems probable that the choir did not survive the accession of Elizabeth and the return of the book of Common Prayer. The Temple had no choral foundation, like the Chapel Royal, the Abbey or St Paul's, although it was a Royal Peculiar and a private chapel. Its services between 1588 and 1840 appear to have followed in general the practice of the parish churches of London. In the Capital the puritan element was always strongly to the fore, and the lawyers' leanings were in that direction. Percy Scholes, in his illuminating article on 'Anglican parish Church Music',[20] says:

'At the Reformation a very considerable party in the Church of England desired thorough reform, on Calvinistic lines, and a good many parish church organs were probably removed or allowed to decay; indeed there is evidence of this.'

Andrew Freeman,[21] without quoting evidence, suggests that there may have been no instrument in the Temple church from about 1570 until 1683 when Father Smith's organ was set up.

It was a common practice to appoint, as an additional member of the staff of a town or country parish, a 'Lecturer' or clergyman whose function was to give sermons on stated days. Lecturers were a thorn in the side of the church before Cromwell's rebellion; such appointments dated from pre-Reformation times and were almost independent of episcopal authority.[22] Such a Lecturer was Hooker's opponent, Walter Travers. Fuller[23] contrasts the two men:

'Mr Hooker his voice was low, stature little, gesture none at all, standing stone still in the pulpit, as if the posture of his body were the emblem of his mind, immovable in his opinions. Where his eye was left fixed at the beginning, it was found fixed at the end of his sermon. In a word, the doctrine he delivered had nothing but itself to garnish it. His style was long and pithy, driving on a whole flock of several clauses before he came to the close of a sentence; so that when the copiousness of his style met not with proportionate capacity in his auditors, it was unjustly censured for being perplexed, tedious and obscure. He may be said to have made good musick with his fiddle and stick alone, without any rosin; having neither pronunciation nor gesture to grace his matter. Mr Travers his utterance was graceful, gesture plausible, matter profitable, method plain, and his style carried in it *indolem pietatis,* a genius of grace flowing from his sanctified heart. Some say that the congregation in the Temple ebbed in the forenoon and flowed in the afternoon... Here might one, on Sundays, have seen almost as many writers as hearers; not only students, but even the gravest benchers (such as Sir Edward Cook and Sir James Altham then were) were not more exact in taking instructions from their clients, than in writing notes from the mouths of their ministers. The worst was, these two preachers, though joined in affinity, (their nearest kindred being married together), acted with different principles, and clashed one against another; so that what Mr Hooker delivered in the forenoon, Mr Travers confuted in the afternoon. At the building of Solomon's Temple (I Kings, vi.7) "neither hammer, nor axe, nor tool of iron was heard therein"; whereas, alas! in this Temple not only much knocking was heard, but (which was the worst) the nails and pins which one master-builder drave in were driven out by the other.'

Eventually Archbishop Whitgift intervened and forbade Travers to preach, on the grounds that he was not lawfully ordained, having received ordination according to the Presbyterian form in a foreign congregation (the Netherlands). Fuller concludes:

'As for Travers his silencing, many which were well pleased with the deed done were offended at the manner of doing it; for all the congregation on a Sabbath, in the afternoon, were assembled together, their attention prepared, the cloth (as I may say) and napkins were laid, yea, the guests sat, and their knives drawn for their spiritual repast, when suddenly, as Mr Travers was going up into the pulpit, a sorry fellow served him a letter, prohibiting him to preach any more. In obedience to authority (the mild and constant submission where unto won him respect with his adversaries), Mr Travers calmly signified the same to the congregation, and requested them quietly to depart to their chambers. Thus was our good Zaccarias struck dumb in the Temple, but not for infidelity, impartial people accounting his fault at most but indiscretion. Meantime his auditory (pained that their pregnant expectation to hear him preach should so publicly prove abortive, and sent sermonless home) manifested in their variety of passion, some grieving, some frowning, some murmuring; and the wisest sort, who held their tongues, shook their heads, as disliking the managing of the matter.'

In 1591 Hooker resigned, 'weary with the noise and opposition of the place,' and retired to the country to write his celebrated *Laws of Ecclesiastical Polity.* He left behind his upright armchair (*ill. 48*) which somehow survived the Great Fire but not, unfortunately, the Second World War. Hooker was succeeded as Master by Nicholas Balguy (or Bagley) D.D., Fellow of Magdalen College, Oxford. Balguy became Rector of St Edmund, Lombard Street in 1593 and of All Hallows the Great in 1595, while Master of the Temple. On his death in 1601 he was administering the Sacrament to members of the Inner Temple before those of the Middle. A joint committee which looked into the matter arranged that each Society should receive the Sacrament first on alternate Sundays. Strype[24] says that it was the custom in Alvey's day to receive the communion sitting, and that Travers had taken Hooker to task for kneeling when he received the Sacrament, and when praying, and for naming bishops in his prayer (it seems that Hooker used the form of bidding-prayers). An interesting feature in the morning service of the Temple is the Bidding Prayer. This is always recited by the Master or other preacher before the sermon, in obedience to the 55th Canon (1604) of the

48. Richard Hooker's chair in the Master's House, lost in the fire of 1941.

English Church, with the congregation standing.

Stow[25] notes in 1603 that 'This Temple Church hath a master and four stipendiary priests, with a clerk, these for the ministration of Divine service there have stipends allowed to them out of the possessions and revenues of the late hospital and house of St John's of Jerusalem in England, as it had been in the reign of Edward VI.' Scholes, of post-Reformation parish churches, says[26] that

'the clerks who had formerly, in the chancel, assisted the priest in the responsive parts of the service, now (perhaps in some places gradually) became reduced to one parish clerk upon whom devolved the leading of the people's verses of the (read) prose psalms and the responses, which latter may, in some places have been chanted to the new adaptation of the old plainsong and in others merely uttered in a speaking voice. A metrical psalm was often included in the service, as what we would today call a hymn, and this was announced, read and led by the parish clerk, sitting at his desk.'

There are references to the Clerk of the Temple church before the end of the sixteenth century In 1581 Richard Baker was permitted to have a life estate in the little house that he had lately built adjoining the church.

For his service in the church he had a yearly offering of 4d from every gentleman of the house.[27] Having built the Clerk's house with certain shops at his own expense, he sold the office of Clerk of the church to one Middleton for £20. This sale of the office was inquired into by a joint committee of the two Inns in 1593. While 'they much disliked such buying and selling of the clerkship,' they allowed the bargain to stand in consideration of the money expended by Baker in his buildings, and confirmed Middleton in the office.[28]

NOTES TO CHAPTER FIVE

[1] Williamson, J. B., *The History of the Temple, London* (1924, 2nd edn), 83.
[2] See Lord Silsoe, *The Peculiarities of the Temple* (1972).
[3] Williamson (*op. cit.*) 127.
[4] Master Worsley's Book (*op. cit.*) 156.
[5] Williamson (*op. cit.*) 83, 89.
[6] *De laudibus Legum Angliae*, trans. John Selden (1616).
[7] Cotton MS. Printed in Herbert's *Inns of Court* (1804) 211-222.
[8] '*Novis organis in ecclesia*' – Inner Temple Act of Parliament, 30 Jan 1519.
[9] Williamson (*op. cit.*) 145
[10] Williamson (*op. cit.*) 144.
[11] Sir William Dugdale, *Origines Juridiciales* (3rd edn 1680).
[12] Walton's *Life of Hooker*.
[13] Strype, *The Life of Matthew Parker*, Vol. I, ch. xxv, 567 (1821).
[14] Williamson (*op. cit.*) 197.
[15] Inderwick ITR, Vol. II. This reference is indexed under 'chorister', but the word 'choir' is clearly used here in an architectural sense meaning an enclosure before the altar where the Benchers and members of the Inns had their seats; there is no express reference to choristers as such in the records at this time.
[16] Inderwick, Vol. I, Intro. lvii.
[17] Walton (*op. cit.*).
[18] *DNB*. Alvey had been installed Canon of Westminster in 1552.
[19] Richard Hooker, *The Laws of Ecclesiastical Polity* (1594). See Book V, ch. 38.
[20] In the *Oxford Companion to Music*.
[21] Freeman, Andrew, 'The Organs of the Temple Church' in *The Organ*, Vol. 3, no. 10, (1923).
[22] Overton, J.H., *Life in the English Church 1660-1714* (1885).
[23] Fuller, *Church History of Britain* (ed. 1845), Vol. 5, 177, and *The History of the Worthies of England* Vol. 1, 289 (1662).
[24] Strype, *Annales* III, 243.
[25] Stow, *Survey of London* (1603).
[26] Scholes, *Oxford Companion to Music* – article on 'Anglican Parish Church Music'.
[27] Inner Temple records 23 May 1585.
[28] Inderwick, Vol. I, Intro. lix.

CHAPTER SIX

The Stuarts

The seventeenth century saw important changes to the status of the occupation of the Temple by the two Societies. Since the dissolution of the Knights Hospitallers, the Societies had leased the Temple from the Crown. The death of Elizabeth I in 1603 marked the end of the Tudor period and the start of the Stuart line under James I. With this change in succession the two Societies became concerned about the security of their tenure, which seemed to have always been guaranteed under the Tudors. They approached their new sovereign pointing out their concern and on 13 August 1608 King James I[1] granted to the two Societies a Charter containing the freehold by letters patent with the designation: *'Hospicia et capitalia messuagia cognita per nomen de le Inner Temple, et le Middle Temple, sive Nove Temple.'*

This gave the lawyers and students of the Societies the freehold to reside and practise law at the Temple, subject to their payment of an annual 'fee farm rent' of £10 to the Crown. Baylis and Williamson[2] mention that as a sign of their gratitude, the Societies presented James I with a cup of pure gold which weighed twelve and a half pounds and cost £666. A second smaller gold cup was also given to the King, and an iron-bound chest (*ill. 49*) was made to keep the Charter. Under this the two Societies were to pay an annual pension to the principal clergyman or 'Master Keeper or Rector' of the Temple Church[3]. However, it was also stipulated that the Crown retained the right to appoint the Master – something that has remained to the present day. This 'Royal Peculiar', as it is known, is a distinction shared, amongst others, with Westminster Ab-

bey. Finally, the letters patent stipulated that the two Inns were jointly responsible for the upkeep and repair of the Temple Church.

Later, during the reign of Charles II, the Middle Temple in 1673 and the Inner Temple in 1675 were able to purchase the rent from the Crown. Under an earlier settlement by the King at the time of his marriage to Queen Catherine of Braganza, the two Societies had been paying this rent directly to her estate rather than to the Crown. This meant that the rent would have to continue to be paid until her death[4].

Until the purchase of the freehold, the Crown seemed to have been an indifferent landlord regarding the upkeep of the church. Indeed, the two Societies felt compelled to undertake some urgent repairs themselves in 1607 and 1608. In the following year, now responsible for this work themselves as a result of their purchase of the Temple, they continued the repairs which in all totalled an expenditure of about £470 over the

49. The iron-bound chest (with the keys for the two Inns) made to house the Charter of 1608.
(Photo Robert Dark)

50. *Martin's monument in the north wall of the chancel: banished to the triforium in 1842 but returned to the Round in 1933.*
From J.T. Smith, 'Antiquities of London' (1791).

three years. Items included in this work were repairs to the roof, pews, protection to the monuments in the Round, work to the windows, purchase of a great brass candlestick to hang in the chancel and two new Communion cups[5].

A famous Middle Temple lawyer of this period was Richard Martin[6]. He was respected for his learning and was a reputed wit which he often directed at other members. This rebounded on him when he used it against John Davies who became so incensed that he attacked Martin one day in the Hall and beat him so hard over the head with a stick that it broke. Martin became a member of the House of Commons and was appointed Recorder of London. When he died he was buried in the Temple Church where his monument can still be seen (*ill. 50*).

There was a general air of laxity at this time which manifested itself in other ways. In 1611 both Inns made an order prohibiting laundresses washing and drying clothes in the graveyard, and directing the removal of a tailor's shop and

certain sheds set up there without authority.[7] The order also described the churchyard as 'a Common and most Noisome lestal'. Myddleton, clerk to the church at the time, had allowed the sheds to be erected. He was also taken to task in the following year for 'storing faggots and other stuff on the roof of the church'. Over many years, general encroachment of buildings up against the church had taken place, even to the extent that the porch itself had been partially blocked up and used as a shop, and chambers had been built on top of the porch itself (*ills 54 & 66*). These had obviously been there for some time for in 1631 the Middle Temple authorities had drawn attention to their dilapidated state[8]. A succession of major repairs to the church took place during this decade. In 1632 there was agreement between the Societies to carry out unspecified urgent repairs. The cost of them was such that the Middle Temple raised the money by a special 'tax roll' of its members. Benchers paid 40s each, Barristers 20s, and gentlemen under the Bar 10s. As could be expected, this odd arrangement of joint responsibility for the care of church frequently broke down. In 1634 the Middle Temple was not prepared to join the Inner Temple in removing some of the buildings that encroached against the church to the extent that they were damaging the walls and obscuring the windows. In the end the Inner Temple proceeded on their own by removing only those buildings that belonged to them. At the same time they asked for further discussions with the Middle Temple with the rejoinder that:

> 'Wherein yf shall refuse to joyne then in regard of the present necessitie thereof this House is forthwith to proceede aloane therein untill some further course shall bee taken thereabouts.'

By 1636 the two Societies were once again in joint agreement about carrying out certain repairs to the church. These were to the east end and were of some magnitude, for the Inner Temple accounts recorded their share of the cost as £182 19s. 10d for masons work, £17 18s. 11d for iron work and £6 9s. 9d for new glass. Disagreement on expenditure took a unique turn in 1637 when Dr Micklethwaite, Master of the Temple, incurred expenditure on the church to which both Societies objected. With the support of the King, Charles I, he rearranged the interior to conform with the King's own chapel[9]. This involved relocating the Communion Table from the centre of the chancel to the east end and repositioning the pulpit. It took a directive from the House of Commons itself to persuade the Middle Temple to pay up their share of the cost of this work. Dr Micklethwaite was at odds with the members of the two Societies on a number of other issues, leading to petitions to the King from both sides. At one point the Middle Temple Benchers refused to pay him his dues. This kind of animosity did not always exist between the Master of the Temple and the two Societies. When Dr William Sherlock was Master in 1688, the Middle Temple presented him with a 'hoggeshead of Clarrett' as a sign of appreciation on their part for his services to them. The Inner Temple not to be outdone, was of a mind the following year to present him with a 'hoggeshead of Clarrett and a quarter cask of canary'. However, they changed their mind and presented him with a pair of silver candlesticks instead[10]. Sherlock unlike Micklethwaite was no great supporter of the monarchy of his day. Indeed it took his wife to persuade him to take the oath of allegiance. A bookseller[11] alluded to this, when seeing him handing his wife along St Paul's churchyard, remarked, 'there goes Dr Sherlock with the reasons for taking his oath at his fingertips'.

Dr Micklethwaite was particularly against the secularisation of the church. This led him to lock it up between services to prevent its being used by the Benchers for committees and other non-religious purposes. This secularisation was not confined to the Temple Inns of Court. It was at this time that Members of the Bench of Lincoln's Inn gave directions that the Communion Table in their chapel was not to be leaned or sat on or to be used as a place to rest hats or books – or even as happened, on one famous occasion, to rest a baby. Further jointly agreed repairs took place in the Temple church in 1638 and 1639.

Again they involved extensive work to the walls as the total cost for masonry work was £308 14s and £432 respectively. Two decades elapsed before the next significant expenditure on the church occurred. In 1658 £400 was spent on repairing the Round. No further work of significance took place for another 25 years. More important matters seemed to arise every time the Societies discussed possible work to the church.

One of the leading lawyers of the first half of the century was John Selden[12] 'the glory of the English Nation'. Born in 1584 he became a member of the Inner Temple. He was a prolific author – his most famous work, *Titles of Honour*, was described as a 'mine of erudition and learning'. He was also a noted linguist and published many books on Jewish history and law. He became a member of Parliament in 1623 and spent a number of years in prison for speaking up against the Crown's interference. When he died in 1654 he was magnificently buried at night in accordance with the Commonwealth custom:

'.... in the Temple Church on the south side of the round walk, in the presence of all the judges, Benchers and great officers. The Lord Primate of Ireland preach't his funeral sermon. His grave was ten feet deep at least, the bottom pav'd with bricks and walled about two feet high, with grey marble coarsely polished..... Into this repository was placed the corpse in a wooden coffin, covered with a black cloth, let down with a pulley or engine. Which being done, a stone of black polished marble six inches thick was let down also and made fast to the repository with clamps of iron yoated in [lead melted in], to the end that in future ages, when graves are dug there, it may not be remov'd. Upon the said marble stone was this engraven *"Hic inhumatur corpus Johannis Seldeni"*, or to that effect. Over this was turned an arch of brick (for the House would not lose their ground) and upon that was throwne the earth &c. And on the surface lieth another faire gravestone of black marble with this inscription: *"I. Seldenis L.C. heic situs est"*.'[13]

A wall monument to Selden was also set up next to his grave, now lost but illustrated in Mrs Esdaile's *Temple Church Monuments*, Plate XVII.

There was much building work in the Temple over the first half of the century. Many chambers had fallen into decay and were replaced. However, the most significant reason for rebuilding in the second half of the century was as a result of a number of major fires in the two Inns. This is not unexpected, as a large proportion of the buildings were either wholly built of timber or contained a considerable amount of it. In addition, rooms were often lined with timber panelling and had open fireplaces. Rooms were lit by candles and chambers were piled high with documents. Buildings stood cheek by jowl with one another and there were no regulations controlling the fire separation between them. Not surprisingly, the Inns were hostage to fortune when fire broke out and once a fire caught hold, it was very difficult to contain it. This problem was not confined to the Inns, as the year 1666 was to show. The year before, the whole of London was laid low by the Great Plague. These events are described by Williamson in his book on the Temple[14]. It was not the first time plague had affected the City and, as a consequence, the Temple. In the summer of 1603 an outbreak occurred and as a result the two Societies closed down until the spring of the following year. But the plague of 1665 proved to be the most devastating of all and by the summer, it began to escalate to an alarming degree. John Evelyn, in his *Diary*, recorded:

'July 16th There died of the plague in London
  this weeke 1100.'
The following month he recorded:
'August 15th.... this weeke [there died] 5000.'

By this time, Evelyn had sent his family out of London and the two Inns had effectively closed down, with members moving out and the entrances into the Inns closed and guarded[15]. The Temple remained pretty well abandoned through to the summer of the following year, at the end of which, early on Sunday September 2nd, fire broke out in a baker's shop in Pudding Lane in the City. The Lord Mayor was called to the scene, but he and others underestimated its danger and refused the suggestion that houses in its path should be pulled down to arrest its progress. Then, from a deadly combination of timber-framed buildings and shops storing inflammable materials such as oil and tallow, the fire took hold of the whole neighbourhood. By this stage there was no holding it, and it was soon swept across the City by a strong east wind. John Evelyn recorded in his *Diary* entry of 3 September 1666:

'The fire continuing, after dinner I took coach with my wife and sonn and went to Bankside in Southwark where we beheld that dismal spectacle the whole Citty in dreadful flames neare ye water side.... The fire having continued all night (if I may call that night which was as light as day for 10 miles round about after a dreadful manner), when conspiring with a fierce Eastern wind in a very drie season; I went on foot to the same place; and saw the whole south part of the Citty burning from Cheapeside to ye Thames.... and was now taking hold of St. Paul's Church to which the scaffold's contributed exceedingly. The conflagration was so universal and the people so astonished that from the beginning I know not by what despondency or fate they hardly stirred to quench it.... So as it burned both in breadth and length the Churches, publiq halls, Exchange, hospitals, monuments and ornaments; leaping after a prodigious manner, from house to house and streete to streete, at great distances one from ye other; for ye heate with a long set of faire and warme weather, had even ignited the air, and prepared the materials to conceive the fire, which devoured after an incredible manner houses, furniture and everything........ All the skies were of a fiery aspect like the top of a burning oven, the light seene above 40 miles round about for many nights. God grant my eyes may never behold the like, now seeing above 10,000 houses all in one flame: the noise and the cracking and thunder of the impetuous flames ye shrieking of women and children, the hurry of people, the fall of Towers, Houses and Churches was like a hideous storme. And the aire all about so hot and inflam'd that at last one was not able to approach it, so that they were forc'd to stand still and let ye flames burn on, which they did for neere two miles in length and one of breadth. The clouds of smoke were dismall and reach'd upon computation neer 50 miles in length. Thus I left it this afternoone burning, a resemblance of Sodom, or the last day. London was, but is no more!'

The fire raged on, progressing west along Fleet Street and through Whitefriars immediately to the east of the Temple. Then, on the third day the wind dropped. But the fire continued for another day, by which time it had burnt down a good part of the Inner Temple buildings. Fortunately, the courtyards and open spaces within the Inns of Court and the recently constructed buildings of brick, helped to arrest the fire. A map of 1677 by John Ogilby (*ill. 51*) indicates how far the fire penetrated into the Inner Temple, and the extent to which buildings were burnt down. This included Sergeant's Inn in the north-east corner of the Inner Temple, and also the tightly packed buildings west of this, immediately outside the Inns of Court, bordering the Temple churchyard and Fleet Street. Included in this was the recently constructed Master's house, built under the direction of the Master, Dr Richard Ball. South of Sergeant's Inn, the chambers of King's Bench Walk were burnt down. To the west of this, Crown Office Row, Tanfield Court, Lamb Building, the Inner Temple Library and the parliament chamber were also destroyed. It was at this point, with the fire beginning to abate, but threatening to consume the cloisters and the very church itself, that the decision was made to demolish some of the buildings built up against it by use of explosives. The fire at its height was so fierce that little could be done to arrest its progress and there was no public organised firefighting at this time. Fighting fires relied on voluntary help or private arrangements within individual organisations. For example when tackling a fire in 1683 in King's Bench Walk, the 'Engeons' of St Bride's, St Dunstan's and St Giles'

were used, as well as those of the Temple[16]. It was not until the end of the seventeenth century that firemen began to be employed in a more general way, when their services could be subscribed to via insurance companies. Apart from a few simple hand pumps or 'engeons', hand chains with use of buckets of water was the most common way to fight fires. In the case of a serious fire, the most effective way of arresting its progress was to demolish buildings in its path, often by use of explosives. In using this last resort to stop the spread of the 1666 fire, part of Fig Tree Court and part of the Round to the church were damaged. It was during this final phase that the Duke of York[17], who was also a Bencher, stayed up all night to help supervise fighting the fire.

As a result of the Fire, the City was cleansed of the Plague. The two Inns, in spite of the devastation, began to function again and by October a committee of six members was formed with the responsibility:

'... to treat with any persons and settle all matters in reference to the rebuilding of the Society.'[18]

Detailed plans for rebuilding were well on the way by the following spring. Included in these was the rebuilding of the Master's House (*ill. 62*). This time Dr Ball put up £400 and as part of this agreement, the two Societies set out leasing details of the house to Dr Ball in recognition of his contribution. In addition, they stipulated that the house was to be built of brick. This was indicative that the two Inns, and indeed London as a whole, recognised that something needed to be done in the rebuilding of London to minimise the effect of fire in the future. Gradually regulations were introduced requiring brick walls to be used between adjoining buildings. Furthermore these walls had to be extended above the roof line to act as fire breaks. Also, window frames had to be set back from the face of external walls in order to minimise the spread of fire between them, as being made of timber they were a particular fire hazard. For similar reasons the distance between windows of adjoining properties was regulated. The two Inns took

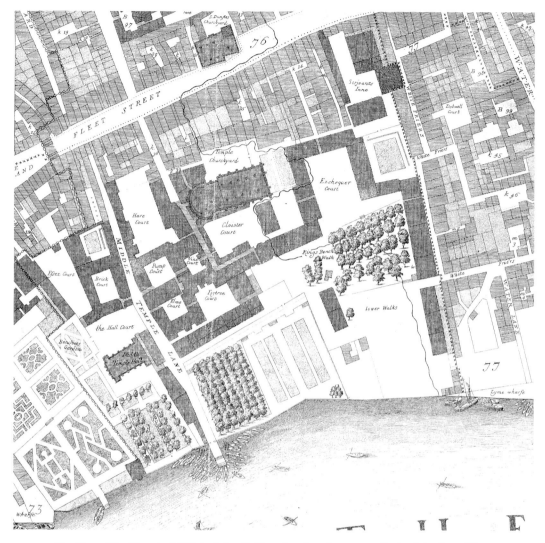

51. Map of the Temple, 1677, by John Ogilby, showing the western limit of the Great Fire.

heir own steps to reduce the risk of the spread
of fire by restricting the height of new buildings.
However, bad practice returned and in time a
motley collection of buildings was once again
hugging the walls of the church (to the west and
south).

New buildings were not only put up to replace
those lost, but additional buildings were erected
towards the river wall. Generally, the cost was
borne by individual Benchers. The representa-
tives of the two Societies controlled the area,
height and materials of construction, and also the

particular use, occupier and leasing arrangements. In addition, the larger spaces such as
King's Bench Walk were laid out with paths and
avenues of trees creating a pleasant aspect from
the chambers towards the river (*ills. 51 & 52*).

By 1675, with the Inns rebuilt, John Playford
(*ill. 53*), clerk to the church, felt confident enough
to write to the two Inns about urgent work to
the church itself with some prospect of its being
funded. He said it was necessary to make the
doors and the screen separating the chancel from
the Round more secure, as the communion plate,

52. (above) A view of part of the Temple, 1671; 53. (below) John Playford, Clerk of the Temple church.

stored in the chancel was at risk. Also, fittings were in a bad state – indeed the pulpit which was in danger of collapse. The bells 'in the steeple' were cracked and needed renewal, preferably with a single bell[19].

Playford had set up a famous music shop in the porch to the Church. He and his son Henry established a virtual monopoly in publishing music in England during the latter part of the century. An advertisement in one of his publications proclaimed:

'At Mr. Playford's shop is sold all sorts of ruled paper for musick and books of all sizes ready bound for musick. Also the excellent cordial called the "Elixir Proprietatis", a few drops of which drank in a glass of sack or other liquors is admirable for all coughs, consumption of the lungs, and inward distempers of the body.'

*54. Stationer's shop in the Porch, c.1678.
From The Gentleman's Magazine Vol. 54, p.911.*

Later the Playfords moved to a shop close by and their original shop was let to a series of other stationers. An engraving of the shop in the porch 1678 (*ill. 54*), when it was run by J. Penn and O. Lloyd, shows how it appeared at the time. The front was built into the northern archway of the porch and the body of the shop in a building against this to the north. This is the lower of the two buildings in this position in the Ogilby map.

Samuel Pepys[20] was a friend of John Playford's and was a frequent visitor to his shop where he bought the latest music. On 22 November 1662 he recorded in his diary:

'...bought the book of country dances against my wife's woman Gosnall comes, who dances finely, and there meeting Mr Playford

he did give me his Latin songs of Mr Deering's which he lately printed.'

Pepys occasionally attended services at the Temple church. He recorded on 13 April 1662:

'.... a boy, being asleep, fell down a high seat to the ground, ready to break his neck, but got no hurt.'

The Playfords were the first publishers of Henry Purcell's music, and when John Playford died in 1686, Purcell set to music an elegy to him by Nahum Tate. Later, when Purcell died in 1695, Henry Playford published Blow's setting of Dryden's *Ode on the Death of Purcell*.

Playford's report on work required to the church needed a joint decision from the two Societies. This took some time, as unfortunately they had to deal with a series of new fires. The first fire occured in 1677 in King's Bench Buildings. Ironically, this was a year after a committee of five Benchers from the Inner Temple had been set up:

'to consider of all necessary meanes to prevent any accidentall fires in this Societie and to view the engeon and to report what further number of bucketts will bee necessary to bee added to the former [ones] now hung in the Hall.'[21]

In 1678 it was the turn of the Middle Temple to suffer the effects of a serious fire. Starting in Middle Temple Lane, it soon took hold, particularly as it was so cold that water froze before it could be properly applied to the fire. It burnt down most of Hare Court, Essex Court, Pump Court and part of Elm Court. The Halls of both Societies were threatened, as well as the cloisters and once again the church. One expedient measure taken by the young members of the Inner Temple to combat this was to fill their engine with beer, as the water was frozen. It took some time for the Benchers[22] to agree to pay the brewer for this unusual use for the common good. Those buildings constructed with brick and stone helped to stop the spread of the fire. More effectively and as a last resort, gunpowder was used once more with the arrival of the Duke of Monmouth and the Earls of Craven and Faversham, who brought officers and soldiers of the Foot Guards to help fight the fire. However, this method of fighting fires was not an exact science! Williamson[23] quotes Roger North, a barrister, who recorded what he saw when it was decided to blow up the Inner Temple Library, that it was done 'with such a vengeance as endangered the murder of many people at great distance'. Indeed in the process of blowing up parts of Elm Court, the Fine Office and the Inner Temple Library, three people lost their lives and the Earl of Faversham suffered a fractured skull. Even after all this effort, the cloisters were burnt down and St Ann's Chapel of the Temple church was damaged by one of the explosions. From this point onwards the chapel remained in a semi-derelict state until it was demolished in 1825 and only the crypt remained in use for the storage of documents. The chapel had not been used for religious purposes for many years.

Christopher Wren was involved in some of the reinstatement as a result of this fire when he designed the cloistered chambers at the eastern end of Pump Court, just south of the church. At first the two Societies could not agree on whether to rebuild the cloisters as part of the replacement building, or to provide more chambers at ground floor level. This was finally resolved by referring the matter to the Chancellor, Sir Heneage Finch who decided that they should be rebuilt. However, in order to respond to the lobby for more chambers, he deemed that the cloisters and the accommodation above should be twice as wide as previously. His decision to have the cloisters rebuilt was mainly influenced by the fact that they were used by students as a place to walk and debate their cases with one another. This decision meant that the association with the Knights was continued in a tangible form. Although the cloisters were destroyed in the Second World War, they were once again rebuilt.

Wren had a previous association with the church, in that his first marriage to Faith, the daughter of Sir John Coghill of Bletchingdon, was solemnised there in 1669.

Seven years had passed since Playford's origi-nal request regarding the need for work to the church, and nothing had been done. However, having addressed the problems arising from the recent fires, the two Societies felt that they were in a position to ask Wren to carry out the work. He had previously inspected and reported that: 'the Church was very ruinous for want of repaire'and estimated the work would cost 'not less than £1400.'[24] The Middle Temple paid from the Treasury House, but the Inner Temple raised an 'air role' on its members, charging Benchers £3 each, Barristers £2. 5s, and Gentlemen £1. 10s. The Inner Temple Treasurer, Sir Thomas Robinson, agreed to advance the money until collected so that the work could start immedi-ately [25]

By the time Wren had finished, much of the church had been 'modernised' to meet the needs of current usage and to the latest fashion. The Classical style used by him was the antithesis of the Gothic style of the church. Delicacy and restraint gave way to flamboyance and cunning.

A new organ and associated loft were placed above a new carved oak screen in the central arch between the Round and the chancel, so that when installed the organ closed off the rest of the arch. This screen is described by Maitland[26], as being very much in the classical style. It spanned right across the the west end of the chancel. In 1703 Edward Hatton[27] described the screen as:

'...of right Wainscot adorned with 10 Pilas-ters of the Corinthian Order, also 3 Portals and pediments; and the Organ Gallery over the middle aperture is supported with two neat fluted columns of the Corinthian order, and adorned with entablatures and compass pedi-ment, and also the Queen's Arms finely carved; the Intercolumns and large panels in carved frames; and near the pediment on the S. Side is an enrichment of cherubims and the carved figure of a Pegasus, the Badge of the Society of the Inner Temple; and on and near the Pediment on the N. Side, an enrichment of cherubims, and the figure of a Holy Lamb, the badge of the Society of the Middle Temple; for though these two Houses have but one Church, yet they seldom sit promiscuously there, but the Inner Temple on the S. and the gentlemen of the Middle Temple Northward from the middle Ile.'

The ornamental front of the organ extended nearly to the ceiling and was adorned with two winged angels with trumpets on either side of the central column of pipes. The side arches above the screen were also plastered over. This was done in such a way that:

'the spaces above it in the side arches were blocked with plaster, so cunningly employed that the very existence of these arches was successfully concealed.'[28] (*ill. 59*)

The lower parts of these and the centre archways were filled up with glass doors and windows (*ill.55*). The justification for this was to prevent the secularisation of the whole building, as:

'The Round had become a convenient rendezvous for lounging, conversation, and commercial transactions, such as were taking place at the same time as in the nave of Old St Paul's.'[29]

Indeed a low partition across the church already existed at this time. An indication of how it might have looked just before Wren replaced it can be seen in the engraving of William Emmett of 1682 (*ill.56*). The new screen, although inevitable, was unfortunate, as it deliberately obscured elements of the original architectural expression of the church and, more importantly, blocked the view of the altar from the Round.

Among other work, Wren furnished the chancel with new box pews, a new altar screen or reredos and a new pulpit, all out of oak (*ill. 57 and back endpaper*). The reredos and pulpit were described in 1703 by Edward Hatton as follows:

'The Altar piece is of the same species of timber but much higher, finely carved and adorned with 4 Pillasters and between them and the columns with entablature of the Corinthian order; also enrichments of cherubims, a shield, festoon, fruit and leaves enclosed with handsome rail and banister. The pulpit is also finely carved and finnier'd

placed near the E. end of the middle ile, the sound board is pendant from the roof of the church. It is enriched with several arches, a crown, festoons, cherubins, vases, &c.'

A detailed account of this work was made as part of the Middle Temple Records by Edward Smith[30], Treasurer, 1682-3 which gives important information about who did the carved work:

	£	s	d
William Phillips, Joyner. Half Screene & Organ Loft.	110	15	0
Pulpitt, Type, Reader & Clerk's seate.	64	10	
Thomas Lowe. Carver's work on Pulpitt, Type & Stairs, &c.	60		
King's Arms and half the Screene	60	2	6
William Rounthwaite, Joyner. his bill for Alter-piece, pillars, pillasters, circular mouldings, rayle and table.	63		
Halfe Screen.	110	15	
Wm Emmett, Carver. for carving work about the Alter-piece, pillar, pillasters, shields, festoons, &c.	45		
Carving work about half Screen & Organ loft.	45		
Sabin the Smith for Ironwork for the type & hinges, rivetts, &c.	10	10	
(moiety paid by middle Temple £285 1s 3d)	£570	2s	6d

Until this account had been discovered by Sydney Harrison, Curator of the Bowes Museum, it was believed that the carving to the altar screen was the work of Grinling Gibbons (1648-1720). This is not surprising because of its particularly fine quality. However, as can be seen by this account it was in fact the work of William Emmett (1641-1693). This is the same William Emmett who did the engravings of the church, as well as a set of fine engravings of St Paul's Cathedral during the course of its con-

55. Interior of the Round showing the doors to the screen and organ above, 1805.
From John Britton, 'Architectural Antiquities' (1805-07).

56. Stylised view of the interior of the Temple church, c.1682, by William Emmett. Note the pointed clerestory windows and open screen between the Round and chancel.

struction giving impressions of how it would look when completed. George Vertue on the authority of Stoakes[31] said:

> 'Wm Emmett, Carver.... was Sculptor to the Crown before Gibons. Phillipps, uncle to Emmett, had that place before him.'

Other carved work by Emmett can be seen at Chelsea Hospital, and St Martin's Ludgate Hill. He also did work at Hampton Court, Kensington Palace, Whitehall and several other London churches. Of the other people mentioned in the above record, William Phillips was the Middle Temple joiner and William Rounthwaite the joiner for the Inner Temple. Emmett had previously been involved with Rounthwaite in work to the Inner Temple Hall.

Of particular note regarding the other work carried out by Wren is that he raised the general level of the floor of the chancel. This was finished with black and white chequered marble (a typical symbol of the freemasons of which society Sir Christopher Wren was a member), and the internal walls in the chancel were wainscoted (oak timber panelled) up to the lower edge of the windows[32] (*ill. 129*). He later 'repaired and beautified' the Plowden and Martin monuments. A plaque dated 1687 immediately behind the effigy of Plowden commemorates this work. A new bell[33] was also installed in the bell turret on the apex of the roof at the west end of the south aisle. This bell now in the roof of the tower on the north side of the church bears the following inscription:

> 'Sir Robt Sawyer Attorny Genall Treasuror
> of the Inner Temple.'
> 'Sir Henry Chauncy, Knight, Treasuror of
> the Middle Temple.'
> 'James Bartlet made me 1686.'

The honour of supplying the new organ to the church became a fierce competition between two organ builders. This lasted for several years and became known as the 'battle of the organs'. A detailed account is set out in Edmund Macrory, *Notes on the Temple Organ*[34]. Initially, in 1682, the two Societies had mind to appoint Bernhardt Schmidt, originally from Germany, who had over the years acquired the nickname of 'Father Smith'. He had become the King's organ builder and had acquired a considerable reputation in this country for building 'sweet sounding' organs. The one in Westminster Abbey was included in his list of completed works. However, representations were made on behalf of a rival builder named Renatus Harris, whose father had returned to this country from France where he had gone for the duration of the Commonwealth. Smith initially protested that he had already been selected but this was not accepted. The two Societies were not able to choose between the two organ makers, so they were asked in 1682 to set up their organs in the chancel of the church so that they could be heard and a choice made. By 1684 the two organs had been installed with Harris's located on the south side, and Smith's

57. A marriage at the Altar showing Wren's reredos, Plowden's monument and the Vestry door. Drawing by R.W. Billings, 1838.

58. Wren's furnishing of the chancel showing pulpit, box pews and Father Smith's organ on the screen. Drawing by R.W. Billings, 1838.

on the north. Dr Blow and Henry Purcell (who had succeeded Blow as organist at Westminster Abbey and at the Chapel Royal), proceeded to play on Smith's organ on agreed days, and Giovanni Battista Draghi, organist to Queen Catherine, played on Harris's organ. The Committee that had been set up to decide between the two could not come to any immediate decision, so the 'battle of the organs' continued for another year. Harris then challenged Smith to make additional reed stops in a given time. This was a cunning move by him because he excelled in making these stops, whereas Smith was more renowned for his Diapasons or Foundation Stops[35]. Nevertheless Smith agreed to the challenge. Burney recounts in his *History of Music*:

'...in the night proceeding the last trial of the reed-stops, the friends of Harris cut the bellows of Smith's organ in such a manner that when the time came for playing upon it, no wind could be conveyed into the wind-chest.'[36]

This was not the only occasion when supporters of Harris, and indeed of Smith, had resorted to dubious tactics in order to influence the decision. This led to both Smith and Harris having their organs guarded. Harris complained to his friends about the cost of the 'extraordinary charges of watchmen', which he said created 'great streights and inconveniences for want of money to supply his occasions'. After representations, Smith was loaned £100 by the Middle Temple in 1685, and Harris a similar amount from the Inner Temple in the following year, for guarding their respective organs 24 hours a day[37].

Even after the challenge of the reed stops, the Benchers could not agree between themselves. The Middle Temple tended to favour the organ of Father Smith, while the Inner Temple favoured that of Harris. Eventually the Middle Temple, fed up with the delay, decided in June 1685 in favour of Smith. It is worth quoting their statement, as it gives the best contemporary description of the competition and the relative merits of the two organs:

'The Masters of the Bench at this Parliament taking into their Consideration the tedious Competicion betweene the two Organ-makers about their fitting an Organ to the Temple Church, and having in severall Termes and at severall Times compared both the Organs now standing in the said Church, as they have played severall Sundays one after another, and as they have lately played the same Sunday together alternately at the same service. Now at the Suite of severall Masters of the Barr and Students of this Society pressing to have a speedy Determination of the said Controversie; and in Justice to the said Workmen as well as for the freeing themselves from any Complaints concerning the same, doe unanimously in full Parliament resolve and declare the Organ in the said Church made by Bernard Smith to bee in their Judgments, both for sweeetnes and fulnes of Sound (besides ye extraordinary Stopps, quarter Notes, and other Rarityes therin) beyond comparison preferrable before the other of the said Organs made by ------ Harris, and that the same is more ornamentall and substantiall, and both for Depthe of Sound and Strength the fitter for the Use of the said Church; And therefore upon account of the Excellency and Perfection of the said Organ made by Smith, and for that hee was the Workman first treated with and employed by the Treasurors of both Societyes for the providing his Organ; and for that the Organ made by the said Harris is discernably too low and too weake for the said Church, their Mastershippes see not any Cause of further Delay or need of any reference to Musicions or others to determine the Difference; But doe for their parts unanimously make Choice of the said Organ made by Smith for the Use of these Societyes – and Mr. Treasuror is desired to acquainte the Treasuror and Masters of the bench of the Inner Temple with this declaration of their Judgements with all respect desiring their Concurrence herin.'[38]

However, the Inner Temple could not agree to this. Eventually in 1687, after much discussion about the appointment of a panel of independent musical experts, the decision was referred to the Lord Keeper, Lord Guilford, but he died before giving any decision. It was left to his successor Lord Chief Justice Jeffreys of the Inner Temple to determine the matter[39]. He decided at the end of that year in favour of Father Smith. At last the five year 'battle of the organs' was over. This was the same Judge Jeffreys who had gained the reputation as a clever but callous and remorseless prosecutor and a fearsome judge. Most infamously he was involved in the 'Bloody Assize', when Protestant rebels were tried for high treason against James II, 'the Catholic King', in six west country towns. Having been found guilty by Judge Jeffreys, many of these rebels were subsequently hanged or deported.

As the choice of the organ had been close, Harris did not lose face and went on to make many more instruments for various churches. His organ for the competition was split up and used as part of the old organ in the Cathedral of Christ Church, Dublin and the remainder was used in St. Andrew's, Holborn[40]. Later, when the Dublin organ was dismantled, those parts of it that were Harris's were used in the organ at Wolverhampton Church. Smith subsequently went on to make the organ for the new St Paul's, although the complete instrument was not installed as some pipes could not be fitted into the case designed by Sir Christopher Wren, who prevented these 'extraneous' pipes being installed. He said that he was not going to allow the 'architecture' of his building to be spoilt by that 'box of whistles'[41].

Father Smith's organ was permanently installed in 1688 at the west end of the chancel, within the central archway and above the wooden screen erected by Wren (*ill. 59*). It consisted of a Great Organ of 948 pipes, a Choir Organ of 366, and Echoes of 401, a total of 1715 pipes. The first organist appointed in May 1688, was Francis Pigott[42] who was given a salary of £50 per year. In 1695, after the death of Purcell, Pigott was made organist at the Chapel Royal but retained his post at the Temple. On his death in 1704 he was succeeded at the Temple by his son John, who also later combined this with the appointment of organist at the Chapel Royal.

The drawing of the chancel (ill. 129) by G.H. Shepherd (1812) shows Wren's classic transformation, before the later invasion by the Victorians. In the course of Wren's restoration, it was recorded in the General Account Book of the Inner Temple (1682-1684) that:

> 'Paid the moiety of a dinner at the Divill Taverne for the entertainment of Sir Xopher Wrenne the whole bill coming to £1. 10s – Paid 15s.'

> 'Paid the halfe of two dinners for the entertainment of Sir Xopher Wrenne att his comeing to survey and giving orders to workemen about the Temple Church £1. 14s 6d, the Middle Temple paying the other halfe.'

The Devil Tavern was probably the best known of the taverns in the vicinity of the Inns and was situated to the west of Middle Temple Lane. It was mentioned in the diary of Samuel Pepys, and had been the haunt of Ben Jonson, the playwright (1572-1637). It was here that Jonson founded the Apollo Club which was frequented by other poets and authors. He was linked to the first great English architect, Inigo Jones (1573-1652), when between 1603 and 1616 they collaborated in putting on a series of court masques. Inigo Jones does not seem to have carried out any work in the Temple, but he created the design for a

59. *Father Smith's organ in its original position on Wren's screen.*
From Macrory, 'A few notes on the Temple Organ' (1859).

masque put on jointly by Lincoln's Inn and the Middle Temple for the wedding of the Lady Elizabeth, the daughter of James I, in 1612. In recognition of this, he was subsequently made a member of the Middle Temple.

After the re-opening of the church Dr Ball, the Master of the Temple, entertained the Bishop of Rochester at his house. The accounts of the two Societies of 11 February 1682-3 record:

> 'For Battalia pie; salad; tame pigeons;
> 2½ dozen of best Pontack at 14s;
> one dozen bottles of best Canary £1. 4s;
> 6 bottles of best Champagne, 9s;
> mum ale and tobacco, etc. £4. 14s. 9d.'

The work to the church carried out by Wren, became the subject of hot debate at the next major 'refurbishment' to the chancel in 1842, when the Oxford Movement was gaining force and all the work of Wren was removed. It was the view of Bruce Williamson in 1924 that the changes carried out by Wren:

> '.... were so flagrantly at variance with the spirit of that transitional Norman and Early English architecture of which the ancient Church of the Knights is so fine an example, that the result must have been a mongrel monstrosity, which only the obsessions of the age could ever have tolerated.'[43]

Williamson also made a wry inference about Wren's work from the text of the sermon celebrating the 'beautifying of the church' which the Rev. John Standish preached on the Sunday following its reopening. His text, Gen. xxviii, 17, included the words: 'How dreadful is this place: Surely this is none other but the House of God!'[44]. It is accepted that many of the original features of the church had been overlaid, imposing a new more flamboyant order of architectural expression that did not relate to the simplicity of the original. However, in its own terms, with a new floor, newly whitewashed stonework, new pews and beautifully carved screens and wainscoting around the walls of the chancel and behind the altar, 'the effect' was surely quite splendid. In some ways it must have looked like the set for a masque that Inigo Jones might have designed.

In the restoration of the church after the Second World War, Wren's reredos, removed in 1840, was reinstalled. Several parts of the screen across the west end of the chancel also survive; a cherubim is now over one of the doors to the vestibule to the Middle Temple Hall and two Corinthian capitals, one carved by Emmett and the other by Lowe, are at the Bowes Museum, Barnard Castle. The Temple pulpit designed by Wren found its way in 1842 to Christ Church, Newgate Street. A photograph of it appears in Plate XLV in Gerald Cobb's *The Old Churches of London* (1941-2). It did not survive when that church was gutted during the last war.

Wren was involved in one other major piece of work at the Temple. This was the replacement of the Great Gatehouse between Fleet Street and Middle Temple Lane. This was at the instigation of Roger North, the Treasurer of the Middle Temple. Wren's Gatehouse, built by Nicholas Barbon, and inscribed with the date 1684, remains to this day as the main entrance into the Temple from Fleet Street. On completion of this and the rebuilding of the cloister, Wren[45] was presented with twelve silver trencher plates in acknowledgement of his services.

In 1684 both Societies made two burial vaults as by now there was little room for burials in the church. Previously in 1654 it had been decided that only members could be buried in the church or churchyard for a similar reason. The vaults are under the garden of the Master's house.

During the reign of William and Mary[46], between the years 1694 and 1695, the exterior walls at the west end and south side of the church were resurfaced with new stone, costing some £400 between them. However, as described by Williamson:

> 'It was during the execution of these repairs that the stone carrying the original inscription which recorded the consecration of the Round church in 1185 by Heraclius, Patriarch of the Church of the Holy Resurrection, was unhappily destroyed by workmen.'[47]

It was not until Queen Anne's reign, after the lapse of another ten years, that further major repairs were carried out to the church. A joint committee formed in 1704 proceeded with substantial works in 1706. These involved repairs to the east and south exterior walls including a new battlement and buttresses. The roof was also re-covered. The interior was 'wholly whitewashed gilt and painted within etc.'[48]. By inference the original highly decorated vaulting was now being whitewashed. Catholic figurative decoration was blotted out as part of the Reformation and all forms of such decoration had probably disappeared by the Interregnum with the onset of a more Puritanical age. In the Round the effigies and the iron railings around them were painted and the pillars wainscoted to a height of six feet (*ill. 80*). The total cost of these repairs was of the order of £1200.

By now the Stuart Period was nearly at an end, during which the two Societies had obtained the freehold of the Temple. The Inns had survived the traumas of the plague and numerous fires. Partly as a result of this, and as a result of general expansion, new buildings abounded. The Inns were well developed on a courtyard principle and the open spaces were laid out with gardens, trees and walks leading down to the Thames where there was a landing stage, the ancient Temple Bridge, for boats to take the lawyers on river journeys. The church was apparently in good repair, but it was hidden behind the mass of buildings erected against it to the south, west and north. Where it was visible, it little resembled the original church as a result of numerous repairs and stylistic changes over the previous hundred years. It was mostly faced with smooth Bath stone. This was very different to the original plastered Kentish ragstone such as still remains on the north side of the Round although no longer with its plaster finish[49]. The buttresses of the Round[50] were now 'classicified' and a classical cornice was added to the aisle-parapets. The south-west door to the Round had a pediment and surrounds. Similarly, classical 'flamming' acorns adorned the gables of the east end of the church. Emmett's engraving (*ill. 60*, which conveniently omits the buildings against the south wall of the church and the building on top of the porch) illustrates these classic additions but it shows the position of the south-west door to the Round in the wrong bay. Its true location is shown in Malton's aquatint of 1792

(*ill. 66*). An interior view of this doorway in its classical form is shown in Pugin & Rowlandson's aquatint of 1809 (*ill. 80*). The doorway was removed in 1827 as part of Robert Smirke's restorations and the absent interior wall-arcading replaced, and apparently incorrectly spaced, in that bay. The external door on the south side of the chancel shown in Emmett's engraving indicates a vestry (*see also ill. 62*).[51] This was blocked up as part of the restoration work of the 1820s when the vestry was removed with other buildings on the south side of the church.

It is difficult to know whether the Round with its battlements had the general overall appearance of the original. It is more likely that the battlements were added in Tudor times. The appearance of the roof to this part of the church has been discussed in Chapter Two. Whether it ever had the appearance as depicted in the Emmett engraving is open to conjecture. Inside, the original coloured decoration to the vaulting had disappeared under numerous coats of

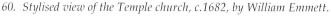

60. Stylised view of the Temple church, c.1682, by William Emmett.

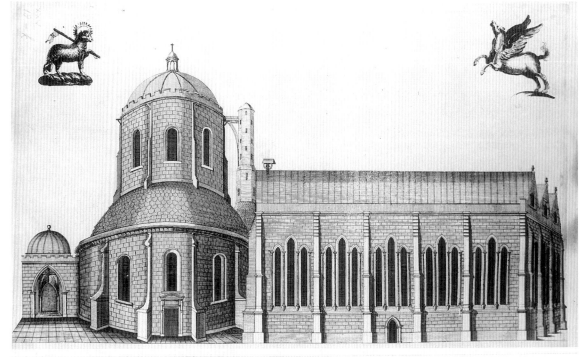

whitewash and the general appearance had been 'classicified' with screens and wainscoting. Box pews had been added and, most significantly of all, the central and side arches between the Round and the chancel had been blocked off.

NOTES TO CHAPTER SIX

[1] Williamson, Bruce, *The History of the Temple, London*, 270 (1925).

[2] Williamson (*op. cit.*), 268.

[3] Williamson (*op. cit.*), 262, 270.

[4] Middle Temple Treasurer's Account Book 100; Inner Temple Records II, 466, Appendix III.

[5] Inner Temple General Account Books. Book I, 17, 18, 31, 32, 40, 41, 48, 49; Inderwick, *Inner Temple Records* II, Introduction xxix

[6] Williamson (*op. cit.*), 214-217.

[7] Williamson (*op. cit.*), 540.

[8] Middle Temple Society Bench Minute Books 1626-1658, 66; 1658-1703, 313.

[9] Williamson (*op. cit.*), 393-394.

[10] MiddleTemple Society Bench Minute Books 1658-1703, 365; Inner Temple Society Bench Table Orders II, 10 Nov 1688.

[11] Lewer, David, *A Spiritual Song*, 65 (1961).

[12] Williamson (*op. cit.*), 454.

[13] Williamson (*op. cit.*), 460 et al.

[14] Williamson (*op. cit.*), 505-507.

[15] Williamson (*op. cit.*), 505

[16] Inner Temple Account Book 1682-84, 1683.

[17] Inderwick, F.A., *A Calendar of the Inner Temple Records* III, 1660-1714, Introduction xiii (1901).

[18] Inner Temple Acts of Parliament IV, 11.

[19] Inderwick (*op. cit.*), 103.

[20] Lewer (*op. cit.*), 53.

[21] Inner Temple Bench Table Orders I, 10.

[22] Inner Temple General Account Book, 16 Feb 1683; Inner Temple Bench Table Orders I, 34.

[23] *Lives of the Norths* III, 42, 43.

[24] Inderwick (*op. cit.*), 173.

[25] Inderwick (*op. cit.*), 174.

[26] Maitland, *The History and Survey of London* (1756).

[27] Harrison, Sydney, 'The Wren Screen from the Temple Church London', reprinted from *The Collector*, Vol. XI, 4.

[28] Inderwick (*op. cit.*), 543

[29] Worley, George, *The Church of the Knights Templars in London*, 30 (1907).

[30] Harrison (*op. cit.*), 1.

[31] Wren Society, Vol. 14, xv (1937).

[32] Inderwick (*op. cit.*), 543.

[33] Ingpen, Arthur Robert, Master Worsley's Book etc, 69 (1910).

[34] Macrory, Edmund, ed. Muir Mackenzie, *Notes on the Temple Organ* (1911).

[35] *English Musical Gazette*, Jan. 1819, 7.

[36] Burney, Dr Charles, *History of Music*, Vol. III, 437 (1776-89).

[37] Williamson (*op. cit.*), 547.

[38] Middle Temple Bench Minute Book, 2 June 1685.

[39] Burney (*op. cit.*).

[40] Macrory (*op. cit.*), 28

[41] *Musical Gazette*, Jan 1819.

[42] Lewer (*op. cit.*), 65, 70, 71.

[43] Williamson (*op. cit.*), 546.

[44] Inderwick (*op. cit.*), Introduction xliii.

[45] Middle Temple Treasurer's Accounts Book 1658-1727, 176; Middle Temple Calendar, 180.

[46] Inderwick (*op. cit.*), Introduction lxxxv.

[47] Williamson (*op. cit.*), 653

[48] Williamson (*op. cit.*), 654

[49] Godfrey, Walter, *A Short Guide to the Temple Church, London,* 1 (1960).

[50] RCHM London, Vol iv, *The City* (1929).

[51] Ingpen (*op. cit.*), 68.

CHAPTER SEVEN

The Georgians

The seventeenth century was shaped by the Civil War of 1642-9, the subsequent Restoration of the monarchy, and the Glorious Revolution of 1688 which ensured Protestant succession with the reign of William and Mary. The eighteenth century saw a gradual transition towards a more 'classical' age where freedom of thought was allowed to develop. It saw the growth of humanitarian and philanthropic feeling and endeavour. The latter is reflected by the history of foundling children in the Temple in the eighteenth century. Accounts of this can be found in both Inns, the most recent of which is by Ian Murray, the Inner Temple Archivist[1]. The Inns were next to the parishes of St Dunstan's and Clement Danes which, unlike today, were highly populated. Some 50% of these people were below the poverty line. It was inevitable that some of the ensuing social problems would impinge on the lawyers. As far back as the early seventeenth century it was a frequent practice to leave or 'drop' unwanted babies on staircases in the Inns. The Benchers displayed 'great benevolence' in paying for the fostering of these children and later for them to be apprenticed. The earliest record of this happening is 1617-18 and the last about 1850. With infant mortality in the country as high as 50%, and because of the additional deprived state of the babies that were abandoned, many died within a short time of being deserted. A review made by the Inner Temple in 1766 records 'dropt 37; died 25; placed out 6; remain 6'. Records kept by the Middle Temple show that the most frequent cause of death was from convulsions, smallpox or measles. Because of frequent early death the babies were baptised in the Temple church as soon as possible after being found and if they subsequently died they were buried in the churchyard. From about 1675 the custom arose of giving the children the surname Temple when baptised. The Christian names were chosen by the foster parents. Typical entries in the registry of finds kept by the Middle Temple are given below:

> 'Elizabeth Temple found 12 December 1749 – Elm Court No. 4 by stairs, baptised 13 December 1749, nurse Mrs Powell, White Fryar's, Ash Tree Court. Died 31 December 1749.'

> 'Catherine Temple, 30 November 1753, Church Yard Court. 1 December Mrs Penny Milford Lane. Put to apprentice to Mrs Ingall embroiderer.'

The numbers of abandoned babies increased so much in the eighteenth century that the Inns gave special instructions to their night watchmen to be especially vigilant to prevent the dropping of any child. They also displayed rewards for anybody who could provide information that might apprehend the person or persons responsible for deserting the children (*ill. 61*) The practice of abandoning children in this way was not restricted to the Temple but occurred all over London. Various public-spirited individuals founded institutions to take these children in and care for them, the most famous of whom was Thomas Coram who established the Foundling Hospital in 1741.

The last century saw the two Societies obtain-

61. A reward notice relating to a child abandoned at the Temple in 1792.

ing the freehold of the Temple, but subject to a rent of £10. At the beginning of the seventeenth century in 1705, with the death of Queen Catherine, the Societies finally obtained the absolute freehold. Later, on 2 November 1732 during the reign of George II, a Deed of Partition and plan regularised the parts of the Temple which the two Societies separately owned and those for which they had joint responsibility. In this document the Inner Temple was made responsible for the upkeep of the southern half and the Middle the northern half of the church. Similarly it regularised the use of the church by the two Societies, with the Inner Temple sitting on the south side of the chancel during services and the Middle on the north side. The Chapel of St. Ann, the vestry on the south side of the church, the Master's House (*ill. 62*) and the various outside spaces associated with the church such as the graveyards were joint responsibilities.

62. The Temple church, south view, with the Master's House. The Vestry was built between the central buttresses c.1662. G. Shepherd, 1812 (Crace Collection, British Museum).

There was a similar arrangement regarding the internal fittings in the church such as the organ, the Communion Table and the bells. As mentioned previously, delays had often occurred when the Societies needed to make a joint decision but could not agree on the necessary action.

General repairs and 'beautification' of parts of the church took place between the years 1732 and 1741. In 1733 the tower over the Round was repaired and in 1736, work was carried out to the eastern end of the Church. This was commemorated by an inscribed tablet inserted in the wall. By 1741 the interior was given 'a thorough scraping, washing, replastering and whitewashing of the walls'. During this period work was carried out to the Benchers' and Master's pews and those occupied by their wives, the pulpit, the organ loft, the Communion Table and the provision of stools and brass candlesticks. Curtains were hung in front of the organ loft, a velvet cushion was made for the Master's pew and the Communion plate was gilded and eight cases made to hold it. A large folio Oxford Bible and eight Common Prayer Books were also purchased[2].

Father Smith maintained the organ until his death in 1708 when his son-in-law Christopher Schreider took over. He was dismissed in 1741 for neglecting his duties and John Byfield was appointed. A number of organists officiated over this century at a salary of £25 per annum. After the resignation of John Pigott[3] in 1733 the two Societies appointed their own organists until 1814. Obadiah Shuttleworth the first Inner Temple organist had in fact been appointed in 1729 because of the frequent absences of Pigott. Shuttleworth[3] was described in the biography of William Boyce as:

> '....A mere harpsichord player who, having the advantage of a good finger, charmed his hearers with such music as was fit alone for that instrument, and drew after him greater numbers than came to hear the preacher.'

A musician and composer of note over this period was John Stanley (*ill. 63*), who succeeded Shuttleworth. Blind from childhood, he became

63. *John Stanley, Organist of the Inner Temple.*

organist at All Hallows church at the age of eleven and obtained his Bachelor of Music at Oxford at the age of sixteen. When he played at the Temple church it was not uncommon to see forty or fifty other organists, including Handel, gathered there to hear him play[4].

Life in the church over this period was dominated by Dr Thomas Sherlock[5] who like his father before him was a powerful preacher. He was Master from 1704-1753. When appointed he was 26 years old and considered too young by many to be able to provide spiritual guidance to the lawyers. But they soon learned to appreciate him. In 1724 the Benchers were so impressed with a series of sermons he gave on 'the defense of the Christian religion' that they wrote to him requesting that he should have these printed. They further showed their appreciation by presenting him with a silver cup costing £49 9s. 6d. In 1747 he was offered the Archbishopric of Canterbury and also a little later the position of the Bishop of London while still Master of the Temple, and an epigram was occasioned by the possibility of either appointment:

'At Temple one day, Sherlock taking a boat,
The waterman asked him, 'Which way will you float?'
'Which way?' says the Doctor; 'Why with the stream!'
To St Paul's or to Lambeth was all one to him.'

After Sherlock retired in 1753 there were six more Masters to the end of the century.

James Boswell was a frequent attender at the church during this period. Two typical records of these visits are:

Sunday 10 April 1763:
'I breakfasted with Temple and then went to the Temple Church and heard a very good sermon on "Set thy house in order, for thou shalt shortly die". This with the music and the good building, put me into a very devout frame, and after service my mind was left in a pleasing calm state.'

Sunday 3 September 1769:
'I then went to the Temple Church. The idea of the Knights Templars lying in the church was solemn and pleasing. The noble music raised my sole to heaven, though it was not Stanley's day, who officiates as organist every other Sunday.'[6]

Boswell's great friend Dr Johnson lived at number 1 Inner Temple Lane from 1760 to 1766. Boswell[7] describes a particular incident that occurred when with him on 28 July 1763:

'As we walked along the Strand tonight, arm in arm, a woman of the town came enticingly near us. "No", said Johnson, "no, my girl, it won't do". We then talked of the unhappy situation of these wretches, and how much more misery than happiness, upon the whole, is produced by irregular love. He parted from me at Temple Gate, as he always does.'

Dr Johnson[8] was 51 when he moved to the Temple and had by then become one of the most eminent literary figures of his day. His famous dictionary had been published five years earlier

in 1755. Whilst at the Temple he formed a group which became known as the Literary Club whose members included Joshua Reynolds and Oliver Goldsmith. Goldsmith was a protégé of Johnson and was becoming a writer and critic of note in his own right. Later at various times Boswell[9] was to describe Goldsmith as:

'...ridiculous, vain, extravagantly dressed, improvident and naive, but also as, tenderhearted, simple and generous, with flashes of brilliance in conversation.'

He lived at number 2 Brick Court for the last nine years of his life, where he died in 1774. He was buried somewhere in the Temple churchyard. It was not until 1841 that a wall tablet to Goldsmith was erected which Mrs Esdaile called a 'gothic object'. This was destroyed in the triforium in the fire of 1941. In 1861, after fruitless inquiry, a plain tombstone was placed in the churchyard inscribed 'Here lies Oliver Goldsmith' (*ill. 64*). After the last war it was moved to a new position. 'He made in his writing but passing allusions, few in number, to the Temple, and the Temple in return neglected him and his grave.' (R.J. Blackman, *The Story of the Temple*, c.1931.) Johnson in his Latin epitaph stated that he 'adorned whatever he touched.'

During the second half of the century numerous small repairs and 'beautifications' were

64. Goldsmith's plain tomb in the churchyard in front of other monuments and the Master's House (1902).

carried out to the church but few detailed records were made of their nature. Two items that give some indication of the finish to the outside of the church are the mention in 1769 that the south side of the church was to be stuccoed and similarly in 1793 when the south side of the church was to be repaired and 'rough cast'. In 1769 consideration was given to repair the crown arch over the Oratory or St Ann's Chapel adjoining the church as it was in a 'ruiness condition'. Mention was made that the records of the Fine Office were stored here. From various descriptions the way through the west end of the church and the area of the porch were narrow and dark and subject to misuse at certain times of the day. Steps were taken in 1769 to overcome this:

'that the wooden rails now belonging to Lamb's buildings should for the present be fixed before the whole western part of the church, to prevent the nuisance by pissing against the same now complained of.'[10]

In 1770 particular arrangements were made for heating the church:

'An iron brazier which will contain a bushel of charcoal to go on casters to be provided, and the same to be filled with charcoal and lighted by the sexton of the Church, and he to place such brazier in the middle aisle of the Church from six of the clock in the morning till a quarter before eleven and then remove it into the Rounds, and after morning service he to place it in the aisle again and remove it into the Rounds a quarter of an hour before evening service.'[11]

In 1779 there was a proposal put to the Inner Temple Bench Committee for a painting on the glass of the east window. It was left to the Treasurer to investigate this idea but no further action seems to have been taken.

The eighteenth century continued to develop the previous century's admiration of the 'Ancient World'. The medieval period, with its 'gothic aspirations and barbarisms'[12], was replaced with a feeling of enlightenment and artistic

taste based on the Greeks and Romans. The classicism brought to the church by the alterations carried out by Wren, was continued by others so that, at the beginning of the nineteenth century, the *Gentleman's Magazine*[13] of 1808 described the church as having:

'18th century buttresses, battlements, tiling and brickwork, a quaint and incongruous belfry, and upon every gable a Wrenean fluted urn with a flame issuing out of the neck thereof.'

'...odious Wrenean overlaying of doorways, windows, entablature and scroll-shores.'

General repairs to the Church were carried out in 1811. At this time, on the orders of the Benchers, the commemorative stone of the consecration of the church, destroyed by workmen in 1695, was remade and placed over the West door. This resulted from an unknown Bencher sending a copy of the original inscription drawn by George Holmes and illustrated in Strype's Stow[14] (*ill. 25*). The new dedication stone was rectilinear in shape rather than the semi-circular shape of the original (*ill. 17*). When Cottingham[15] carried out a survey of the condition of the church in 1840 (Appendix Four), he was very disparaging about the quality of the work carried out in 1811. He noted that they had repaired the six free-standing clustered columns of Purbeck marble in the Round with Roman cement and encased the bases with slabs of Portland stone. He commented on their repair of the chalk groins as follows:

'I have no doubt the builders employed at the Church in 1811, were aware of the insecure state of the inner roofs, though not to the full extent that actually existed, but they were probably not instructed to go into the matter beyond a kind of Churchwarden's "lick and promise" which left the building quite as bad as they found it.'

Up to this point in time, the stability and old ways of the eighteenth century still held sway, Sir Joseph Jekyll, Treasurer of the Inner Temple, described his elderly fellows in 1816 as 'fogrums' opposed to all modern fashions, including new-fangled comforts[16]. Dickens reflected this *laissez-*

faire feeling in *Barnaby Rudge* (Chapter XV) when he wrote:

> 'There are still, worse places than the Temple, on a sultry day, for basking in the sun, or resting idly in the shade. There is yet a drowsiness in its courts, and a dreamy dullness in its streets and gardens; those who pace its lanes and squares may yet hear the echoes of their footsteps on the sounding stones and read upon its gates, in passing from the tumult of the Strand or Fleet street, "Who enters here leaves noise behind".'

The beginnings of the industry and human endeavour that characterised the nineteenth century began now to have their effect in the Temple. In 1819, at long last, work commenced on an ambitious programme of removing the clutter of buildings nestling up against the church to the south. In particular, it was carried out with a view not to let these buildings creep back again as had happened before, and it signalled that the old order of things was at an end. This was a significant year in other ways, as both the Inner and Middle Temple Societies appointed their own architects for the first time. In the past surveyors had been employed. The Inner Temple chose Robert Smirke, and the Middle Temple, Henry Hakewill. Smirke, noted for his Greek Classical Revival architecture, was patronised by the Tory party and had come to notice on account of his work on the Royal Mint in London (1807-09), and Covent Garden Theatre (built in 1809, but burnt down in 1857). He had also been appointed in 1815 as one of the architects to the Board of Works, joining Soane and Nash. In 1825, as a result of the removal of the buildings, he was asked to submit proposals for general repairs for the Inner Temple side of the church. These were recorded as a Bench Table Order on 11 February 1825:

> 'Mr Smirke having made a Sketch of the appearance which the Temple Church will exhibit when the proposed Improvements shall have been made.'

Work commenced in 1826, partly to redress serious problems of decay. It was done as a rolling programme of separate commissions, the sum total of which was a major replacement or removal of important parts of the historic church which went beyond the simple repair of the south side of the church where the buildings had been removed. What he did and the way he did it led to considerable controversy. It was carried out at a time when James Wyatt's approach to such work still held sway, even though much criticised by some antiquarians such as John Carter and the Rev. John Milner. This involved, amongst other things, the excessive removal of historic additions, features etc. as part of a general simplification, tidying up and opening up of the interiors and exteriors of churches. It went beyond the principles of removal or replacement of the later, more scholarly, Gothic Revival Movement of the 1840s, and far beyond the minimalist approach expounded by Ruskin and Morris from the 1847s onwards.

During the actual work carried out by Smirke, the stair to the corner of the cloisters that Wren had designed south of the church was rebuilt, in order to provide a less encumbered view of the church. More significantly, as part of the removal of buildings to the south, the house built into the ruins of St Ann's Chapel which had been shattered by gunpowder in 1678 to stop the spread of a fire, was demolished. In September 1825, Sir Robert Smirke[17] recommended that the chapel '...was in so ruinous a state that it must be pulled down and the records therein must therefore be removed.'

The records referred to were those of the Fine Office and were kept in the crypt of the chapel. Smirke requested that these should be removed to the vestibule of the church. The Sub-Treasurer wrote to the Chirographer of the Court of Common Pleas, who was in charge of these records, but he refused to move them or hand over the key as he did not think the new location was suitable. Following this the door to the crypt was forced open and the contents removed to the church vestibule. The remains of the chapel were immediately demolished and carted away. The Fine Office records had been stored there since

1678 when a fire destroyed the original Office in Hare Court. The removal of the remains of St Ann's Chapel was later denounced as 'an unpardonable outrage'[18]. The appearance of the chapel, after the removal of the house before demolition, is depicted in the watercolour drawing by John Buckler of 1826, previously referred to in Chapter Three (*ill. 81*). Disquiet about its demolition continued to the extent that Robert Smirke's brother Sydney felt that he needed to defend his brother's action when he was involved in further restoration work twenty years later. In a joint publication with Essex of 1845[19], he again explained his brother's reasons for his actions by pointing out that the chapel was later than the main church. When demolished, ashlar work to the Round had been found behind and therefore the chapel formed no part of the original intention. He said:

> 'It was clearly posterior to the church and formed no part whatever of the design. It deformed the symmetry and encumbered the exterior of the church, without possessing any intrinsic architectural beauty or interest; for its features were plain and the whole had undergone considerable mutilation and change.'

He refuted those who had said that the chapel had been a structure of exquisite beauty and accused them of not actually having seen it. If they had they could not have agreed with this exaggerated description. He went on to say that any rebuilding would only have been conjectural and would have created 'a small and mutilated excrescence, for the mere gratification of curiosity.' Later research suggests that although built later than the Round, it was probably built at about the same time as the enlarged chancel of 1240, less than fifty years later. From the description written just before the chapel was demolished, reproduced in Chapter Three, and from the details that can be ascertained from the Buckler painting, it is hard to believe that it was plain and devoid of any architectural beauty. All that remains today is the undercroft to the chapel.

It is interesting to speculate what line the ecclesiologists of the Gothic Revival Movement would have taken, if the decision regarding the chapel had been made some twenty five years later. They would have been torn between getting back to the purity of the original intentions – as perceived in the nineteenth century – and accepting that it was as contemporary to the Round as the chancel. If they had decided to retain it, they would have had the confidence that it could be rebuilt in a style as good as the original – indeed probably better! If the decision had been made twenty five years further on, after the Gothic Revival Movement had nearly run its course, it would have been very different. Then it would have been made on the basis of the principles of The Society for the Protection of Ancient Buildings (SPAB). This was set up by William Morris in 1877, as a reaction to the 'vandalism' by wholesale alteration or rebuilding of original features to cathedrals which was occurring across the country under the guise of the Gothic Revival Movement. SPAB's approach was not to '*repair, restore, or improve*' with implications of removing and renewing, but to '*conserve*' what was found with an absolute minimum of replacing what was there, and then in such a way that the repair could be distinguished from surrounding original work. SPAB also wanted to respect the work of all ages as part of the total history of a building and its use. With this approach, the house built into the ruins of the chapel would not have been removed in the first place. However, if this had already happened, then the ruin of the chapel would have been left with the minimum of work necessary to make the ruin safe and to slow down further decay of the fabric. Today the approach would be very similar to that of SPAB, and can be seen in the restoration work to the church after the fire damage of the last war – described later in this book. Having made the decision to remove it, it is a pity that it was not customary then to make a record of what had been taken away.

Robert Smirke continued with this and other work until 1828. He describes the work to the south wall of the chancel and to the lowest part of the Round where the chapel was removed, in a letter dated 10 February 1826 saying:

'...I have fortunately been able to discover fragments remaining of the ancient fabric sufficient in every part to restore it correctly, and I have in no respect deviated from the original forms.... in clearing away the ruins of the vaulted building [ie. the chapel], the remains of the surface of the original walls of the Round church were perceived and I have carefully preserved them. In the same manner I have discovered parts sufficiently to enable me to restore with certainty nearly the whole of the great pointed windows on the south side of the church upon one of which the workmen are now employed.'[20]

It is difficult to say what was exactly meant by this. By today's standards, it sounds ominous. Rather than saving and conserving what was there as original fabric of the church, he was embarking on a programme of removing and replacing it with a replica in dressed Bath stone, which was a different stone from the original. St Aubyn, who made alterations to the Round in the 1860s, gave much more detailed information about the finish to the original external walls. His discoveries indicated that they were of rough coursed Kentish ragstone finished with a thin layer of plaster. The Inner Temple Bench Records of this period show that Burnell the stone mason was paid over £1000, indicative of a substantial amount of work being carried out.

Smirke also replaced the tiled finish to the roof on the south part of the Round with lead, and the upper part with stone 'which was plastered over, a few years ago'. In carrying this out, the battlemented finish to the top parapet was replaced with a plain one (compare *ills. 66 and 67* showing the Round before and after this work). The old rotten belfry was removed from the roof over the south side of the chancel (*ill. 65*) and

65. *The Temple church from the cloisters. By J.R. Herbert, 1804.*

66. South-west view of the Round church, 1792. Aquatint by Thomas Malton.

67. The Temple church as restored, 1828. Drawn by Thomas H. Shepherd.

the bell was placed inside the roof[21]. Brickwork to the south west gable was removed and the gable 'restored'. The 'classical' urns to the top of the gables to the chancel were replaced with crosses[22].

Robert Smirke's work inside the church was limited to the Round. By this time it was generally in a dilapidated state. Stone surfaces were greatly repaired and encrusted with plaster and built up with layers of whitewash, and wherever possible covered with monuments. The Purbeck columns were crudely patched up, as described above, as part of the work of 1811. He arranged for the paving to be taken up, renewed where necessary and relaid on bitumen to overcome dampness. Smirke proposed to re-lay any stones that were removed from the floor which had a monumental or other description on them in a line against the wall. The extent to which he carried out this intention is not clear[23]. The stone seat and the arcade were renewed as well as the capitals to the columns to the arcade and the grotesque heads of Caen stone. Typically, without any thought for the original, Portland stone

was used for the replacement heads rather than the original type of stone. Some of the monuments on the freestanding columns were removed. The two door openings on the south side were blocked up. Finally, the heating stove and flue in the Round were repaired. By the time the work had finished, over £4,000 had been spent. Two stone tablets commemorating this work can still be seen, one on the inside and one on the outside of the south part of the Round. Billings in 1838 gave a good indication in his drawing of what the Round looked like after Smirke had finished, although the artist has left out the monuments in the interior views (*ill. 17*). The grotesque heads referred to above were the ones mentioned so fondly by Lamb a few years earlier in 1823 in *Essays of Elia*:

'...the grotesque Gothic heads (seeming to me then replete with devout meaning) that gape, and grin, in stone around the inside of the old Round Church (my church) of the Templars.'[24]

This was in his essay *My First Play* which described the first plays he was taken to see when a child. Charles Lamb (1775-1834) was born in the Temple in Crown Office Row, where his father was clerk to the lawyer Samuel Salt.

Billings[25] when later describing the renewal of the heads in his book of 1838, said that as all the grotesque heads and capitals to the arcade were more or less decayed, they were taken down and replaced with new carvings. However, a few original ones were put up again. There were also six heads and capitals on the north side, either hidden or destroyed by monuments placed against them. He said:

> 'The masterly manner in which the restoration of the arcade is effected, reflects great credit to the workman, and proves our capability of executing these works equal to the most approved examples of antiquity.'

However, not everyone shared this view. Again, like the demolition of the chapel, concern was expressed, particularly when it was discovered that some of the original heads were used as cart wheel crutches[26]. Richardson[27] in his book of 1845 wished to establish more clearly exactly what work had been done as far as the grotesque heads were concerned. He interviewed the people actually employed in the work and established that some heads at the time of the restoration retained their leading characteristics, but were worn to a greater or less degree, while others were of a sufficient condition to make a good likeness to the original. They were all renewed except the six on the north side which were behind monuments and which Richardson renewed as part of the 1840s work.

He ascertained that the heads on the south side and a few on the north were the work of:

> 'a young man who had been a fisherman and quarryman and then a mason. He copied the originals as far as they furnished him with authority, but had no knowledge of such subjects to guide him when they were doubtful or defective.'

The remainder on the north side (except the six previously mentioned) and four on the east side:

> '...were executed by a carver who it is feared studied more for effect than accuracy.'

These comments are in direct contrast to the rosy picture painted by Billings.

The compartment arcades were carefully restored after drawings and measurements were made. As the work involved blocking up two doors on the south side, additional heads were required. This could explain why in this area, two or three heads are repeated. Some heads appear to be in the style of a much later date than the original designs, with at least one resembling the head of King Charles I. (*ill. 68.*)

68. A head resembling Charles I.

Richardson also established:

> 'The directions of those employed was to copy the original work as closely as possible and the author was assured that there was no intentional deviation – *but by some inadvertence the heads were with a few exceptions put up without regard to their previous order!*'

It is clear that Richardson's concern was more to do with historical authenticity and quality of the carving of the replacement than with the ethics of whether they should have been replaced at all. It should be remembered that he was quite happy to replace six of them himself as part of the 1842 work. However, he would have claimed that his work would have been historically accurate and more skilled. The approach today would have been to keep the

69. *Engravings by R.W. Billings in 1838 of the replacement grotesque heads. Numbers 2 and 3 are similar to originals shown in ill. 70*

70. The unrestored arcading, showing the original heads in their original order and the matrix of Lucy Hare's brass (1601) on the floor. Etched by J.T. Smith 1811.

original heads, and 'conserve' them.

A current look at whether any of the heads are replicas of the originals can be attempted by examining a series of engravings by Smith of 1811 (*ill. 70*) and by Nash published in 1818 (*ill. 18*), i.e. before the renewal of the heads. On comparing these twelve heads with the present fifty, the four furthest on the right of the Smith engraving are indeed similar to existing ones either side of the West doorway. This confirms Richardson's findings in that some of the present heads were copies of the originals (compare the heads in ill. 70 with those of ill. 69) – but as can be seen from the Smith engraving – not in the original position. None of the ten (out of 56) carved capitals, and the two (out of ten) capitals to the Purbeck wall shafts illustrated by Nash in 1818, match any of the present ones. On this evidence, it can be concluded that the majority of the renewals were freely carved. Again this was a tragic loss of a unique set of early carvings.

To this must be added the frustration that no record was made of the original heads before they were removed. It is also lamentable that, contrary to Billings' assertion, there did not seem to be any skilled stone carvers to do the work. William Morris raised this point later, regarding the work of many Gothic Revivalist craftsmen who were no match compared to the original craftsmen. He accused them of producing sterile replicas and at the same time debasing the craftsmens' art.

By 1828, when he ceased work on the church, Robert Smirke was running a large, well organised practice. He had completed Canada House (1824-1827), and had designed and started on site the British Museum (1823-1847). He later built up a reputation for restoration work on historic buildings, including work to Westminster Hall, the Chapel Royal at St. James's Palace and the Banqueting House of Inigo Jones. He was knighted in 1832 for his work for the Board of Works. He also carried out further work at the Inns of Court, two notable surviving examples of which are the lower King's Bench Walk (1829), and Paper Buildings (1839). More significantly, he designed several new churches in the Neo-Greek style, for which he was much criticised by Pugin, who felt the only true style for church building was Gothic.

In conclusion, and accepting that work had to be done to make the church wind and weather tight, most of the work on the church carried out by Smirke during the 1820s was highly questionable by today's standards. Although he replaced some of the worst excesses of the classical embellishments, he did not display a real understanding and sympathy for the architectural style of the medieval building. Gilchrist, in his *Life of Etty*[28], said:

> 'Sir Robert Smirke, a competent Builder-Architect, of small real sympathy with Gothic, and superficial knowledge of it.'

Smirke's work to the church even falls short of standards that were beginning to be expressed only twenty five years after the work was completed. One can only be thankful that money ran out and the Benchers did not agree to further works that he suggested. It is appropriate that John Ruskin has the last word, particularly when considering the destruction of St Ann's Chapel and the grotesque heads much beloved by Charles Lamb. He said:

> '...*Restoration*.... means the most total destruction which a building can suffer: a destruction out of which no remnants can be gathered: a destruction accompanied with false descriptions of the thing destroyed.... It is impossible as to raise the dead, to restore anything that has ever been great or beautiful in architecture.... And as for direct and simple copying, it is palpably impossible. What copying can there be of surfaces that have been worn half an inch down? The whole finish of the work, was in the half inch that is gone; if you attempt to restore that finish, you do it conjecturally; if you copy what is left, granting fidelity to be possible... how is the new work better than the old? There is yet in the old some life, some mysterious suggestion of what it has been, and of what it has lost; some sweetness in the gentle lines which rain and sun has wrought. There can be none in the brute hardness of the new carving... Do not let us talk then of restoration. The thing is a lie from beginning to end.'[29]

In 1829 Robert Smirke was asked to comment on whether it was appropriate to put stained glass into the church windows. Subsequent to his recommendation it was decided not to proceed with this work. At the time of giving his views he reported that there were a number of ominous cracks in the building. This foreshadowed the next major works to the church in the early 1840s.

NOTES TO CHAPTER SEVEN

[1] Middle Temple Archives, 'An Account of Children Exposed in the Middle Temple'; Murray, Ian, *The Little Temples*.

[2] Roberts, R., *A Calendar of the Inner Temple Records*, Vol IV, 1714-1750 (1933).

[3] Lewer, David, *A Spiritual Song*, 71 (1961).

[4] *Op. cit.*

[5] *Op. cit.* 66

[6] *Boswell's London Journal 1762-63* (ed. 1950); *Boswell in Search of a Wife, 1766-69* (ed. 1957). John Jones was the alternate organist for the Middle Temple (1749-96), R.J.S. Stevens, a noted composer of glees, succeeded Stanley as the Inner Temple organist (1786-1810).

[7] *Op. cit.* 327.

[8] Bellot, Hugh, The Little Guides – *The Temple*, 79 (1914).

[9] *The Oxford Companion to English Literature*, 402 (5th edn, 1985).

[10] Roberts, R., *A Calendar of the Inner Temple Records*, Vol V, 1751-1800 (1936).

[11] *Op. cit.*

[12] Trevelyan, G.M., *English Social History*, 296 (1978).

[13] *The Gentleman's Magazine* Vol lxxvii, pt2, 1000 (1808) and Vol. lxxxi, pt 1, 100 (1811).

[14] Esdaile, Mrs Arundell, *Temple Church Monuments*, 7 (1933).

[15] Cottingham, Lewis Nockalls, *Report on a Survey of the Temple Church*, in Middle Temple Archives, 26 Oct 1840.

[16] Baker, J.H., *The Inner Temple*, 9 (1991).

[17] Inner Temple Bench Table Minutes (ITBTM) 1801-1826, Sub-Treasurer's Report 8 Nov 1825.

[18] *Athenaeum* 1843, 301.

[19] Essex, W.R.H., Smirke, Sydney, *Illustrations etc. of the Temple Church London* (1845).

[20] ITBTM *op. cit.*, 10 Feb 1826.

[21] *Op. cit*, 24 Nov 1826.

[22] Billings, R.W., *Architectural Illustrations and Account of the Temple Church London,* 47 (1838).

[23] Esdaile (*op. cit.*), 11.

[24] *The Works of Charles and Mary Lamb*, Vol. II, 99 (1903).

[25] Billings (*op. cit.*), 55

[26] Crook, J. Mordaunt, 'The Restoration of the Temple Church: Ecclesiology and Recrimination' in *Architectural History*, Vol. 8 (1965).

[27] Richardson, E., *The Ancient Stone and Lead Coffins etc The Temple Church* (1845).

[28] Gilchrist, A., *Life of Etty* pt I, 279 (1855).

[29] Ruskin, John, *The Seven Lamps of Architecture* (1849).

CHAPTER EIGHT

The Early Victorians

The restoration and repairs to the church started by Robert Smirke in the 1820s came to an end when the Middle Temple Benchers were not prepared to fund any more work[1]. Ten years later in 1838, the Middle Temple was again in a position to do further repairs, but Sir Robert Smirke was too ill to carry this out and as a consequence, James Savage (1779-1852), who had succeeded Hakewill in 1830 as architect to the Middle Temple, was asked to advise. Savage had designed Plowden Buildings for the Middle Temple and in his own private practice many other buildings in the Gothic Revival style including St Luke's, Chelsea. The request to carry out more work on the church came at a time when the Benchers now accepted that the Inns of Court had been sorely neglected over the years. This general state of disrepair was captured by Dickens who wrote in *Pickwick Papers* in 1836:

> 'These sequestered nooks.... the public offices of the legal profession.... are for the most part, low roofed, mouldy rooms, where innumerable rolls of parchment, which have been perspiring in secret for the last century, send forth an agreeable odour, which mingled by day with the scent of dry rot....'[2]

It was also at a time when the population of London was rapidly increasing, having almost doubled since the turn of the century, from 865,000 to 1,500,000. It would continue to increase another threefold by 1900 to 4,500,000. With business booming as a consequence there was now the money and commitment for refurbishing buildings, as well as for building new ones.

As a result, by the end of the second half of the nineteenth century, a large part of the two Inns was rebuilt. It included a new Hall and Library for the Inner Temple, as well as Harcourt Buildings, Dr Johnson's Building, parts of Hare Court, Crown Office Row, Paper Buildings, Goldsmith Buildings, Tanfield Court Buildings, additional chambers and a new grand gate at the southern end of Middle Temple Lane. This work was carried out by some of the most eminent architects of the day, in a variety of Victorian styles. But not all of it was a reflection of changing times, as the Inns continued to be plagued by fires – the rebuilding of Paper Buildings, for example, was attributed to the carelessness of William Maule Q.C., leaving a lighted candle by his bedside.[3]

As far as the church was concerned, in May 1838 James Savage was initially asked to make improvements to the organ. However, the work was not carried out immediately, and a year later the Middle Temple decided to embark on more general work to 'repair and beautify' the church[4]. They sought agreement with the Inner Temple who, in turn, wanted to improve the heating. As a result a joint committee was formed in May 1839 to agree and administer these works[5]. The Committee, on inspecting the church, recommended a number of repairs to the roof, walls, pews, heating and, more significantly, the stripping of stonework columns and vaulting back to the original surfaces. They also urged opening up the two side arches between the Round and the chancel, which had been blocked up and secured with doors since the end of the seventeenth century. This request reflected the changing use of the church from that time. The Round was no longer seen as having a mainly secular use and the chancel a religious one. Nor was the Round seen any more as a collecting point for undesirables who were likely to run off with the church plate from the chancel. The Master separately requested the removal of the monuments from the church. In the following year James Savage was asked to proceed with the work.

Three years and 195 meetings later[6], after stripping back to the surface of stonework revealed massive decay and years of poor repair, and timber fittings were judged to be rotten beyond repair from rising damp, a virtual complete restoration of the church had taken place.

As a result of the ever increasing amount of work, as more decay was discovered, the initial estimate of cost of £4,215 had risen to £51,896 by the end of the contract in 1842[7]. The *Gentleman's Magazine*[8] of 1843 claimed that the true cost exceeded £70,000. Half way through the contract the escalating liability caused the members of the Committee to ask the architect to investigate certain expenses. This led to the stonemason, Burnell, being dismissed for false accounting, and Barrett the carver was employed in his place. Then the architect in charge, James Savage, came under scrutiny as costs continued to increase. Sir Robert Smirke was asked to investigate the accounts on behalf of the Committee. He was also asked to take over the supervision of the works, which he declined to do. On his recommendation the work was stopped on 20 April 1841 until he could report on the matter, but in view of his ill health he asked his brother, Sydney Smirke and Decimus Burton to help him. As a result of this investigation James Savage was rather unfairly dismissed for lack of cost control[9]. In his defence Savage had explained that the increases were caused by difficulties in getting accurate costs for the masons' work and the overcharging for this, the additional and unforeseen work necessary once areas were stripped back revealing extensive decay, extra work to the foundations beneath the Round, the change in style of joiners work after research into historical

accuracy, the need of expensive reference models for the carvers, and the cost of accommodation on site for the huge workforce. The pressure to complete the work as soon as possible made it difficult to cost every item ahead of it being carried out, and would have substantially delayed the work. L. Cottingham, who was asked to carry out an independent Condition Survey of the church when costs started to escalate, was asked whether they could have been predicted. He supported the view of Savage that until areas were stripped back it would be difficult to accurately cost work (*Appendix Four*). However, members still proceeded to dismiss Savage. This 'scandal' was effectively buried until J. Mordaunt Crook wrote about it in *Architectural History* in 1965[10]. Savage said about the prospect of being dismissed:

> 'My dismissal will be an act of the greatest injustice to me and certainly without any apparent or probable advantage to the progress or successful completion of the works.'

Subsequently Savage appears to have carried out few commissions until his death ten years later.

Of particular note in Cottingham's survey report of 26 October 1840 was his concern about work carried out in 1811, when settlement of stone ribs was supported with iron rods passing through the ribs into timber beams above. Equally the chalk to the groins was wedged up with tiles, slates, and stopping in the joints. As an aside he mentioned that the original round window had been discovered above the west doorway. However, this could not be properly explored until 1860 when the building over the porch was removed.

Cottingham is of some interest. He was an architect working in the Gothic Revival style who was involved in restoration work and had worked on Rochester Cathedral, where he replaced the central tower, and on a number of abbey churches. He lived in Waterloo Bridge Road, Lambeth, where he had a museum of medieval architecture which contained examples of medieval woodwork, Gothic carvings, plaster casts of capitals, bosses and sculpture. With so few examples of genuine medieval work left, Savage drew extensively on these when considering replacement work in the church. He borrowed upwards of 200 specimens of early English work to use as models for the carvers to help with the design and execution of the bench ends, capitals etc.[11]. In the end Cottingham felt that he should be paid for his advice and the borrowing of fragments from the museum. When he died in 1847, an application was made to the Government to buy his collection for the nation. This failed and it was subsequently auctioned off. Eventually some of the items were acquired by the Victoria & Albert Museum.

After the departure of Savage, the architects involved in investigating the costs, Sydney Smirke and Decimus Burton, were appointed in July 1841 to complete the works. This was mostly to the designs of Savage. Sydney Smirke (1798-1877) was Robert's youngest brother and both of them owed much to Tory patronage. Irrespective of this Sydney was a scholarly architect and was confident in both Renaissance and Gothic styles. He was also skilled in the use of cast-iron which he used to great effect in the construction of the great dome at the British Museum. Decimus Burton (1800-1881) was the tenth son of James Burton. He designed a number of the villas in Regents Park and a wide range of other buildings. He was more interested in Greek Revivalist architecture than Gothic.

Twelve months after the appointment of Smirke and Burton, excluding furnishing, completion was achieved in June 1842[12] (*ill. 85*). The words of Savage above proved to be prophetic – the final cost exceeded the estimates of Smirke and Burton, as extensive additional work was undertaken – the very same problem that had led to Savage's dismissal. The increase was despite using a very detailed system of cost control recommended by Sir Robert Smirke, which involved using standard rates for work and obtaining estimates before each piece of work began. Ironically, the Benchers approved this last increase in their final summary report in the same terms used by Savage in his own defence:

'... the increase has arisen almost wholly from difficulties which could not have been anticipated.'[13]

A study of this report indicates a huge set up for the works, with over 130 workmen on site in the autumn of 1841. It is curious to note from the report that, on the one hand modern steam driven stone cutting machinery was in use, and on the other there was the need for thousands of candles in order to see when working. Other items of expenditure were for beer for the stone carvers, and beer and spirits for workmen 'on account of removal of coffins at night'.

Cottingham, commenting on the work of Robert Smirke to the Round in the 1820s (*Appendix Four*), said 'it was to be deeply regretted that... greater research was not made to ascertain more correct detail'. This was not the case in 1840-42 as much scholarly research into historical accuracy was carried out. Furthermore some of the finest craftsmen in the land were used to execute the work.

The beginning of the 1840s, when the work started, was at the point of a major change in architectural thought and expression. The Classical style of architecture was still used for most important buildings but soon the Gothic Revival Movement, which mixed religious fervour with a belief that the Pointed Gothic style of architecture of the fourteenth century was the best for all buildings, gained popularity.

At the commencement of the restoration of the Temple church, the Cambridge Camden Society, one of the main instigators of the Gothic Movement, had only just been formed (1839). Its journal, *The Ecclesiologist*, was not commenced until 1841. In its first issues were set out the Movement's principles for restoration work to churches. Although Pugin had already published his book, *Contrasts,* on the use of Gothic architecture in 1836, the Society republished this in 1841 together with his book *The True Principles of Pointed Christian Architecture*. These were to have considerable influence in the use of this style of architecture. As a result, J. Mordaunt Crook in his article in 1965, said that the work to the Temple church of Savage, Smirke and Burton:

> 'Never won the full approval of thorough-bred ecclesiologists. The Cambridge Camden Society considered it a misfortune that Savage had set to work before the principles of ecclesiology had attained the status of an exact science.'[14]

However, it is clear that the work followed in broad terms, the principles that were later formulated by the Society. As stated in *The Ecclesiolgist* of 1842:

> ' To restore is to revive the original appearance.... lost by decay, accident or ill-judged alteration.'

Of course, in most cases, 'restore' meant remove and replace. Sydney Smirke in his account of the work rather ominously stated:

> 'The whole of the interior fittings were removed, together with the screen, and every vestige of modern work throughout the building.'[15]

As has been seen, 'modern' meant anything built or installed after the middle ages, such as Wren's work. It seems that the more valuable items removed were auctioned off and 'Wren's' altar screen was sold to the Bowes Museum, Barnard Castle, as 'Lot 24'.

In 1845 Sydney Smirke and William Essex[16] gave a detailed description of the work carried out. In summary, all of the fixtures and fittings were removed. The floors were renewed and that in the chancel was lowered by fifteen inches to the original level. Most of the wall surfaces, inside and out, vaulting and the Purbeck marble columns and wall shafts were renovated except where this had already been carried out by Robert Smirke or where surfaces were still encumbered by buildings. New roofs were placed over the Round and the staircase tower. The original inscription was recut around the top of the West doorway and the door itself was renewed (*ill. 71*). A new font was made similar to that at Alphington, Exeter. Heating ducts were constructed below the floor.

Some aspects of the work warrant a more detailed description and this is given below.

Ancient Coffins and Effigies

In the process of carrying out the work in the Round a number of stone and lead coffins were discovered under the Round (*ills 28-30*). These are described in more detail in Chapter Two. Whilst work continued these were removed to a temporary building where they were seen by thousands. Edward Richardson[17] said that although the skeletons and wrappings in the coffins were in good condition when found, on being exposed to the air and light they rapidly deteriorated and much of the contents were reduced to dust. Similarly parts of the lead became so oxidised as to 'crumble to pieces in the hand'. When the structural work to the Round was finished they were re-interred in a concrete vault in the centre of the Round.

Like the coffins, the effigies in the Round were stored in a shed whilst the major works to the Round were being carried out. They were then restored by the sculptor Edward Richardson as they were badly defaced and had successive coats of paint up to ½in thick which concealed the original shape and finish.

Smirke describes the work to the effigies as:

> '... being done with much success, and the more prominent parts that had been broken off are so effectively reinstated, that it is hardly any longer possible for even a critical eye to distinguish the old from the restored parts.'[18]

He stated that a description of this restoration was published by the sculptor[19] 'so that future antiquarians will have no reason to complain of any want of good faith'. A judgement on this can be made after reading about the post war work carried out to the effigies, described in Chapter Fifteen, when the extent of these repairs was revealed, showing the level of conjecture involved in the restoration.

From the above description the restoration of the effigies appears to have been carried out with considerable care but *The Dictionary of National Biography* reveals a further scandal, for in de-

The Organ and Views to the Altar

Originally it was intended to open up the two side arches between the Round and the chancel and remove the screen under the organ. In so doing it was found that the organ structure was so dangerous that it was also removed together with the organ, and for the first time in nearly 200 years, the central two halves of the church were visibly connected. Savage and others were so struck by this new vista that they urged the Benchers to place the organ elsewhere to allow this view to be retained. The Benchers sought the opinion on this matter from a number of eminent architects and artists. These were Sir Robert Smirke, Sydney Smirke, Cottingham and Blore, architects, and Etty and Willement, artists. They were asked to give their views on various locations for the organ – its present position between the Round and the chancel; in the arch at the western end of the Round; against or beyond the eastern end of the chancel; or in a chamber built out from the middle of the north side of the chancel. The key question was whether it should be returned to its previous position in the central arch. Only Blore seriously considered putting it back, as he thought it was the best musically. The others wished to keep the central arch clear. Savage in his report of 23 July 1840, said:

'As a matter of principle there is no doubt that a good central view of the East or Altar end of the Church from the entrance was always a main object in the older times and never considered secondary.'[21]

Sydney Smirke on 17 July 1840 reported:

'There is so beautiful an effect produced by clearing away all the obstructions that have been hitherto interposed between the circular and quadrangular portions of the Church, that I would strongly recommend the former site of the organ to be left perfectly clear and open.'[22] (ill. 72).

The most favoured position was to put it on the north side of the chancel and this was the one adopted by the Benchers (ill. 95).

71. The handsome West door (1842) which survived the fire of 1941.

scribing the work of Richardson it says:

'He incurred some opprobrium by his restoration of the effigies of the Knights Templars in the Temple Church in 1842, and was refused admission to the Society of Antiquaries. The effigies had suffered before he began to restore them, by being left in a damp shed in Hare Court during the winter of 1841-2.'[20]

It is significant that when Richardson described the work to the effigies he said that it was impossible to preserve the original colours and gilding 'because of their adhering to the paint, and owing to the moist and perishing state of the stone and marble'. The storage of the stone coffins in damp surroundings also helps to explain their rapid deterioration. This criticism did not deter Richardson as he went on to restore other effigies and monuments including those in Chichester Cathedral.

72. *The Temple church as restored in 1842 showing the renewed Purbeck marble columns in the Round, Smirke's stone altar reredos, candle-lit candelabra, Minton floor tiles and railings round the effigies. A sliding brass rod can be seen on either side which was closed at the commencement of the service; latecomers had to remain in the Round.*

Decoration and stained glass

Richardson and Willement[23,24], both commented on the traces of early decoration on the chancel spandrels when the limewash was removed. Decoration was also found on the inside of blocks of stone that had been used, at some time in the past, to block up several openings in the triforium. Details of these decorations are described in Chapter Three. It was noted that there were no figurative representations. Sydney Smirke said:

> '....the certainty that the original building was so finished left no alternative to the architects, whose duty was that of simple restoration, except where necessary or convenience required them to deviate from their model.'[25]

It was claimed that it was not possible to discover enough of the details of the original designs to reinstate them. It is more likely that what was found was of curiosity value only, and no serious attempt was made to reconstruct or save what was found. It was sufficient to discover that the vaulting was decorated in earlier times. A scholarly replacement 'in the style of that period' would be made. Thomas Willement (1786-1871), an heraldic expert, was appointed to carry out this work. He submitted a detailed, well-researched report on proposals for painting the ceilings to the Committee in November 1840[26]. This traced the history of such work from early Christian worship up to Norman times and made the point that most early brightly coloured decorations from this period, which had not already been destroyed by fire or alterations, were whitewashed over in the seventeenth century with the rise of a more puritanical approach to religion. He said that it was appropriate to put this style of decoration back as a way of expressing a more reverential feeling which was then increasing. His designs were founded on examples that remained from the same period as the church, and resembled those found in contemporary illustrated manuscripts. He included in the designs the arms used by the two Societies of the Inns of Court and the emblems of the Holy Evangelists. The west wall of the chancel was decorated with six enthroned figures representing the monarchs connected with the history of the Knights Templars and the church (*ill. 84*).

The designs for the stained glass to the east windows were also carried out by Willement and were again based on existing examples of the same period. A distinguished artist in stained glass who is credited with reviving the art., he advised George IV and later Queen Victoria in this capacity, designing the windows for St George's Chapel Windsor. He justified the use of stained glass at the Temple church rather than simply replacing the existing clear glass:

> '...to produce subdued light, which would produce a religious feeling and calm devotion for the worship of God, and the representations on it for the unlearned, to provide the most powerful impressions of those events, judgements, and mercies which are recorded in the Holy Scriptures.'[27]

He described his design as:

> 'like early mosaics of small pieces arranged in regular panels, containing subjects from the Holy Writ, the intervening spaces filled by foliage ornaments, and the whole, when there was sufficient space, enclosed with a rich and elaborate border.'

In addition he incorporated illustrations of the arms of the two Societies, famous Knights Templars, royal arms and various Templar symbols such as two Knights riding the same horse (*ill. 83*).

Altar Screen

The design for the altar screen, or reredos, was by Smirke & Burton (*ill. 82*. It was made of stone and was a highly coloured Gothic extravaganza. The length was broken down into a series of arches, flanked by strongly articulated columns and triple curved heads. The central five arches were set forward of the others and were emphasised by steeply pointed tops and crockets (leafy knobs along the sloping edges). They were surmounted with foliated crosses. The middle arch was decorated with an ornamental gilded cross, while the two side arches on the north contained the Decalogue and the two on the south the Lord's Prayer and Creed.

Encaustic Tiles

Unfortunately all of the early encaustic tiles found in the chancel were taken up.   However, Richardson recorded a number of the original tiles (described more fully in Chapter Three). New encaustic and partially vitrified tiles manufactured by Minton were laid in the chancel and the Round. Smirke[28] said that the designs by Willement (*ill. 73*) were based in part on the medieval tiles found on the church floor and from contemporary remains in the Chapter House at Westminster. Subsequent to the fire of 1941 some of these were relaid in the triforium. A comparison between these and the medieval tiles

drawn by Richardson does indeed show a similarity in the design of the griffons and knights, but the modern tiles do not have the crude vitality of the earlier ones, nor the patina of age.

Pews

The general design of the oak pews was by Savage and that of the carved elbows was based on existing medieval examples loaned to him by Cottingham. The fine carving of the elbows was by S.A. Nash who had carried out many commissions in Suffolk and London (*ills 74 & 75*). The cost of these was considerably more than Savage had originally estimated and was one of the reasons that led to his dismissal.

Members wished the pews to provide as much seating as possible and they were so arranged that the free-standing pillars in the chancel were clear of the pews. This led to the provision of

73. Detail of the Minton encaustic floor tiles, relaid in the triforium after the last war. Photograph by Robert Dark.

74 & 75. Oak elbows to the stalls in the chancel (1842), carved by S.A. Nash. The cost was very heavy.

two side aisles along the line of these pillars and no central aisle (see back endpaper). It is strange that after all the effort to open up the view from the Round to the altar, by not having a central aisle the pews partially blocked it (*ill. 72*). The other disadvantage was that arrangement did not allow a direct processional route to the altar, a point made by the ecclesiologists. The request for a central aisle was repeated by others at regular intervals but nothing happened until after the pews were destroyed during the Second World War.

The Wall Monuments

The original request to remove the monuments from the church came from the Master. Their number was such that in the words of Smirke[29] 'they had accumulated to such an extent as greatly to impair the beautiful effect of the building'. Another problem was revealed when they were taken down. 'The removal of the Monuments has disclosed the great damage done to the walls, and especially to the pillars by their fixture'[30].

The 92 monuments and the oak wainscoting were removed and the walls behind them repaired. A few monuments were refixed, but the majority were put in the triforium (*ill. 76*). This decision was made after several alternative locations were suggested to house them including converting the Exchequer Office, placing them at the east end of the church or constructing a monumental cloister in the churchyard. The latter was rejected by the Master, who said it would encroach too much on his house and garden if located there.

Mrs Arundell Esdaile[31] was particularly scathing about the removal of the monuments to the triforium as they were one of the most historic collections in England. She blamed the architects for banishing them to this cramped and unsuitable location. Her criticism seems unfair when it is recalled that it was the Master who requested that they were removed from the church and it was he and the Benchers who decided to reject the various alternatives suggested by the architects.

76. Entrance to the triforium showing monuments removed from the church in 1842. The monument to Sir John Witham (1689) seen on the right of the doorway survived and is now on the south wall of the chancel. Drawing by Herbert Railton.

At the conclusion of the restoration of the church Smirke praised the Benchers for supporting it for:

'... it may be confidently said that the Church would have been a ruin before many years had expired, but for this timely interposition. The main external walls were pushed out towards the north, south and east; the vaulting was fissured to an alarming extent; and the pillars were mutilated and corroded to their core. The whole fabric was, in truth on the verge of dissolution.'[32]

The Ecclesiologist[33] in turn praised the Benchers for repairing the church 'on a scale of costliness and magnificence which has no parallel within the last few centuries'. Gone was the 'field of monuments of the most heterogeneous and unseemly character' that covered every flat surface of the church as well as all the signs of 'comfort and smugness, which our more imme-

diate ancestors seem to have valued so highly'. Whilst praising the 'beauty and propriety of the whole' it did list thirteen points[34], mostly to do with the internal arrangements, which would make the work complete. The most important of these were the previously mentioned lack of a central aisle and the fact that the roof of the Round was not conical.

After all this, the church must indeed have looked magnificent. Its overall beauty and composition could be appreciated for the first time in centuries, with the long view made possible by opening up the arches between the Round and the chancel. In addition the elegant proportions of the chancel could be seen, now that the floor had been lowered to its original level and the high box pews replaced by open benches. The columns were no longer hidden by monuments or wainscoting and there were now, as in the earliest times, highly decorated ceilings and a patterned encaustic tiled floor. There was a new polychromatic altar screen and stained glass inserted in the east windows where none had existed. The broken parts of the effigies of the knights had been cunningly repaired, and these were offset by the grotesque grinning heads on the surrounding arcade – even though they were replacements of the 1820s.

However, the result of the 'restorations' undertaken by Robert Smirke in the 1820s, and by Savage, Sydney Smirke and Burton in the 1840s, was finally to have replaced or scraped away virtually all of what remained of the medieval work and that of subsequent centuries. Walter Godfrey, who was responsible for the conservation work after the fire of 1941, said:

'Nothing could have been more thorough than the way in which every ancient surface was repaired away or renewed, so that in the end, the result was a complete simulation of this superb monument.'[35]

It has been pointed out that this scraping away was unlikely to have happened after 1877, when new principles for conservation work on church buildings were formulated by SPAB, advocating the retention of original features and 'conserving' what was there, with the absolute minimum removal of original material. The Society was formed by William Morris as a direct result of concern over the kind of work carried out at the Temple Church, where the presumption was to remove and replace rather than to keep and conserve. In SPAB terms what happened at the church was 'vandalism'. Morris said:

'These old buildings have been altered and added to century after century, often beautifully – always historically; their value lay in that; they have suffered almost always from neglect; also, often, from violence, but ordinary.... mending would have kept them standing; pieces of nature and of history.

'But of late years a great uprising of ecclesiastical zeal, coinciding with a great increase of study, and consequently knowledge of medieval architecture, has driven people to spend money on these buildings, not merely with the purpose of repairing them.... but also of restoring them to some ideal state of perfection; sweeping away, if possible, all signs of what has befallen them, at least since the Reformation, and often dates much earlier.'[36]

Although the work was carried out because of the parlous state of the church, Morris would have said that it could have been 'conserved' without the need to 'replace'. Jane Fawcett, in her book *The Future in the Past*, looked afresh at what had happened and formed a very similar view to that of Morris. She concluded that:

'One of the ironies of the Gothic Revival is that it largely destroyed the very buildings from which it drew its inspiration. Considerably more medieval architecture was lost through restoration than through demolition. Why did the architects of the medieval movement show so little understanding for medieval buildings? The answer is surely twofold: over-zealousness and over-confidence.'[37]

It is difficult to understand how these architects, with all their knowledge and love of this period, placed no lasting historic value on what

they removed. It was seen more from the point of view of curiosity, to be admired for a short time and then to be 'carted away' to the scrap heap. They had the supreme confidence that they could either reproduce a perfect facsimile of what was removed or create something better. This would explain why in most cases no record was made of what was discovered or removed.

Jane Fawcett concluded that, while lamenting what was removed and restored in churches all over the country during this period, the best work is now accepted with the passing of time and it can stand comparison with that of any other period in history. Unfortunately, because of the devastating fire of 1941, apart from photographs and the memories of the ancients, such as David Lewer, we are denied the opportunity of testing her opinion as far as the Temple church is concerned. In particular we are unable to see the work for ourselves, 150 years on, when it too would have started to mellow with age.

With all the enthusiastic 'carting and scraping away' by those carrying out the work of the 1840s it is difficult to know if anything of the original now remains. Richardson[38] in 1845 was of the opinion that the two (gilt) heads with crowns, on each end of the springing of the label moulding over the central east window, may well be original. He said one resembled the portrait of King Henry III on the effigy in Westminster Abbey, and the other either his queen, or Eleanor, queen of Edward I. There is also a finely carved medieval corbel head of a woman with a wimple or head-dress in the Museum of London said to have come from the church. From its size it could be one of the other heads missing from the label mouldings to the aisle windows at the east end of the church. Richardson also mentioned as possibly original the four upper corbel heads of Saracens and Christians between the Round and the chancel (*ill. 38*). These were coloured at the time he described them and had blue glass beads inserted for eyes. With the scraping away of the layers of limewash the heads in these positions now have no colouring or glass eyes so it is difficult to determine if these are the original ones which he described or are replacements.

Perhaps one of the only remaining features of the medieval church which gives an indication of the sublime beauty of the original work, is the corbel head on the most southerly pier of the south arch between the Round and the chancel. The authenticity of this is based on one of the few descriptions made during the works of 1840. Richardson describes this head as being enriched with colour and gilding:

'The cheeks and lips were red, the eyes grey, the brows and long flowing hair gilt, and the fillet band across the head blue. Some of this colouring remains but the greater portion came away with the thick coatings of limewash and common colour covering it.'[39]

Illustration 91 shows a photograph of this head, with the colours mentioned by Richardson clearly discernable. Its serene beauty is something to be admired and more is the pity that nothing else of this period remains in so complete a form. As a footnote to this Savage complained about the difficulties of researching and obtaining examples of carved work of the period of Henry III (1216-1272). He also experienced the same problems that Richardson commented on regarding the new grotesque heads of the 1820s in the Round. Savage said, when investigating the work of the first mason Burnell, that:

'...to my astonishment I found a great number of Capitals and Bases carved by a Man who knew nothing of Gothic work.'[40]

This explains the need to use so many models of gothic carved work mentioned previously for the stone masons to copy. Subsequently, he found the work of Barrett satisfactory.

In conclusion, in spite of reservations today about the work of Savage, Smirke and Burton, in its day the restoration caused considerable excitement and interest. The *Gentleman's Magazine* of 1843 said:

'Above 20,000 persons must have visited the building by the benchers' orders since it opened in November last, including the greater part of the royal family and nobility, and for some months hundreds were refused admittance daily, not having orders.'[41]

NOTES TO CHAPTER EIGHT

[1] Inner Temple Bench Table Minutes, 24 November 1826 and 30 November 1830.

[2] Dickens, Charles, *The Posthumous Papers of the Pickwick Club,* ch. XXXI.

[3] Baker, J.H., *The Inner Temple: A Brief Historical Description,* 30 (1991).

[4] Final Report of the Church Committee of the Two Societies, 12 April 1843, 1. (Middle Temple Library).

[5] *Op. cit.* 2

[6] *Op. cit.*

[7] *Op. cit.*

[8] *Gentleman's Magazine* XX, Jul-Dec 1843.

[9] Final Report (*op. cit.*), 11.

[10] Mordaunt Crook, J., 'The restoration of the Temple Church: Ecclesiology and Recrimination' in *Architectural History,* Vol. 8 (1965).

[11] Letter from Cottingham to Savage, 19 March 1841 (Middle Temple Library).

[12] Final Report (*op. cit.*), 13.

[13] *Op. cit.* 14.

[14] Mordaunt Crook (*op. cit.*).

[15] Essex W.R.H., Smirke, Sydney, *Illustrations of the Architectural Ornaments etc. of the Temple Church* (1845).

[16] *Op. cit.*

[17] Richardson, Edward, *The Ancient Stone and Lead Coffins etc. of the Temple Church* (1845).

[18] Essex (*op. cit*)

[19] Richardson, Edward, *The Monument Effigies of the Temple Church with an Account of their Restoration etc.* (1843).

[20] *DNB*, Vol. XVI, 1110 (1900).

[21] Savage, J., *Report on the Position of the Organ,* 23 July 1840 (Middle Temple Library).

[22] Smirke, Sydney, *Report on the Position of the Organ,* 23 July 1840 (Middle Temple Library).

[23] Richardson, Edward, *The Ancient Stone and Lead Coffins etc. of the Temple Church* (1845)..

[24] Willement T., Report on the Painted Ceilings etc., 2 November 1840 (Middle Temple Library).

[25] Essex (*op. cit.*).

[26] Willement (*op. cit.*).

[27] Willement (*op. cit.*).

[28] Essex (*op. cit.*).

[29] Esdaile, Mrs Arundell, *Temple Church Monuments,* 16.

[30] *Op. cit.*

[31] *Op. cit.* 1.

[32] Essex (*op. cit.*).

[33] *Ecclesiologist,* July 1842, 41

[34] *Ecclesiologist,* Vol. 2, Feb 1842, 98.

[35] Godfrey, W.H., *Recent Discoveries at the Temple, etc* (1953).

[36] Fawcett, Jane, *The Future of the Past,* 76 (1976).

[37] *Op. cit* 75.

[38] Richardson E., (*op. cit.*).

[39] *Op. cit.*

[40] Savage, J., *Comments on Work of Mr Burnell,* 19 March 1841 (Middle Temple Library).

[41] *Gentleman's Magazine* XX, Jul-Dec 1843.

CHAPTER NINE

The Surpliced Choir

It was George Warne, the second blind organist, who introduced a rudimentary choir in 1827 when two ladies, stationed in the former organ loft, were appointed to sing during the service. A year later a male singer, presumably a baritone, was added. Finally, a bass joined them in 1838. Dr Hopkins recalled those days at the Temple before he was appointed there as organist:

> 'When I first went, there were only two ladies and two gentlemen in the choir, and they used to sing in the organ gallery. The curtain would be drawn aside for a few minutes, the singers would sing, and everybody would turn west to look at them; then the curtain was banged to with a rattle of brass rings. What queer ideas they had of music and organists in those days!'[1]

Christopher Benson, (ill. 77) Canon of Worcester, succeeded Thomas Rennell as Master of the Temple in 1826 and enjoyed a high reputation as a preacher of the broad evangelical school. He criticised the views of the Oxford 'tractarians' and was no great lover of church music or of anything which he considered to be 'trappings.' In a letter to the Benchers during a dispute in 1843 he wrote:

> 'When I first came to the Temple, it was an unpretentious church, and to a sober rational service of the Almighty, in which all might join in the responses, and nothing was wanting to answer the demands of seriousness and piety but an improvement to the psalmody, which was miserably deficient from the improper appointment of a clerk who

77. Christopher Benson, Master of the Temple.

could not sing. To remedy this defect some male and female singers were unhappily introduced whose exhibitions in the organ gallery were offensive to many.'

Benson added that a psalm sung by the congregation was superseded by an anthem 'in which they could not join – and that anthem not so performed as much to gratify either devotion or taste.' However, the 'exhibitions' continued in the organ loft until they were brought to a sudden end with the closing of the church in 1840 for renovations.

With the restoration of the church nearing

completion in 1842, it seems that the two Societies had given little thought to the services which were soon to be resumed, though the salaries of the organist, organ-blower and the four singers were paid throughout the two and a half years that the church was closed. But ideas for a very different Temple service were beginning to form in the minds of those who felt the Oxford Movement in their hearts. William Burge, QC, and the Church Committee, if not the majority of the Benchers, became alive to the fact that here, after the break occasioned by the closing of the church, was a unique opportunity for introducing the Cathedral Service and for establishing a surpliced choir in the ancient tradition. The independent status of the Temple church ensured against any possible episcopal disfavour. The *Musical World* of 25 August 1842 announced

> 'the imminent reopening of the Temple Church in all its pristine appropriateness and splendour. A choir of about fourteen voices, including six boys, has been engaged to perform the regular cathedral service under the direction of an efficient choirmaster. This is an example that deserves to become a precedent.'

It is a curious fact that the Temple Church Choir came about almost by accident, or at least by the acceptance of a *fait accompli*, as many of the Benchers had left London for the Long Vacation. The Master had accepted the idea of a choir, not without some misgivings but in preference to the retention of the gentlemen and ladies. It was he who put forward the name of John Calvert, a deputy lay-vicar of St Paul's, as a person who could form a choir. Calvert was asked to provide a choir for the opening Temple service on the understanding that no guarantee could be given that the Societies would make it a permanent arrangement, but he was nevertheless ready to do this at his own risk and he provided an estimate of cost. He would obtain for the opening service two experienced trebles and four juniors, two altos supporting the boys, and a tenor. He was to sing bass himself and

be Master of the Choir. The cost would be £230 per annum, compared with £800-900 at St Paul's. He suggested abolishing the office of Clerk, 'as his duties are performed by the Choir,' and reducing the salary of the organist from £80 to £60, on the grounds that he would not have responsibility for the choir, thus saving costs.

After long discussion by the Benchers, it was ordered

> 'that it having resolved to open the Temple Church for the performance of Divine Services on Sunday next, the Church Committee of both Houses to be requested to open it in such a manner as they shall think right for that day only.'

The postponed service[2] took place on Sunday, 20 November 1842, with the little band of six choirboys and three gentlemen. They were Enoch Hawkins (alto), John Hobbs (tenor) and John Calvert (bass), with James Turle, organist of Westminster Abbey, at the console and 'with Mr Goss of St Paul's in attendance.'[3] It is not surprising that the *Hallelujah Chorus*, sung at the rehearsal, was quietly dropped and that Tallis' *Hear the voice and prayer* was sung instead. At the evening service (3 pm), Purcell's *I was glad* was the anthem. On the previous day *The Times* stated that

> 'Mr Warne, the organist of the Temple Church, will play a voluntary on the organ, which, by the addition of pedals, pedal-pipes and several new stops, is now considered to be one of the most exquisite instruments in Europe.'

W.H. Cummings, then a chorister who continued as a tenor at the Temple and became Principal of the Guildhall School of Music, remembered the Temple organ without pedals because Mr Warne used sometimes to lift his left leg and hold down a bass note with the knee-bone. He also recollected the introduction of the first pedal stop which was 'so tremendous in its effect that it used to shake the spectacles on the noses of the Benchers.'

William Burge, one of the prime movers in the architectural restoration, published in 1843 his book *On the Choral Service of the Anglo-Catholic Church* which contained detailed recommendations to further the new regime. As to chanting he stated

> 'there ought to be a careful rehearsal of the chants at which the organist should attend; he will then arrange with the choir those verses in which he will employ the Swell, so that their voices may swell with it.'

Cummings was asked by Master Burge to give the name of the chant which the choir had just sung. Knowing that W.B. disapproved of Spohr, the Victorian composer, the boy boldly said he thought it was by Byrd, whereupon the old gentleman exclaimed 'Ah, beautiful: There's nothing like Elizabethan music!'

On the second Sunday, 27 November, George Cooper junior, assistant at St Paul's, was at the organ and he continued to act as organist for six months. It was said that his playing of Bach was 'simply unsurpassed.'[4] The Benchers could hardly reverse the acceptance of the highly popular choral service though it was still not finally approved as permanent. George Warne was still officially organist at the Temple, but it was thought that his blindness would not enable him to conduct a fully choral service. He protested, was offered 'a fair trial', but understandably declined and resigned. He was given a pension which continued until his death in 1868. There were many candidates for the new post, but the contest ultimately lay between Edward Hopkins and George Cooper. Hopkins got the job, having lost his previous post in his absence, and the name of the organist for 7 May 1843 is recorded in Calvert's register book as 'Mr Hopkins.' This date was later to be remembered as an historic occasion, as being the first day of his 55 years as organist of the Temple church (*ill. 78*). Three Sundays later a royal party of princes, princesses, dukes, duchesses, the Greek Ambassador, Lord Brougham and Lord Morpeth was present at Morning Service when the church was densely crowded. It must have been a great day for young Hopkins at the organ.

On 1 April 1843 Prince Albert caused some

78. *Edward John Hopkins, Organist and later also Director of the Choir.*

consternation by turning up unannounced to attend a rehearsal for the choir, coming by foot, attended by only one servant. The choristers sang several compositions, for which he was highly gratified and after staying half an hour, he returned home, again on foot.[5]

Edward John Hopkins was born in 1818 in Westminster and came from a musical family.[6] He became a chorister in the Chapel Royal, St James's and learned the organ with T.F. Walmisley at St Martin-in-the-Fields where the young lad would play the outgoing voluntary.[7] In 1831 he sang at the Coronation of William IV in Westminster Abbey but his voice broke before Victoria's accession. At an early age he gained access to the Abbey organ loft where James Turle was organist. Turle told the members of Mitcham parish church that he had no hesitation in letting Hopkins take the whole of an elaborate service in Westminster Abbey by himself. Hopkins was appointed organist at Mitcham when he was only seventeen. Four years later he found improved conditions at St Luke's, Berwick Street.

The question of a permanently established choir and the possibility of daily service was still undecided when attention was diverted by a broadside from the Master. In a long letter of 20 January 1843 to the Treasurer of the Inner Temple, he objected to the mode of 'admitting persons to the seats of the painted Church as if it were a painted Theatre.' More seriously, he found that it was nearly one o'clock before he got into the pulpit, as a result of the singing of everything – chanted psalms, the Litany, Responses, the *Te Deum* and the *Jubilate*. A short anthem might be admitted 'for the lovers of Ecclesiastical Music', but he thought that none of this constituted worship. He added that the Temple had no choral foundation 'and a choir there has never been, I believe, until now.'

Benson might have received some support in this attack upon the new choral service, had he not made the mistake of implying his authority on the services of the Temple church. The Benchers replied with a most conciliatory letter, and hoped to satisfy the Master by ordering the omission of the Litany. This subject found its way into *The Times* and a Memorial signed by 205 members of the two Societies was presented to the Benchers, 'protesting against the sudden and by them most unexpected suppression of a considerable portion of the Choral Service.'

Meanwhile, the Benchers set up a committee to consider the rights and privileges of the Master of the Temple, and no doubt the ghost of Dr Micklethwaite attended on its sittings. In continuance of their reply to Benson they said that they had acted on the conviction that he consented to a choir in the church. Furthermore, the Bench hoped that the Master would not persist in requiring any investigation into the respective rights of the Master and the Bench, considering that such rights could only be ascertained by inquiry into remote antiquity. Whatever they might be, they could not be enforced by either side without injury to those great interests which all parties were desirous of pro-

tecting. The Master would seem to have accepted this advice, as no further correspondence was exchanged on this particular subject. Benson had won his point on the choral Responses, though only temporarily, as by December 1844, he was again complaining about the chanting of the Responses in the Litany.

The church was closed from 6 August 1843 for three months for 'further beautifications' including the provision of a pulpit and choir stalls, the latter, 'ornamented with carved figures of angels with wings expanded.' When reopened in November it was noted with satisfaction that 'the choir has been removed from the objectionable place in the gallery to each side of the church, so as to exhibit both visibly and audibly the antiphonal nature of the service.'[8] By March 1843 a 'double choir' with six choristers and three gentlemen on each side had been made permanent by the Benchers. It is astonishing how heady was the news of choral service and a surpliced choir in the Temple church. It was little short of a sensation and so was the spectacular architectural restoration.

With the summary dismissal of John Calvert in January 1844, the road was suddenly cleared for Hopkins to take sole charge of the choristers and music. Trouble arose from a protest by James Bennett, then the principal tenor, against his being given notice by Calvert. Prompt investigation uncovered the fact that the choirmaster, having regularly received a lump sum from the Benchers in accordance with his contract, had withheld payment to the members of the choir. Furthermore he had ordered large quantities of music, charged to the Temple, much of which was for his own personal use. In the circumstances and following a report by the Committee, Calvert went off rather hurriedly to become choirmaster to the Cathedral, in Spanish Town, Jamaica[9] where he set up a surpliced choir.

As a result of this unfortunate affair, on 7 May 1844 the Benchers appointed a permanent committee 'to have the superintendence and regulation of the Choir of the Temple Church as recommended by the joint committee in their report of 19 April.' This was the original 'Choir

Committee' whose successors have ever since, under that designation, been responsible for ordering the affairs not only of the choir but also of all matters connected with the church.

Hopkins was delighted to be informed that he would be master of the choristers. He was also told to carry out his new duties 'in the manner that seems best to yourself.' He hurried home with the news for his father and mother, and he 'formed the inward resolve that I would not rest until the Temple Choir had become one of the best in London.'

Matters settled down now that the new committee had taken over the appointment and payment of the gentlemen of the choir and arrangements for the monthly music 'scheme' in consultation with Hopkins. For many years the entries in the Choir Committee minute book largely consisted of the problems with the gentlemen of whom many came and went rather more frequently than desired. But some remained at the Temple for many years, including Thomas Young (1844-72), J.H.B. Dando (1844-73), both altos, Henry Parkin (1875-98), tenor, and Lewis Thomas (1857-85), bass – all of whom were there in Hopkins' time.

In April 1845 Christopher Benson resigned the Mastership, perhaps like Hooker 'weary with the noise and opposition of the place' and it is obvious that he was never happy under the new regime. The Benchers sent him a letter regretting his resignation and trusting that he might speedily be restored to health. In acknowledging their good wishes Benson replied that he had not felt so well for years.

The new Master was Thomas Robinson, DD, Preacher at the Foundling Hospital and a Professor of Arabic at Cambridge. Hopkins recalled that

> 'he was a rather learned and uninteresting preacher, but a wonderfully good *reconteur* and after-dinner talker. On one occasion a certain wit – Sir George Rose – remarked: "Yes, I agree with you all. I greatly prefer him at the bottle than in the wood"; wood, of course, referring to the pulpit.'

Robinson elected to live in the Master's House which Benson had not occupied and had let to the aged and impecunious Reader, the Rev. W.H. Rowlatt, and his family of nine, which included several spinster daughters. Rowlatt had to move out after thirteen years there, and was a continual source of worry to the Bench regarding his circumstances.

Hopkins was soon recognised as a first-class organist. He was a frequent visitor to organ factories, and he gave the first organ performance of Mendelssohn's *Wedding March* at a recital at Walker's factory in 1844. This was a day or two after its first British orchestral performance under the composer at a Philharmonic Concert. The fashion for the *March* has continued ever since. For five years Hopkins had been hard at work in laying the foundations of the Temple Choir. The corner-stones were the Psalms and the perfection of their performance became well known. A letter in *The Guardian* in 1848 said:

> 'If the visitor lay down his Prayer-book he will not miss it, for he will hear every word distinctly pronounced, every sentence clearly and reverentially enunciated.'

This tradition of psalm-singing continued for more than a century and was accompanied with consummate art by subsequent Temple organists.

From the beginning there was a series of notable choristers. The Duke of Wellington often attended the Temple service and, at his funeral in St Paul's on 18 November 1852, it is said, though without evidence, that Henry Sanders, the Temple head boy, sang a solo over the open 'grave' before the coffin was lowered into the crypt.

For ten years after the formation of the Temple choir, the education of the choristers was unsatisfactory. They had been drawn from various London schools,[10] and their journeys to choir-practice led to 'idle and truant habits.' The choir of Lincoln's Inn Chapel was founded about the same time and in 1854 a joint school for the choristers of both choirs was established at 10 New Boswell Court (*see front endpapers*).[11]

Canon Lonsdale resigned the Readership in 1865. The Benchers now preferred 'a Gentleman

He proposed the appointment of a choir master, but the Benchers decided to appoint him as Director of the Choir as well and to increase his salary by £40 to £290 per annum. At the age of fifty Hopkins felt that he had achieved the success which he sought when he first came to the Temple. The appointment was confirmed in 1869 and he was presented with 50guineas, in recognition of his services as organist for 26 years. But there were more triumphs to come.

79. Alfred Ainger, Reader and later Master of the Temple. Portrait by George du Maurier.

who can intone the choral parts of the service' and, from a list of six candidates, the Rev. Alfred Ainger (*ill. 79*) was appointed.

'Once having listened to his voice, the assembly elected him unanimously. His rare beauty of tone, low and vibrating – his manner of reading, vivid without being dramatic, impressive without the slightest striving for effect – were indeed unique, drawing many to the Temple for nearly forty years to come.'

It is evident that Hopkins found himself increasingly handicapped in his lack of official authority over the gentlemen of the choir who were nominally responsible to the Choir Committee. He was organist and master of the choirboys but not in control of the whole choir.

NOTES TO CHAPTER NINE

[1] 'A talk with E.J. Hopkins' by Raymond Blathwayt in *Great Thoughts*, Dec. 1900. George Warne had succeeded George Price in 1826 who in turn had been joint organist to the two Societies since 1814, and previously to the Inner Temple in 1810. Emily Dowdling had been organist to the Middle Temple since 1796 but dismissed in 1814 for non-attendance.

[2] The reopening of the church for 6 November was delayed until the 20th on account of the incomplete floor tiling because of the Staffordshire Potteries strike.

[3] The choir was at first 'crammed in the little stone gallery in front of the organ', no choirstalls having been provided. The console was at first placed well back within the organ chamber.

[4] Prestige, G., *St Paul's in its Glory*, 1831-1911, 22 (1953).

[5] *The Times*, 3 April 1843

[6] Pearce, C., *The Life and Works of E.J. Hopkins*.

[7] Hopkins, E.J., Reminiscences read before the College of Organists (1886). See also Bumpus, T.F., *English Cathedral Music*, Vol. 2, 420.

[8] Jebb, J., *The Choral Service* (1843).

[9] Clarke, B., *Anglican Cathedrals outside the British Isles* (1958). The Cathedral at Spanish Town was extended in 1848-53 and the architect is given as John Calvert!

[10] Of the first six choristers, it is known that W.H. Cummings attended the City of London School, then in Milk Street. Charles Sowerby was grandson of James de Carle Sowerby, of *Botany* fame. Aynsley Cook (b.1835), the grandfather of the oboist Eugene Goossens, followed. He sang solos at the opening of St George's R.C. Cathedral, Southwark, and at concerts directed by Mendelssohn and Spohr. Later he was 'Chamber Singer' to the Marquis of Anglesey, one of the heroes of Waterloo and a great amateur musician. Cook was with the Carl Rosa Company for many years and declared his repertory to be 92 operas.

[11] Boswell Court was one of a maze of alleys on the north side of the Strand which were swept away to build the Royal Courts of Justice, 1874-82

CHAPTER TEN

The Later Victorians

The second half of the nineteenth century was heralded in 1850 by a near disaster when a fire started in the boiler chamber situated under the floor of the music room. This was caused by the ignition of faggots placed on top of the furnace. Fortunately the fire was put out before much damage was done.

By 1857 E.J. Hopkins, the organist to the Temple church, had persuaded the Benchers that the organ needed major repairs and adjustments.[1] These were carried out by T.J.F. Robson of St Martin's Lane, at a cost of over £400. Hopkins had previously reported that the mechanism was 'worn and noisy as to cause its rattling motion to be distinctly heard in the church'. Larger bellows, new wind trunks, soundboards and key movements, a larger swell box and 'new wrought-iron actions' were provided. Dents were taken out of the pipes and their tops repaired, and finally 'sliding glass doors were provided for protecting the whole'. In 1859 Hopkins[2] was allowed to complete this work by employing Robson to extend the Swell, make further mechanical adjustments and add a few further stops. In addition a number of very fine stops were added. These were obtained from Edmund Schultze, a distinguished organ builder from Germany who personally supervised their installation. The number of pipes had been increased to 3,333 from 1,715 when the organ was first completed in 1688. There were now 1,384 pipes in the Great organ, 1,011 in the Swell, 668 in the Choir and 270 in the Pedal. One other important addition to the Temple organ, made during the alterations of 1859, was the provision

of 'Joy's Patent Hydraulic Bellows Blower'. This machinery gave some trouble at first and, while adjustments were made in 1861, the organ was once again blown by hand. The organ blower since 1842 had been James Quint, a workman who had suffered an injury while engaged on the restoration of the church and who had been given the job in compensation; this was now his swan-song. The installation of these engines had meant that the machinery had to be accommodated in the vestry beneath the organ, which brought a complaint from the Master that the furniture and robes were exposed to serious injury 'from accidents that have more than once occurred and the consequent escape of water.' He suggested that a new vestry might be built on the ground freed by the demolition of the old buildings on the north-west side of the church. This request was not immediately taken up by the Benchers, as they were more concerned to complete the restoration of the church resulting from this demolition. It was not until 1868 that they acted upon the Master's request.

Sir Robert Smirke had cleared away the buildings against the church to the south in the late 1820s. By 1860 the removal of the buildings to the north-west meant that the perimeter of the church would at last be free of all buildings, something that the Benchers had been trying to achieve for a very long time. Finally the chambers above the porch (*ill. 85*) were removed revealing the outside of the beautiful wheel window set into the west end of the Round (*ill. 90*).

This demolition meant that the major refurbishment to the church of the 1840s could finally

80. Interior of the Round church, 1809. Aquatint by Pugin and Rowlandson.

81. St Ann's Chapel before demolition, 1826 (notice the rat). Watercolour by John Buckler.

82. Elevation of Altar Piece, 1843, Smirke and Burton (R.H. Essex delt.).

83. East windows in the chancel 1843, by Thomas Willement.

84. The Temple church after restoration, 1842-3.

85. Church porch from the south, June 1861, before demolition of the chambers above. Watercolour by J. Wykeham Archer.

86. The Temple church, April 1862. Watercolour by J. Wykeham Archer.

87. Churchyard Court, June 1860.
Watercolour by J. Wykeham Archer.

88. Church porch, June 1861.
Watercolour by J. Wykeham Archer.

89. Two original capitals in the porch, 1861. Watercolour by J. Wykeham Archer.

90. Circular window over the porch, revealed on demolition of chambers above, 1861. Watercolour by J. Wykeham Archer.

91. A corbel head with seraph, probably original. Photograph by Robert Dark.

92. The Temple church from the south, the porch added in 1954. Photograph by Robert Dark.

93. The Round church, showing the effigies. Photograph by Geremy Butler, 1997.

94. A view towards the altar and Wren reredos. Photograph by Geremy Butler, 1997.

be completed. J.P. St. Aubyn acted as architect for the Middle Temple and Sydney Smirke in the same capacity for the Inner Temple. With the clearing of the picturesque timber houses to the north, some of which had survived the Great Fire, (*ill. 87*) the old Dickensian atmosphere that had permeated the area for so long at last disappeared. A photograph of this area was taken in 1858 before the demolition (*ill. 96*). This and other photographs taken between 1858 and 1861 are a remarkable historical record and more so when it is considered that, less than twenty years earlier, Daguerre and Fox Talbot had produced the first permanently fixed pictures using a camera. It would be another twenty years before photographic plates with improved sensitivity were being mass produced.

Before describing the restoration work it is useful to consider what was revealed when these

95. The chancel after the restoration of 1842 but showing the organ case when brought forward of the chamber in 1868. Photo Gilbert Benham.

buildings were removed as one can gain some idea of how the church might have looked in earlier times. The open area north of the church was still an ancient churchyard, although crossed with a paved pathway, and was less of a public space or route compared with the south which looked onto one of the main courtyards of the Temple. As a result, this side of the church had not been altered over the years as much as that on the south. Areas of the lower parts of the external walls of the church were revealed when six feet of soil which had accumulated over the centuries was carted away. St Aubyn described what was discovered by these removals in a lecture at the RIBA on 16 May 1864 titled *An Account of the Repairs Lately Effected at the Temple Church, London*. A photograph, taken at the time in 1861, recorded what was revealed (*ill. 97*).

At the same time, between the years 1860 to 1862, a series of exquisite and detailed watercolour drawings were made (*ills 86-90, 98 and dust jacket*) by J. Wykeham Archer (1808-1864). Born at Newcastle-upon-Tyne, Archer was a painter of water colours and an engraver. His principal works included a series of drawings of ancient edifices and streets in Edinburgh and London. Those of London were published in the William Twopenny collection and were over a hundred in number. If his painting of the north-west side of the Round is compared with the photograph of the same area, it can be seen how faithfully it reproduces what was there. With this evidence, it is reasonable to assume that the other paintings are similarly accurate (*ills 86-90, dust jacket*). Together with the photograph they make a wonderful historical record, particularly as these areas were to be altered so drastically. Archer's paintings also convey the excitement at the time of making these discoveries, especially in his painting of the wheel window above the porch. With the piles of rubble in the foreground, it is as though the window had been freshly revealed and we are sharing what was seen. Of particular note is the delicacy and simple beauty of the stone tracery to the window and original patches of rendering or 'plastering' to the stonework on the wall adjacent to the window. His

96. North side of the church before demolition of ancient buildings. The shored-up building was replaced by Goldsmith Building (J.P. St Aubyn, architect). The iron post marks boundaries in the churchyard between the two Inns under the Deed of Partition, 1732. (Photograph 1858).

other paintings show similar traces of render to other areas of exposed walling. The stone beneath this was rough finished, with ashlar or dressed stone framing the windows. This can be contrasted with the patch repairs of brick infill to the Round at parapet level above where the buildings had abutted the church (*ill. 88, dust jacket*).

St Aubyn, in his address to the RIBA in 1864 gave his observations on what was discovered:

'The walling is of Kentish rag stone, in irregular or random courses.... abundant proof remains to show that the whole external face of this walling was covered with a thin coat of plaster, filling in the hollows and just covering the surface of the rough stone.'

He went on to describe how this was restored. The ragstone was made good 'as nearly as possible to harmonise with the old work.' However, he admitted he was not bold enough to re-adopt the original method of plastering over the stone. He said that the new pointing had been done in such a way that it would not prevent rendering being applied in the future. He similarly made good the ashlar surrounding the windows which he identified as fire or Reigate stone. Bath stone was used for the new dressed stone. This was carefully shaped and worked with a stone axe in the medieval method. In the course of carrying out this work, stone masons' marks were found on the outer surface of some of the stones.

The use of a rubble wall with a plaster finish

97. North side of the Round after removal of earth revealing ancient stone coffins (1861 photograph).

for the majority of the external walling was common for buildings of this period. One explanation of this is that in the twelfth century, at the time of building the church, transport was still rudimentary so local building materials would have been used for most buildings. London did not have a ready source of stone so it would have had to be transported from another region and, as a consequence, would have been very expensive. Good quality finished stone was used for the church but it seems to have been limited to areas where it would achieve maximum effect or was to be carved. Examples are the Purbeck marble for the internal columns, the Reigate stone for the window surrounds and the Caen stone from Normandy inside the church. A cheaper approach was then used for the large areas of external walling. Ragstone from Kent would have been relatively inexpensive as it was one of the nearest sources of stone and could be conveniently shipped up the river Thames.

Now that the three buttresses on the north side of the church could be seen together, it was noticed that the off-sets were all different (*ill. 86*). St Aubyn felt that the eastern one had probably been rebuilt on the original plinth at the beginning of the seventeenth century. The newly exposed ones to the west had been much mutilated and the dressed Reigate stone on the faces

had perished in places. In reconstructing these he felt reasonably certain that by careful examination, stone by stone, of the overlaying parts as they were removed, they were being rebuilt to the original profile. They have three off-sets compared with the buttresses on the south side of the Round which only have two. The northern ones are probably a more accurate reflection of the originals, as it is known from previous illustrations and descriptions that those on the south were 'classicised' at about the end of the seventeenth century and then 'restored' by Robert Smirke in the 1820s. St Aubyn also discovered that the front faces of these buttresses were curved in sympathy with the curve of the face of the Round. One other detail to note is the small nook shafts to the window reveals. These were in a very poor condition and were renewed with red Mansfield stone.

By now the Cambridge Camden Society was closely watching what was happening. This meant that detailed written descriptions of what was exposed were also being recorded on a regular basis in their journal *The Ecclesiologist*. For example, in June 1862 it recorded that when the porch was exposed to the north:

'...it was clearly open arched, and it gabled north and south, as well as westward, if, indeed, as is most probable, it did not project with one or more additional bays in that direction, – thus forming a species of narthex. It was once roofed with a lead roof, directly laid upon vaulting: the marks of the boards to which the lead was fixed being to this day visible in the portions of the Norman plastering which still adhere externally to the groins, and have been brought to light. Thus the very graceful wheel window over the doorway was once – as it is again, and will, we are glad to say, continue to be – open to the daylight. The capitals of the nook-shafts of the north arch of the porch are of a unique and peculiarly elegant design; one of them seems to represent a coronal of tubular flowers, probably honeysuckles, set vertically, with the mouths turned outwards.' (*ill. 89*)

98. North side of the Round after demolition of buildings there, but before the removal of earth. Note the remains of plastered rubble walls. Watercolour by J. Wykeham Archer, December 1860.

St Aubyn[3] discovered the foundations of two buttresses and their top course under the eaves of the Round where it meets the porch. This can be seen from a study of Wykeham Archer's paintings. St Aubyn concluded from this that the porch was of a later date than the Round. It was his view that it was built sometime between the building of the Round in 1185 and the second chancel in 1240. There has been some disagreement as to whether the buttresses were built as part of the original church[4]. His discovery would suggest that they were constructed, if not at the time that the Round was built, then certainly very soon afterwards. He also felt that the great West door, with its exquisite carving, was part of the original Round of 1185. From his inspection of the ornamental details of the

wheel window and their similarity to those of the capital of the porch, he concluded that it was inserted at the time the porch was built. When describing the window he said:

> 'The wheel window is both curious and beautiful. Observe the cusps, caps, and bases; and the mode of fitting the work together, with a wedge piece fitted between each voussoir. On each stone of the enclosing circle a centre line was scratched, which would show, I think, that the shape of each stone was drawn on the flat and then cut to the lines, instead of using a template or mould, as is the modern practice.'

This is the first time that such a detailed historical record was made when carrying out works to the church; it involved written, photographic and drawn information. It is unfortunate that the architects of the 1820s and the 1840s did not make similar records of what they discovered or did when much of the historic fabric was exposed and later covered up, altered or removed.

By the 1860s the Cambridge Camden Society had established its principles for restoration work to churches. Expressed simply, it considered that there were three types of restoration – destructive, conservative and eclectic. The last of these was the one preferred[5]. Earlier volumes of *The Ecclesiologist* set this out in more detail:

'We must, whether from existing evidences or from supposition, discover the original scheme of the edifice as conceived by the first builder, or as begun by him and developed by his immediate successors; or, on the other hand, we must retain the additions or alterations of subsequent ages, repairing them when needing it, or even carrying out perhaps more fully the idea which dictated them.... For our own part we decidedly choose the former.'

It can be seen from this that *The Ecclesiologist* did not only describe what was discovered as a result of the demolition – this was incidental to advice on the form that restoration work should take. With the principles set out above, the form of the Society's advice for the work to the Round of the Temple church came as no surprise:

'A question has arisen how the sloping lead roof is to be finished. It is clear that originally it merely overhung; but modern requirements would not be satisfied without some expedient to carry off the water. The choice lies between three alternatives:- to imitate the parapet which Sir R. Smirke erected on the other side, to make a stone gutter, or to make a lead one. Of these the first is intolerable, as it would wholly disfigure the one portion of the building which is happily still capable of being restored to its primitive aspect. The third is the simplest, the most sightly, and the nearest to the old treatment; so we most sincerely trust that it may be adopted; otherwise the Templars will have

earned themselves the just reputation of being thirty years behind their age in architectural knowledge[6].'

Who could have resisted this pressure in the climate of the ascendant authority of the Camden Society! Thus the parapet to the low pitched roof to the Round was removed and the pitched roof behind was relaid in lead and taken over the top of the external wall. It was finished with an external gutter made also of lead. St Aubyn even paraphrased the opinion expressed in *The Ecclesiologist* in his lecture at the RIBA in 1864 which described his work to the church. When talking about the gutter to the Round he said:

'An iron or lead gutter, resting on the table course, was then suggested; and the result is the cast lead gutter which you now see.'

The article in the June issue of *The Ecclesiologist* concluded with a plea that the Round should be finished with a conical capping. This advice was duly taken by St Aubyn. The almost flat roof and parapet to the clerestory to the Round were removed and replaced with a conical roof pitched at 65% and finished in lead. This was surmounted with an iron finial with a weather vane in the shape of a cockerel. The overall appearance was similar to the changes made by Salvin to St Sepulchre, Cambridge[7] (*ill. 14*) in spite of the lack of any real evidence that it had ever been like this before. It was still fifteen years too early for the views of William Morris and SPAB to have been felt. No doubt they would have been very concerned regarding both the Camden Society's view about what should happen to the existing roof of the Round and the actual work done. In William Morris's terms, all the history and patina of time of this part of the building had been swept away at a stroke. The Round had undergone the most dramatic changes to its physical appearance over the years when compared with other parts of the church. Illustration 99 shows how it appeared after the work of the early 1860s. *Illustrations 66 & 67 show* how it appeared in 1792 and in 1828, first with a crenellated top to the parapet and then with a plain one. More intriguing is a comparison with the William Emmett etching made in the late seventeenth century (*ill. 60*) which shows curved pitched roofs to the Round. St Aubyn's steep pitch of 65% made the clerestory roof more of a spire than a dome and its steepness worried even the ecclesiologists[8].

During the course of this restoration work the architects for the two Societies appeared to be about to demolish and rebuild the porch. This over-enthusiasm for an 'authoritative historically accurate replacement'[9] concerned some Inner Temple Benchers so much that they summoned the architects to a special Bench Table meeting in May 1862 and subsequently asked George Gilbert Scott to advise them on the porch. He said:

'I see no room for a moment's question as to its preservation. The porch is a most valuable specimen of the most interesting period of Mediaeval architecture. Although built later

it is an integral part and by the way it is bonded in was probably effected by the original architect. As regards its restoration, I would certainly recommend it, though with the utmost care to preserve and recover its perfect design at least as far as it extends.'[10]

As a result of this advice, the Benchers gave the two architects clear instructions to follow the guidelines set out by Scott. St Aubyn said in his lecture at the RIBA that he was able to save the northern arch, which he thought was original, as well as the north west pier and the original groining that covered one half of the porch. As part of this work the floor was lowered to what was considered its original level, revealing the bases of the columns of the West doorway and those of the buttresses to the porch.

In removing the accumulated soil to the north of the church, a number of stone coffins were discovered. None of them was in a very good

99. The Round church 1862, the parapets removed and steep pitched roofs introduced by J.P. St Aubyn.

condition and when opened were found to be filled with a mixture of bones and rubbish. It was decided to leave these in the positions where they were found. These can be seen in one of Wykeham Archer's paintings (*ill. 86*), and are still in the same positions today. Numerous other fragments of bones were found in the general area of the graveyard.

In the end the ecclesiologists congratulated 'Mr St Aubyn heartily on the skill and judgement displayed in this most important work'[11] . They described the transformation to the Round as 'at once harmonious and picturesque'. The one note of criticism was that the parapet to the porch was too plain and not of the right proportions. Their final comment was a plea for the central block of seating in the chancel to be divided up to provide a central aisle so that there was an uninterrupted view of and approach to the altar from the round nave.

It is worth balancing these comments with a more contemporary view of the approach of the ecclesiologists given by Jane Fawcett in 1976 in her book *The Future of the Past*:

'The architect has always had the moral choice of adaption or replacement... No one should expect moral judgement over the styles of other periods: yet this is precisely what architects over the years have always done... what are the options open to them?

'Owing to the iconoclasm of the seventeenth century and the neglect of the eighteenth, the nineteenth century inherited these problems of evaluation in an extreme form. The conservative repairs recommended by Ruskin and the Society of Antiquaries and later by Morris and SPAB are, we hope, accepted today as the only moral solution, but to architects they have seldom appealed. To the ecclesiologists such arguments did not exist, and it was their introduction of stylistic and liturgical theories that proved so disastrous to nineteenth century restoration, and led architects to employ stylistic effects which were often quite out of character with the buildings to which they were attached.'[12]

The iron-bound chest made to contain the Charter of 1608 (*ill. 49*) was kept under the Communion Table in the church. Over the years this had been forgotten. In 1865 it was forced open[13], as the keys had been lost, in order to establish what it contained. There was an inner box which contained a parchment with the great seal of James I in Latin about the grant from the King. It was still in good condition. There were also two other documents signed by the King of a similar date, one about the office of lecturer and one concerning a petition to the King.

During the latter part of the 1860s, Hopkins[14], the church organist, requested that the console and organ should be moved forward further out of the recess in which they were housed. The sound was not being properly diffused into the church, and the reverberations within the recess were such that he often had to get a friend to play the voluntary after morning service so that he could retire from the din of the organ in order to be fresh for the afternoon service. In 1868 the alterations were carried out (*ill. 95*) and in the following year a new practice-room for the choir and a vestry were completed. For several years the provision of improved accommodation for the clergy and choir had been under consideration but, with the demolition of the old music room and the extension of the organ machinery down into the vestry, the matter became urgent. There was disagreement between the two architects. St Aubyn[15] proposed a new vestry against the north wall of the church, east of the organ. Smirke wanted a detached room, linked to the church by a covered way. The Committee was asked to decide the matter, and in July 1868 St Aubyn's plan was approved, subject to modifications. The extension, built against the east wall of the organ chamber, consisted of a long open-raftered room with a line of small lancet windows in the north wall, and a larger three-light window at the east end which was partitioned off by robe cupboards to form the Master's vestry. A flight of steps down from the Master's garden gave access to a door at the end, and there was direct access to the church from the practice room which formed the western part of the new addition (*see back endpapers*). Gas lighting was installed to light the new accommodation.

In January 1872 a report on the lighting of the church was submitted by the Societies' architects together with George Gilbert Scott[16]. Gas lighting was not recommended as it was felt that it would damage the coloured decorations. Instead, thicker wax candles, protected from draughts by cylindrical glasses, were installed in new positions to get the best distribution of light. The softer light must have provided a warmer glow during winter evenings than would have been the case with gas lighting. A disadvantage to the use of candles was that they could drop hot wax over the choristers! George Ripley[17], a chorister from 1893-1901, recalled 'the candle-wax all over our Eton suits – usually taken out by a hot pen-knife and a piece of paper'. Eventually in 1886 the candles to the church were removed, except those that lit the choir stalls, and replaced by electric lighting which was placed around the top of the free standing pillars.

In 1877 and 1880 there were further works carried out to the organ. The first involved the renewal of the hydraulic engine and blowing system and the addition of eight new stops. It was in the course of this work that another serious fire was narrowly avoided. During the alterations, when the practice room was full of organ-builder's materials, Hopkins, who was rehearsing with the choir in the church, suddenly became aware of the smell of burning:

> 'Looking hastily towards the organ, he observed that a carelessly-left lighted candle had already set fire to some of the tracker work. A frantic rush to the instrument, and a successful tearing down of the burning wood at great personal risk, were the means of saving not only the organ, but the historic pile itself from a terrible destruction.'[18]

The second was in response to a report that 'rats were doing mischief to the organ.'

The nineteenth century was drawing to a close. At the beginning the church had been in a very poor state of repair. By the end it had been restored to such a high standard that major works would not be required for a considerable period of time.

NOTES TO CHAPTER TEN

[1] Lewer, David, *A Spiritual Song*, 146 (1961).
[2] *Op. cit.*, 146-147.
[3] St Aubyn, J.P., 'An Account of the Repairs Lately Effected at the Temple Church London', 16 May 1864 (RIBA).
[4] Billings, R.W., *Architectural Illustrations etc Temple Church*, 40, 47 (1838).
[5] *Ecclesiologist* 1842.
[6] *Op. cit.*
[7] *Op. cit.*, 41
[8] *Op. cit*, June 1863.
[9] Inner Temple Bench Table Resolution, 16 May 1862.
[10] Scott, George Gilbert, letter in Middle Temple Library, 24 June 1862.
[11] *Ecclesiologist*, June 1863
[12] Fawcett, Jane, *The Future of the Past*, 100 (1976).
[13] Inner Temple Bench Table Orders, November 1865
[14] Lewer (*op. cit.*), 153.
[15] Lewer (*op. cit.*), 157, 158.
[16] Scott, George Gilbert; St Aubyn, James Piers; Cotes, Arthur, Middle Temple Library, 5 Jan 1872.
[17] Lewer (*op. cit.*) 191
[18] Lewer (*op. cit.*), 170.

CHAPTER ELEVEN

The Director of the Choir

In 1869 Thomas Robinson retired as Master of the Temple and was succeeded by Charles John Vaughan, MA, DD, (*ill. 100*), who had been Headmaster of Harrow between 1844-59, where he had raised the number of pupils threefold. He accepted the Bishopric of Rochester but then withdrew, and became vicar of Doncaster where he had the gift of preparing young men for ordination. Before he left there were over one hundred ordinands who became known as 'Vaughan's doves'. 'He delighted in sarcasm and his smile was even more dreaded than his frown.'[1] He denied the Apostolic Succession and held low doctrine on the sacraments. 'His sermons were always carefully written in a tense and nervous style, but his voice and manner gave the impression of unreality.' Vaughan was somewhat autocratic and crossed swords with the Benchers, wanting recognition of his place in either Hall to be next to the Chair, as indeed had been the custom. Once more a committee was set up to examine the position of the Master's precedence, and it was resolved that the office had no such right when dining in Hall.

A curious echo of the medieval situation remains to this day in the administration of the Temple church. The priest has assumed the title of Master of the Temple but, contrary to the implications of his letters patent, he has in reality no jurisdiction over the church – the management and care of the building and the ordering of its services being in the hands of laymen (the Benchers of the two Societies, its owners), who are responsible only to the Sovereign as Head of the Church. Exemption from episcopal and

100. Charles John Vaughan, Master of the Temple. Portrait by George Richmond.

archiepiscopal jurisdiction has also survived and has continued within the framework of the Church of England. The Temple church as stated before is a Royal Peculiar and the Master receives his letters patent from the Crown appointing him 'Custos' or 'Keeper' of the Temple. He takes office without institution and proceeds to his stall without induction.

The Master of the Temple, in spite of his unique and independent office, finds himself in a position of little authority. The late Canon

Anson wrote of the Mastership:

'If one consulted the letters patent, one might suppose that this office was of a more magnificent nature than in fact it is. To be "Master and Keeper of our house and church of the New Temple", "to preside over, rule and govern the house and church aforesaid and the ministers of the same church whether clerks or laymen", to have "all manner of tithes, oblations and obventions of the church aforesaid", all sounds very grand.'

In fact neither the Temple nor its church are his to govern. The letters patent describe the Temple as a Rectory, which it has never been (it has no parish, apart from the precincts), and the tithes to which they refer are non-existent, the Temple, as a religious house, having been specially exempted from tithe by numerous papal bulls.[2] It is small wonder that more than one Master of the Temple has had to be reminded of his true status by the Benchers, but a greater wonder that so many Masters have filled the post so well and have been on such amicable terms with the Societies in this curious relationship.

Dr Vaughan became concerned with the welfare of the choristers and saw to it that they were provided with a cold lunch between the two services on Sunday. They had hitherto fended for themselves. Hopkins took part in the meal but seldom talked and was said to have eaten as much mustard as beef. Vaughan also thought that the boys' education was wanting, as the choir school had too few pupils to make it viable. The Reader, the Benchers, the Warden and Preacher of Lincoln's Inn were all in agreement with him, and in 1875 the school was closed after 21 years. The choirboys were then sent to the Stationers' Company's School which had been opened in 1861 in Bolt Court on the north side of Fleet Street (*see front endpapers*). Dr Johnson had lived in the house adjoining the playground from 1765-76 which was now the headmaster's residence. Mr Chettle, the headmaster, often came to the Temple service, and Henry Humm recalled that, on the first occasion of his singing the solo in *Hear my Prayer* he was somewhat

overawed to see the headmaster sitting in one of the front pews. He was afterwards heard to observe: 'Yes, he may sing like a little angel but in school he's a little devil.'

Henry Humm, remembered by some as the greatest treble soloist, at least in Hopkins' day, wrote of his time at the Temple:

'Very little was new and nothing very ambitious, but much of it was beautiful. Was there ever a more charming anthem, of its kind, than Wesley's *Wilderness* with its perfect quartet "And sorrow and sighing shall flee away"?'

Regarding Hopkins and the choristers he said:

'Apart from his penchant for "clumping" little boys, I do not remember that he was actively unkind; at the same time I have no recollection of his ever doing or saying anything calculated to bring him into friendly touch.'

About this time the Prince of Wales often attended the Temple service. Mr Gladstone was seen occasionally in the church and it is reputed that César Franck lunched with Hopkins after a visit.[3]

Another celebrated visitor was Jenny Lind 'the Swedish Nightingale', who was then in her sixties. Her last public performance was in 1883. Hopkins was one of her favourite accompanists at her Exeter Hall concerts. E.H. Lewis, then a chorister, remembered her often coming to the Temple practice-room to run through their part with them, always bringing packets of sweets in sugar-loaf bags for them. Hopkins recalled how in earlier days at the Temple 'Jenny Lind amazed the people who didn't know her by joining in the hymns and singing most exquisitely.'

In 1879 Vaughan became Dean of Llandaff, but the Benchers were happy for him to continue at the Temple. Humm remembered him as:

'a benign old gentleman who wore nice black gaiters, as befitted his shapely legs and ecclesiastical dignity. On rare occasions, we were invited to take a very uncomfortable tea at his house.'

Canon Ainger, a bachelor, was always welcome at the Master's House by Vaughan and his wife, for the Master loved good talk and good literature, and anyone who promoted them. Ainger was an authority on Charles Lamb and in many respects resembled him.

Although weddings at the Temple were extremely rare,[4] there were of necessity many memorial services for departed Benchers. There are two ceremonial staffs, one mounted with a silver Pegasus for the Inner Temple and one with a gilt Lamb and Flag for the Middle which are clamped against the respective Treasurer's stall during a service. In former times on the Sunday following a memorial service, the staff was draped with black crape, and at the conclusion a Dead March was played, all standing.[5]

In 1880 the second edition of the *Temple Church Service Book* appeared, which included the *Temple Hymn Book* and with Hopkins' scholarly preface. Three years later came the handsomely-bound *Anthem Book and Psalter*. Dr Pearce wrote that Hopkins' system of pointing the Psalter was greatly in advance of any previous one. He added that Hopkins sometimes extemporised his outgoing voluntary, and enjoyed quite a continental reputation as an organ player.

'During the entire period when he was organist, the Temple Church could only be described as a veritable Mecca for church organists and musicians of all denominations.'

In 1882, at the age of 64, Edward Hopkins received his MusD diploma from the hands of the Archbishop of Canterbury – the Lambeth Degree, long overdue. Dean Vaughan was happy to present Dr Hopkins with his gown and hood. It was not generally known that he refused a knighthood.

The seventh centenary of the Consecration of the Round church was celebrated in 1885 in the presence of the Prince of Wales, Prince George and the Princesses Louise, Victoria and Maud.[6] The Archbishop of Canterbury's text was *Testis sum Agni* – 'I am a witness of the Lord – one of the ancient mottoes of this House.' He said 'Work for the future. Build for this time to come.

Yes, lay the foundations deep and strong.'

In celebration of Queen Victoria's Golden Jubilee (1887), a masque was held at the Inner Temple, at which Master Henry Humm made the greatest hit of the evening with the song *Orpheus with his Lute* by Sullivan.

'A rapturous encore brought the youngster back to the stage... A procession then led the way along draped corridors and through ornamental alcoves, to the Temple Church where Smart's *Festal March* was played and Handel's *Coronation Anthem* was sung by the choir. The Treasurer and the Benchers were congratulated on the brilliant success of a gathering which had no parallel in the present generation.'[7]

Dr Hopkins' own jubilee – his fifty years at the Temple – came in 1893, when for Sunday 7 May he composed an anthem *The Lord is full of compassion and mercy*. In his morning sermon, Vaughan was fulsome in his references to the Temple organ and its greatly talented organist.[8] On the following Tuesday a crowded congregation attended a recital by Dr Hopkins and afterwards in the Middle Temple Hall, the Societies presented him with a magnificent silver tea and coffee service together with a purse of one hundred guineas to mark his completion of fifty

101. Dr Hopkins and the Temple Choristers, 1897. Note that the four senior boys wear bow ties with their Eton collars. From 'The Quiver'.

years, during which he had presided at the organ of the Temple church and as Director of the Choir. At the same time, three of the choristers came forward and on behalf of the whole of their number presented him with a handsome scarf-pin of twelve pearls with a diamond in the centre, which the senior choirboy felicitously said was emblematic of their twelve selves and their master.

Another 'little bit of silver' – a handsome inkstand – came from his old friend, Canon Ainger, the Reader. On his accepting a Canonry at Bristol in 1887, Ainger had exchanged appreciative letters with the Bench who did not wish to lose his services and who gladly approved his providing a deputy during his periodic absence when in residence. But he was finding it a strain and in 1892 his resignation was accepted with regret by the Bench, who voted him a testimonial of £300. Ainger was succeeded by the Rev. S.A. Alexander, but shortly after, Vaughan had a severe illness and in 1894 resigned the Mastership. The Benchers felt a deep sense of loss, and a testimonial to him of £300 was voted by the two Inns. The much-loved Dean died at Llandaff in 1897; he left in his will a strict injunction that no biography of him should be attempted.[9] On Vaughan's resignation, the Prime Minister offered the Mastership to Canon Ainger, much to his delight. The dignified Master's House, so long already a home to him, was now to become officially his.

In 1893 the Stationers' School moved out to Hornsey, whereupon a new school was found for the choristers at King's College School in the Strand, but four years later K.C.S. itself moved out to Wimbledon and the Benchers had difficulty in finding another school near at hand. Finally, the choristers were transferred in 1900 to the City of London School, which had moved from Milk Street to a new building on Victoria Embankment in 1883. There they remained for the next century (*see front endpaper*)

On the occasion of the Diamond Jubilee in 1897 the Temple choristers led the procession onto the steps of St Paul's. Dr Hopkins, at 79, was among the tenors. This was one of his last engagements as early in 1898 his resignation was

accepted and he was granted a pension of his full salary (£340) as Honorary Organist of the Temple Church (*ill. 101*). He was also presented with a gold hunter watch by the Benchers and a beautiful silver salver, suitably inscribed, from the Temple ladies.

His farewell on Sunday 8 May, was the 55th anniversary of his first Sunday at the Temple organ. All the music sung and played were his own composition, and Canon Ainger in his sermon paid him a graceful tribute, tracing the influence of the Temple church upon church music in London. At the end of the afternoon service and his postlude, a great crowd gathered in the porch and beyond to salute Dr Hopkins as he proceeded from the church to the Inner Temple gate.

NOTES TO CHAPTER ELEVEN

[1] *A Dictionary of English Church History* (3rd edn. 1948).
[2] C.G. Addison, *The Temple Church*, 34 (1843).
[3] Capell, Richard, 'Franck in London', *Daily Telegraph* 19 Mar 1949.
[4] In 1958 Dr Macdonald, rector of St Dunstan-in-the-West, expressed his opinion concerning Temple Church weddings. He maintained that the old marriage registers were not registers at all as the Church was not licensed for weddings. Recent marriages had been by special licence of the Archbishop of Canterbury, then costing £20, and the entry then had to be made in the register of St Dunstan-in-the-West, in accordance with a direction by the Archbishop "of some years ago." There was a move to license the Temple Church but the Choir Committee thought that this would come within the jurisdiction of the Bishop of London, though Dr Macdonald thought that this would not be so.
[5] On the death in 1891 of Sir Thomas Chambers, QC, Recorder of London, a valued friend and benefactor of the choir, a special memorial service was held on the day of the funeral (29 December). Each choirboy received a shilling and a miniature photograph. Dr Hopkins played the *Dead March in Saul* by Handel, and "couldn't the old boy play it!", exclaimed Walter Minnion. "On one occasion, of fourteen Sundays, thirteen saw the crape, and EJH told me that he thought of fitting a handle to the organ, as he knew what the result would be if he turned it."
[6] *The Times*, 2 Feb 1885
[7] *The Daily Telegraph*, 21 Jun 1887.
[8] *The Times*, 8 May 1893.
[9] The explanation may be found in the biography of John Addington Symonds by Phyllis Grosskurth (1964); also in J.A. Symonds' *Memoirs*, edited by the same author (1984).

CHAPTER TWELVE

The Twentieth Century

Henry Walford Davies (*ill. 102*) was born in 1869. He was a chorister at St George's, Windsor, and when his voice broke, became a pupil assistant to Walter Parratt. His first appointment was at St Anne's, Soho and he then secured a post at Christ Church, Hampstead, where he remained organist until coming to the Temple.

It was the turn of the Middle Temple to appoint the new organist, and from about a hundred candidates, three were selected to play the organ and accompany the choristers who, when they were asked which choirmaster they liked best, all shouted together 'Mr Davies!' They said that they had elected the 'Doctor' – he was about to become Doctor of Music in the University of Cambridge. On 25 February 1898, Walford Davies was appointed Organist of the Temple church with a salary of £250 p.a. Dr Colles[1] observed:

> 'Thus his responsibility was solely to the Choir Committee and not subject to any clerical direction, and to an outsider this must have been seen as an unusual arrangement. The church was closed during the Long Vacation (August and September) so that the duty consisted substantially of Sunday services and weekday practices through only ten months of the year. No wonder that the Temple was regarded as a "plum" amongst organists' appointments.'

On New Year's Day 1901 Dr Hopkins was taken ill; on 22 January the death of Queen Victoria was announced, and on 4 February came the news that Hopkins had passed peacefully away.

102. Sir Walford Davies.

With the departure of an old man of eighty, now came a revolution. A chorister wrote:

> 'We had a young man of 28 who soon proved to be a real friend to all and called us by our Christian names or appropriate nicknames. The old upright piano gave way to a first-class Grand, and form-desks were made which enabled the boys to 'half-sit' at practice (*ill. 103*) The Doctor was not a disciplinarian, but discipline was perfect as far as he was concerned.'

An occasional assistant[2] was not so lucky.

133

103. Walford Davies taking practice, 1904. Note the half-sitting desks which he introduced. The vestries were built in 1869 (J.P. St Aubyn). Electric light had replaced gas-holders, seen on the right.

It was not until the beginning of the twentieth century, after a lapse of over twenty years, that further changes were made to the church. The first of these concerned the Benchers' 'creature comforts'. During the long vacation of 1901, the heating system was renewed and the church did not reopen until November. In a letter to Mr Horace Smith, the Master, Canon Ainger, wrote:

'We open our Church on Sunday, and should be glad to see a good muster of Benchers on the occasion. A lovely short anthem of Wesley's, and services to match. I hope we shall be warm, after spending so much time and hard-earned money on the new machinery. I had thought of preaching from a text good old Bishop Lonsdale used to quote - "Hot water! Ah! – a very good thing in a church – a very bad thing in a parish!"'

Walford Davies soon introduced new music at the Temple. The Benchers agreed that once a month the Sunday afternoon evensong would be shortened without a sermon, and a cantata would replace an anthem. Alexander, the Reader, at first disapproved of the arrangement, for he was the afternoon preacher, but was won over by Davies' persuasion. Arnold and Greene gave way to Bach and Brahms. Dr Colles remembered hearing for the first time 'How lovely is Thy dwelling-place' from the *German Requiem*[3]. Then came *St Paul, Messiah,* the *Christmas Oratorio, St Matthew Passion* and the *Mass in B Minor.* Unaccompanied 'Carols in the Round' left unforgettable memories in the minds of many worshippers at the Temple church.

Full practices with the Gentlemen were at 5 pm on Fridays. R.G. Minnion wrote:

'Doctor sometimes held us spell-bound. He talked not only of the Sunday's music but also of the attitude we should have towards Church music generally, of phrasing, rhythm and of the technique required for singing the psalms and anthems. Yet we were free to sing as the spirit moved us. He taught more by his manner than by precept. His eloquence at these rehearsals secured Sunday performances which attracted many of the eminent musicians and artists of his day to the church. I remember Ellen Terry sitting in the congregation and weeping during a certain boy's solo. Long before Master Lough's time there was a succession of boy soloists trained by Doctor which testified to his power of inspiring a singer with the right technique without spoiling his natural gifts.'

There were two outstanding adult singers in the choir, Gregory Hast, solo tenor, and William Forington, solo bass, 'as splendid a man as he was a singer.' The two, together with the Abbey lay-vicars Sexton and Norcross formed the famous Meister Singers Quartet. Hast was a superlative singer and his greatest distinction lay in the beauty and clarity of his English. In 1902 he took the solo part in Walford Davies' new oratorio *The Temple* at the Three Choirs Festival at Worcester, with great success. Davies' *Everyman* became very popular for many years, following its first performance at the Leeds Festival in 1904. However, in later years he was overshadowed by Elgar in this respect. But the Temple church remained the ideal setting for his unique music-making, and Walford Davies' oratorio *St Francis*, his anthems *God Created Man* and the unforgettable *The Walk to Emmaus* are among his finest compositions. He hardly ever composed for the organ, yet vied with Hopkins in his time as an accompanist.

In 1902 G.E. Newsom MA replaced Alexander as Reader and struggled to attain Davies' ideal in the matter of intoning, accepting his censure with unruffled good humour. Everyone was sad when Ainger, the Master, passed away on 8 February 1904 and, at the Temple memorial service, Davies played his old friend's favourite Schubert song – the beautiful *Litanie aller Seelen*.

The new Master of the Temple was H.G. Woods DD, formerly President of Trinity College, Ox-

ford. The Benchers took the opportunity to review the position and salary of the Mastership, pointing out that by their Charter the Inns were responsible to pay fees to the Master amounting to £17.6.8d a year jointly, the Crown also undertaking to pay him £20. Payment had subsequently been increased to £100[4] by each Inn who also had to find the Master a house which he had to maintain at his own expense. The new Master pronounced himself quite happy with the findings of the Committee. Relations with the Benchers were friendly, and Dr Woods soon found himself under the spell of the Temple. He was also a historian and assisted Master J. Bruce Williamson in compiling the list of Masters of the Temple. He also made a fine collection of portraits of former Masters, which hung on the staircase wall of the Master's House. They were unfortunately destroyed in the fire of 10 May 1941.

Alfred Capel Dixon was one of Walford Davies' first new choristers, the eldest of six brothers who followed one another in the choir[5]. It was said of him by a colleague: 'He was the greatest chorister both as man and boy that I have ever known. I have treasured memories of Dick singing *I know that my Redeemer liveth* and, decades later, of his tenor solos.'

By 1908 the close-knit choir reached its peak of achievement (*ill. 104*). By then a number of boys had left the choir, but few wished to leave

104. Walford Davies and the Temple Choir in the north churchyard. Note the voluminous 'Cathedral' surplices, without cassocks.

Temple which seemed a second home to them. The 'Templars' Union' of old choristers filled this need and survived two terrible wars.

The Union flourished from the start. Cricket and football teams were formed and in 1913 a Camp hut was established at Angmering, partly paid for by the Doctor, which the choristers could also attend in the summer holidays. This was a great advance following the only annual one-day outing to Brighton paid for by the Benchers in Hopkins' day. Another innovation was the magazine, *The Templar*, which has survived to this day.

The 'Templars' Quartet' was formed in about 1910 and consisted of Capel Dixon and Norman Stone, tenors, and Frank Hastwell and John Halford, basses. They attained considerable eminence at public concerts, and the four were able to join the Temple Choir as supernumaries, for the choir could well do with this reinforcement, in view of the heavy programme of singing which appeared month by month in the bulky service forms.

These years were full of music both within and without the church. In 1908 the choir took part in the commemoration service for the tercentenary of the birth of Milton at the church of St Mary-le-Bow. Walford Davies was responsible for the music and composed a setting of *Ode on Time* for the occasion.

> 'At the last minute he discovered that he wanted something in the nature of a Voluntary for strings and organ, and dashed off *A Solemn Melody*, which exactly filled the purpose. Later he offered this to Henry Wood for the Promenades and, greatly to his surprise, it was received there with such vociferous applaud that Wood had to break his rigid rule against encores and repeat it. It became a regular feature of every Promenade season, and beyond doubt Walford's most popular work.'[6]

In the midst of all this choral activity in 1908, the architect Reginald Blomfield made important alterations to the altar area that had been designed as part of the 1840s work (*ill. 82*). He raised the altar platform by one step and also altered the central arcade of five panels to the altar screen. The pointed tops to the four side arches to these containing the Decalogue were removed and replaced by a plain finish. The ornamental gilded cross to the central arch was replaced by a plain white Latin cross surrounded by golden rays. Similarly the coloured patterning to the front surface of all five arches and also that within the recesses of the set back arcading was redecorated in plain white. The heavy framework of the sanctuary was replaced by a lighter one of Purbeck marble with shafts of Irish fossil stone. Blomfield also designed a new altar cloth. In the course of carrying out this work the eastern wall behind was exposed. This revealed the much altered aumbries described in Chapter Three. In their altered form they consisted of three divisions with round-headed arches set above the floor level. The backs had been filled in so that they were now only four inches deep. These were further investigated in the 1930s.

A year later in 1909, major repairs to the organ were carried out at a cost of over £2,000. During most of this time the organ could not be used and the choir sang unaccompanied. The work was carried out by Frederick Rothwell and included the renewal of the blowing system and a new patent pneumatic tracker system controlled by rows of ivory tabs (*ill. 105*), a unique invention by the organ builder. In addition eleven new stops were added. The work of Father Smith and Schultze was carefully repaired and preserved. On completion, it was a balance between the old and the new. Master Muir Mackenzie[7] said:

> 'The old work has been dealt with and revoiced in such a manner as to bring out all its beauty to the best advantage, and the new stops designed and put in by Mr. Rothwell are of exceptional beauty.'

In 1911 the bell tower and turret were rebuilt. At this time the porch was found to be in a poor state of repair, with several cracks in the stone. The Temple surveyors proceeded to renew the stone facing of the interior of the north-west and south-west pillars of the porch, including new caps, shafts and bases to the grouped columns. Portland stone was used and, in order to blend in with the old work, it was stained with blackened oil. This meant that some of the original medieval work that had been carefully preserved fifty years earlier was removed. The Benchers at this point realised, as they did fifty years before, that it was not acceptable to remove original work without careful consideration. They asked the conservation architect, W.D. Caröe, to supervise the next stage of the work which was to the West doorway itself. He described this work in a report to the Choir Committee in 1912:

'Soon after work had commenced it appeared that old original carving of merit existed under the surface and that it had been covered with paint and putty and dirt so as to present to the eye little more than a black mass of decayed stone. By careful work this carved stone was cleaned and hardened. It appeared that one or two of the outside pilasters on the north side of the West door had been renewed and had been coloured black, apparently to match the door. Probably this was done in 1840. Beyond this and a small patch of stone inserted in one place, no evidence was discovered that the doorway itself had ever been restored.'

He was horrified that the surveyors had put artificial colouring on the new work to the porch and he tried to remove this as well as the black colouring on parts of the pilasters to the West door. Caröe dramatically changed his mind about the authenticity of the West door carvings for in 1927 he said:

'I have pointed out before that this doorway is not ancient but a last century construction, and probably an attempted imitation of a decayed doorway that it now replaces.'

The second summer camp at Angmering had just ended when the Great War broke out and life would never be the same again. The Temple church and its services continued much as usual, but many members of the Templars' Union joined the Forces in advance of conscription in 1917. However, *The Templar* magazine was kept going, and was much appreciated by those who were now scattered far and wide.

Sir Edward Grey[8] and Sir Henry Newbolt[9] were both drawn to the beauty and quiet of the Temple church, as was Hubert Parry to the music who came to hear his cantata *Voces Clamantium.*

'I was quite thrilled with wonder at the performance... the sound of their voices is so pure and good... The whole service impressed me very much.'

But not everyone approved of the Temple service. Martin Shaw criticised a remark made by Professor Hadow in a 1916 pamphlet:

'It is refreshing to find that his standard musical service is neither at St Paul's Cathedral nor Westminster. But why does he select the Temple Church? The choir is undeniably one of the best in London, and if he means that the best standard of singing is to be found there I would not dispute it. But it must be confessed that the musical atmosphere is decidedly "stuffy".... No; honour to whom is due; and with all the good will in the world the Temple Church service cannot be quoted as a standard to Londoners, beautiful as it is in many ways.'

The Organist and Choirmaster (January 1917) commented:

'We cordially agree with Mr Shaw. For a Collegiate church – as it is – the Temple Church is destitute of everything which a devout Anglican churchman desires to have provided for him in the reverential conduct of Divine Service – with the exception perhaps of the mere singing of the choir. Its mean unadorned altar, its uncassocked choir, its out-of-date seating, its utter want of anything in the shape of ritual, the depressing influence of its mere concert and lecture-hall atmosphere, etc. Many a church in the poorest parts of East-end London could have been more appropriately and more wisely held up as a reliable standard for imitation.'

The lines written by M.A. Clutton in 1898 still held good:

No superfluous decorations here;
No raised 'altar' forbidding to 'draw near',
Sublime in its simplicity adorned,
Christ's 'Table' is for sweet communion formed.

Another loss to the Temple was the death of the Master, Dr Woods, whose funeral service took place in the church on 22 July 1915. He was succeeded by Ernest William Barnes MA DD FRS, Fellow of Trinity College, Cambridge, who soon became a close friend of Walford Davies. Horace Dixon's chief recollection of Dr Barnes was of his habit of swinging about, very much like the Master's own parrot.

Parry and Walford Davies were together on the platform to inaugurate the 'Fight for Right' movement. A few days later, Parry gave him a song, saying 'Do whatever you like with it.' It was the manuscript of *Jerusalem* which soon became almost a national anthem.

On 11 December 1917 General Allenby entered Jerusalem. In view of the historical association, a special service took place in the Temple church on the 16th. The effigies of the Knights in the Round were crowned with laurel, 'a gracious and beautiful gesture', commented Edith Simon, 'and an accurate one, not assuming too much.'[10]

On 12 December the following year, by permission of the Benchers, 'the duke of Connaught, as Grand Master of the Order of St John of Jerusalem, was present with more than 500 members of that Order, 'all wearing their quaint regalia, at a solemn service of thanksgiving for the deliverance of the Holy Land from Turkish rule.'[11] The collection was devoted to the fund which had been opened for the rebuilding of the Hospital of St John in Jerusalem, bombed by the Germans.

It came as a great surprise when Walford Davies was invited to become first Director of Music at the University at Aberystwyth as from 1 April 1919, but he continued to oversee the music at the Temple church. The Directorship in

Wales was not entirely successful and eventually, following a serious operation, he resigned and took up an appointment as Organist of St George's, Windsor in 1927. By then he had become well-known at the BBC and had given his first broadcast, with the help of some Temple choristers, to school-children on 4 April 1924. 'His gift of communication, so evident in all his personal teaching, did not evaporate before the microphone.' *Music and the Ordinary Listener* for many years was not to be missed by thousands of eager music-lovers.

As soon as Walford Davies had told the Benchers of his departure to Wales, consideration was given to the appointment of his successor and it was thought that one of his assistants would be chosen. But Master Muir Mackenzie, himself a musician, had another name to put before the Choir Committee, that of a brilliant young organist at the Royal College and in due course George T. Ball, ARCM, was offered the post as Acting Organist under Walford Davies. At the Inner Temple on 6 March 1919 it was moved by Master Bankes, and seconded by Master Acland, that the recommendation be adopted, subject to the consent of the Middle Temple (although in fact it was the Inner's turn to appoint). Thus was the young genius most fortunately netted for the Temple Church, and its music continued to prosper for sixty years under his guidance and inspiration.

George Thomas Thalben-Ball was born in 1896[12] and soon showed musical ability of great promise. At the Royal College of Music he won an open scholarship and was soloist in the first performance in England of Rachmaninoff's *Third Piano Concerto* in D minor. He studied the organ with Sir Walter Parratt and at the age of sixteen became a Fellow of the Royal College of Organists. After his appointment in 1916 as organist of Paddington Parish Church, he came to the Temple three years later. One of the choristers wrote:

'I wonder whether anybody remembers the first time Mr Ball took a full practice at Temple? I was in the choir at the time, and was in my place ready to begin. After a few moments, in walked Mr Ball. We looked at one another and waited to see what would happen. Mr Ball did not wait: he carried on as though he had always been our choirmaster.'

It was indeed a formidable task for such a young man to take over the work and great inheritance of such a musician as Walford Davies at the Temple. However, the transition was remarkably smooth. Thalben-Ball became an enthusiastic admirer and disciple of the Doctor's and entered sympathetically into the Temple atmosphere. At the same time he had his own positive contribution to make and was not afraid to do things tactfully in his own way if he thought it an improvement. But there were no violent changes and in any case Davies, still officially Organist of the Temple, continued to take some of the services, Wales permitting.

In 1919 the Templars' Quartet were together again, and became permanent members of the Temple Choir, making a total of four basses, four tenors and two altos. In number, the choristers remained as six on each side, *decani* and *cantoris*, with several probationers.

Soon after coming to the Temple, Thalben-Ball started a series of short organ recitals, given every Thursday at 1.30pm (*ill. 105*). These continued without a break, except for the Long Vacation, until the summer of 1923 and gave a splendid opportunity for him to learn every possibility of the wonderful organ. It was also an opportunity for musicians and Temple habitués to get to know the young organist's fine playing. His early compositions included the fine *Sette of Carols*, the epitome of carols in the Round. The monthly cantatas continued as before, with Bach, Mendelssohn, Brahms and the Handel Chandos Anthems. Further works by Parry and new ones by Vaughan Williams were introduced, with carols by Warlock, Howells and Darke. Walford Davies' *The Five Sayings of Jesus*, *Grace to you and peace*, *God created man* and *St Francis* remained sure favourites under the new regime. Wesley's *Wilderness* remained one of the great anthems of the year's music, but Mendelssohn's *Hear my Prayer* was absent for some time, only

105. *George Thalben-Ball at the Temple Organ c.1930. Note Rothwell's patent stop-tabs. (Photo: Gilbert Benham)*

to return with vigour in 1926. On 7 June 1925 the tercentenary of Orlando Gibbons' death was marked by four of his anthems sung in the Round, followed by Walford Davies' *Let us now praise famous men*. As before, the Psalms continued to be given the most careful preparation and to hold pride of place in all the Temple music.

Early in 1920 Dr Barnes resigned the Mastership. He was succeeded at the Temple in 1920 by William Henry Draper MA, who remained there for ten years, and became a good friend of the choir, not least of the choirboys who looked forward to his excellent tea-parties. On 3 December 1923 Dr Draper dedicated the War Memorial tablet in the practice-room. He spoke to the parents in sympathy, with reference to his own three sons whom he had lost in the War, and he said a prayer not easily forgotten.

In Lloyd George's last Honours List a Knighthood was conferred on Walford Davies, to everyone's delight, on 12 December 1922. Dr Colles

106. Ernest Lough, the famous Temple chorister. He recorded Mendelssohn's 'Hear my Prayer' with George Thalben-Ball and the choir for HMV in 1927, at the age of fourteen.

remarked that it 'marked the termination of his work at the Temple, not any particular achievement in Wales.'

At a concert given in the Inner Temple Hall on 10 July 1923, the proceeds going to a fund for East End children's holidays, Lord Justice Bankes announced Sir Walford Davies' official resignation. On 19 July Mr G. Thalben-Ball was appointed Organist and Director of the Choir of the Temple church, as from the following Michaelmas. Davies expressed his deep sense of gratitude to Mr Ball for all his work at the Temple during the past four years, and his happiness at leaving this work in his hands.

The Benchers were delighted with the high standard maintained by their young organist and his choir and, following the new developments in electrical recording, the idea of a permanent gramophone record of the choir's singing came to be assessed. After some hesitation, HMV was commissioned to record *Hear my Prayer*

in the church, with Lough (*ill. 106*) singing the solo *O for the wings of a dove*. The result was phenomenal, as all the world knows. The fame of the record remained, and in 1962 HMV presented a Golden Disc to Dr Thalben-Ball and Ernest Lough to celebrate the selling of the millionth record, unsurpassed by any other. *Hear my Prayer* (March 1927) was soon followed by 'Hear ye, Israel' (Elijah) – considered by some and by Lough himself to be his best. '*I know that my Redeemer liveth*' (Messiah) '*I waited for the Lord*' (Hymn of Praise) and '*Oh come everyone that thirsteth*' (Elijah) were also recorded. The last two were duets sung with Ronald Mallett.

The issue of *Hear my Prayer* produced results which were felt almost at once at the Temple. Crowds swarmed into the services, some to hear the renowned music at first hand, others to gaze at the chorister who had won so many hearts through the medium of the celluloid disc. The Benchers were somewhat embarrassed at the unexpected publicity, and tickets of admission to all services had to be introduced, or the church would have been overwhelmed with its huge influx of visitors. Tickets remained in force until July 1929 when Lough had left the choir. He recalled many amusing anecdotes such as the belief that 'that boy' expired when he came to the words 'and remain there for ever at rest.'

More gramophone records followed in 1930 when Denis Barthel, another soloist with an expressive contralto voice, sang, among other works, Parry's *Jerusalem*. At the Aldershot Tattoo of 1934, tens of thousands heard a recorded verse of *Abide with me* sung by a Temple choirboy, Dennys Lake, whose voice had an unusual quality. Sadly, in the Second World War, he failed to return from a bomber attack in 1941. Ronald Mallett, who had sung with Ernest Lough, also died tragically in a Japanese prison camp.

As time passed Smirke's stone altar-screen of the 1840s was considered increasingly out of character with the building, even though it had been simplified by Blomfield. It was removed in 1929. At the same time the Choir Committee employed the architect Sir Charles Nicholson and later Sir Aston Webb, to design a new altar arrangement. Various ambitious ideas were put forward including the recurring suggestion that a central aisle to the altar be created by removing some of the pews. In the end, in 1933, the Committee opted for a simple alteration. A plain low table was used and a deep blue curtain patterned with a fleurs-de-lys was hung behind the table against the east wall.

The removal of the stone altar-screen allowed further investigation of the recesses in the east wall which had been rediscovered by Blomfield in 1908 and are described in Chapter Three. These consisted of two small and one large central recess. The opinion of the Council for the Care of Churches (C.C.C.) and the Ministry of Works was that these were aumbries or cupboards. Further research suggested that the central arch was originally two smaller ones similar to the others and they had been altered in the seventeenth century to contain a mural monument. There were also signs that the trefoil-headed side recesses originally had a projected label or had moulding above them, which had been roughly hacked away. The design of these was probably similar to those above the aumbries on the north and south walls of the Chancel. From these discoveries it was decided to reconstruct the two central aumbries and restore the two side ones (*ill. 107*).

The C.C.C. recommended in their report that several of the monuments which were in the triforium should be brought down, as well as a brass outside the building, as they were particularly fine and would add interest to the interior of the church. Mrs Esdaile, the leading authority on monuments, should be asked to prepare a report 'on the wonderful series of monuments and their respective merits.' The Choir Committee took this advice and the Martin and Plowden monuments in the triforium and the Littleton floor brass outside were placed in the church. In 1933 Mrs Esdaile completed her report in the form of a book entitled *Temple Church Monuments* being a Report to the Two Honourable Societies of the Temple.

In the same year J. Bruce Williamson,[13] the Bencher who wrote the definitive book on the history of the Temple, wrote to the Choir Committee hoping that:

> 'they will reach some decision regarding the east end of the Temple church and at last get rid of that funereal curtain we have stared at so long!'

Eventually, in the 1930s the curtain was taken away and the rough rubble wall remained the austere background to the Communion table until Wren's altar reredos was brought back in 1953 after more than a century's banishment. An earlier attempt had been made in the 1930s to return it to the church when it was rediscovered at the Bowes Museum. However, at the time it was considered by some too 'high church.' In the words of Williamson:[14]

> 'I do not doubt the excellence of Wren's work in the case of the screen designed by him on purely classical lines and quite therefore out of keeping with the Early English character of the interior of the choir of the church, as it now exists, but to erect it again in the church as it exists today would I think be a disastrous mistake.'

He went on to say 'the church is a place of worship not a museum'.[15]

These comments take the argument full circle and bring to mind the comments of Jane Fawcett quoted in a previous chapter about moral judgements upon the styles of earlier periods.

After ten years as Master of the Temple, Dr Draper resigned in January 1930 and died shortly afterwards. He was a well-loved Master and took a keen interest in the choristers and the Union. He was succeeded by Canon Spencer Cecil Carpenter, DD, 'a man of learning and culture, and apparently of democratic ideas.' If he was democratic, he was also distinctly High Church in his leanings, somewhat to the consternation of the Benchers. He considered that the altar lacked dignity. Though they wanted religion, they did not want 'ornaments', whether cross or candlesticks, and the Master's efforts in this direction met with a polite but firm rebuff. As a foil, the Rev. John Francis Clayton, a 'low

107. *The Temple church in the 1930s after alterations to the Altar, revealing the ancient aumbries. The brass memorials to the members of the two Inns lost in the Great War became past repair after the 1941 fire. High up in the clerestory can be seen the stained-glass window presented by Willement who designed it in 1842.*

church' preacher, was appointed Reader in the same year in place of the Rev. R.F. Rynd. Tall and active, he had been a keen cross-country runner in his time. His reserved manner was partly due to shell-shock suffered in the War. He presented a distinctly Victorian figure on his way to his flat at the top of Goldsmith Building after service, with his top hat, tail coat and a tiny attaché-case so out of proportion to his large figure.

At St Paul's, the Temple choristers took part in the annual performance of *Messiah* and *St Matthew Passion*.

The last camp at Angmering took place in 1929 as, unfortunately, the lease of the bungalow ran out. However, a very different holiday was made possible in 1931 when, through the efforts of Thalben-Ball, a boat trip to the Mediterranean was organised.

Later, Captain Alfred Dewar, a regular member of the Temple congregation, who was also a distinguished historian, gave up his time to take over the organisation of the choir's summer camps and arrange other activities for them, including football and cricket matches.

Since the break-up of the Quartet, Dixon had formed the Templars' Male Voice Choir drawn from old choristers. He was an inspired conductor and the choir soon became known as one of the best in London. Their singing culminated at the Command Concert at the Albert Hall to celebrate George V's Silver Jubilee in 1935. This was devised by Walford Davies as Master of the King's Music.

On 5 March 1935, much to his surprise, Canon Harold Anson (*ill. 117*) found himself Master of the Temple, after Dr Carpenter's move to Exeter. Anson was a man of remarkable charm, and his friends were devoted to him. His influence in the Temple was soon felt, and with his sympathetic understanding both of people and of situations – including his own as Master of the Temple – he rapidly made many close friends among the Benchers and the choir.

The degree of Lambeth Doctor of Music was conferred upon George Thalben-Ball by the Archbishop of Canterbury in the Inner Temple Hall on 27 November 1935. The honour was timely and most surely deserved, for he had for many years been recognised as the leading organist of the younger generation, as well as for his great work at the Temple – 'my first love', as he himself had called it. On 16 June 1933 the BBC Concert Organ had been opened by Sir Walter Alcock, Thalben-Ball and G.D. Cunningham. These three famous organists also played at the formal opening of the reconstructed Royal Albert Hall organ on 23 January 1934. With Marcel Dupré, who played there later, the press referred to them as the ABCD of organists. In 1936 Thalben-Ball was the first English organist to be invited to give a recital to *Les Amis de L'Orgue* at St Eustache in Paris, by courtesy of M. Joseph Bonnet. From this period dates his *Toccata in the French style*. At the Queen's Hall he always had a great reception each year when he played at the Promenade Concerts. At the Organ Music Society in the Temple Church in 1936, J.A. Westrup commented:

> 'The registration had clearly been devised by one who not only plays but also listens intently to the actual sounds produced. Equally outstanding was the taut, clear rhythm and the immaculate execution. Dr Thalben-Ball's staccato is an object-lesson in itself.'

Dr Ball's practices at the Temple were always stimulating. He continued to employ many of Walford Davies' maxims such as 'look ahead', 'don't strain', 'the softer the tone the clearer the words', and in the Psalms, 'as fast as you can and as slow as you must.' There were the three Ts – Time, Tone and Tune. Time was the framework, of first importance, upon which everything else was built, and without which the whole structure fell to pieces. Tone was never to be forced, but maintained through the full value of a note – 'Sustain!' was the key to produce 'Temple tone.' Tune was something which should not worry anyone who listened to himself and his neighbour. Dr Ball often drew a parallel from some architectural feature of the church to illustrate a point in singing: the arches between the pillars were phrases, rising and falling, and the pillars themselves were barlines, occurring at equal intervals.

Temple music remained much the same as in former years. 'Ah yes, very beautiful,' commented Sir William Harris (who had succeeded Walford Davies at Windsor), 'but a very limited repertoire – not much of the glorious Tudor school.' This was true, but inevitable in a church with no daily choral service. In addition, its special requirements as the private chapel of the Inner and Middle Temple had to be borne in mind. The music for the month was still submitted to and approved by the Choir Committee, at least in theory.

As for the 'dress' of the choir, black cassocks did not appear until 1929, the voluminous 'cathedral' surplice being thought adequate. Mortarboards had gone out after Hopkins' time, and City of London School caps were usual – although in the 1930s CLS straw hats appeared during the summer. On Sundays the choristers wore Eton suits and collars, but the Marlborough suit known as 'blacks' came in about 1930 and gradually ousted 'Etons' though not the collar.

As there was no sub-organist, Thalben-Ball could not conduct the service or anthem unless it was unaccompanied. Otherwise the head chorister was essential for success as he virtually led the choir by watching the organist in the mirror. The other three corner-boys would constantly be 'looking-across' diagonally, with the result of complete unity and harmony if all went well. The men behind watched across too and never conducted anything. It was a remarkably successful arrangement and had persisted since Hopkins' time.

Tom Meddings became head choirboy in 1937 and his singing was outstanding. His 'Ye now are sorrowful' (Brahms' *Requiem*) was especially memorable. Two other excellent soloists followed in 1938. Alan Young had a rich, contralto voice, which suited 'He was despised' (*Messiah*). Kenneth Kedge had a plaintive higher tone. His unsophisticated artistry was very moving, for example in the duet *The ways of Zion do mourn* (Michael Wise) which he sang with the baritone Tom Budgett, formerly a chorister of the 1920s. He also sang 'My Saviour Jesus now is taken'

(*St Matthew Passion*) with another choirboy Alan Polgrean, who had a cool, even voice which was shown to advantage in Mozart's *Benedictus qui venit*. By 1939 the choir had achieved a very high standard, not forgetting Alfred Capel Dixon's inspiring tenor solos and his intoning of the Litany on Good Friday, which rivalled that of Hast's in bygone years.

All this glorious music in hallowed architecture was soon to be shattered.

NOTES TO CHAPTER TWELVE

[1] Colles, H.C., *Walford Davies* (1941).
[2] Among Davies' pupils were Henry Colles and Leopold Stokowski (there is no truth in a statement that his original name was Stokes). Other young organists who would gather at the Temple on Saturday afternoons to improvise on the organ with HWD included W.H. Harris, Harold Darke, Gerald Bullivant, Rutland Boughton, Sydney Toms and George Dyson.
[3] 'German' was dropped from the title of Brahms' *Requiem* in 1914.
[4] The Master's salary was increased by the two Inns in 1913 from £400 to £600 p.a.
[5] There were also six brothers of the Capener family. HWD seems to have favoured families of choristers.
[6] Colles (*op. cit.*).
[7] Macrory, Edmund, *Notes on the Temple Organ* 53 (3rd edn, 1911).
[8] Colles (*op. cit.*). 'A Foreign Secretary who could come back from announcing war in the House of Commons and drop into his chair with the exclamation "I hate War", was the man to convince such as Walford.'
[9] Author of *Songs of the Sea* and *Songs of the Fleet* (Stanford), the solo sung by many a Temple baritone, not least by Ernest Lough.
[10] Simon, Edith, *The Piebald Standard* (1959).
[11] *The Times*, 13 Dec 1918.
[12] See Jonathan Rennert, *George Thalben-Ball* (1979).
[13] Ref. letter in Middle Temple archives.
[14] Ref. letter 1935 to Choir Committee in Middle Temple archives.
[15] Ref. letter to Middle Temple Choir Committee, 15 Dec 1935.

CHAPTER THIRTEEN

Destruction

When on 3 September 1939 Chamberlain gave the grave news on the wireless that we were at war again, the sirens wailed immediately. It was a false alarm, although everyone was half expecting bombs at any minute. In the event, the 'phoney war' continued into the next summer, with little happening until the fall of France. But preparations for war in London steadily mounted. These had begun in the Temple since the Crisis of 1938, and the choristers were ready that autumn for evacuation with the City of London School at which they attended. *The Templar* magazine of April 1939 recorded that:

> 'the Munich Agreement came just in time to prevent trenches being dug in the Gardens, for they were all pegged out in readiness. One of the balloons of the barrage scheme was stationed there for a time.'

With increased uneasiness it was learned that

> 'the railings round the south side of the church[1] from the porch to the Master's garden have been removed for the War Effort.'

The war became a reality in the middle of the Long Vacation of 1939. The choirboys were camping at Bryanston School at the time and their stay was cut short for their return to London and evacuation with the City of London School at Marlborough College on 1 September.

The Benchers decided to reopen the Temple church in October as usual, and services continued to be held with men's voices in the choir. The choirboys (with their gasmasks handy) were able to sing again in the church during school holidays at Christmas and Easter. But by the summer of 1940 the war was ever nearer and the Blitz began in earnest. The boys came home again at the end of the summer term and sang valiantly for several Sundays, services continuing through the Long Vacation. Occasionally the sirens sent the choir to the air-raid shelter under Goldsmith Building and they sang there to members of the congregation By mid-September the situation was getting too dangerous and it was a relief to know that the boys had returned to Marlborough. On 15 September there was a warning during morning service and another in the afternoon which lasted until 3.15 p.m., when a short service followed with a congregation of four. It was at this point that the Benchers suspended services until further notice.

At 3.45 a.m. on Thursday 19 September the first bomb fell in the precincts. It hit the corner of the Inner Temple clock tower causing grievous harm to the Library. Six days later at 2 a.m. five bombs fell in the Temple, the first in the Gardens and the second on the north entrance to the Inner Temple Hall, blowing out every window in the building though breaking hardly any glass in the church. The third bomb fell in Crown Office Row, the fourth south of Pump Court and the fifth in Essex Court, all causing much damage. Fortunately there were no casualties and the few people on duty or sheltering there were safe. Then at 10.30 p.m. on 15 October a parachute-mine fell in Middle Temple Lane, bringing down the east wall of the Hall and its fine Elizabethan screen.[2] The precincts rocked with the blast, windows being broken as far away as the Master's

House. In the church many windows were broken, though the three at the east end and some in the Round remained intact.

Though air-raids continued nightly, there were less by day and there was a lull at the Temple until Christmas. Services were resumed for a while from 22 December and carols were sung on Christmas Day. On the 29th nine of the choristers were back to sing at a heart-felt service – the Temple was probably the only City church where a full choir could be heard that Christmastide. The precincts escaped comparatively lightly in the big incendiary raid in the City that night, but on Wednesday, 1 January 1941 another land-mine fell on Harcourt Buildings and on Crown Office Row, blowing in many more of the church windows and their temporary coverings. The custodian had spent weeks getting everything straight and dusted again for services, and now it was in a worse state than ever. On the following Sunday, ten choirboys arrived for a restricted service which took place on a very cold day for a congregation of thirty people. On the following Sunday, 12 January, the choir arrived to find yet more damage. A heavy bomb had fallen at the north-west corner of King's Bench Walk, demolishing the east wing of the Master's House. Fortunately the Master was not in residence but he arrived from Kent to survey the wreckage. The church had had a lucky escape, though Willement's east windows had been badly shattered. Dr Thalben-Ball was very upset about the damage and remarked to a Bencher who was present that he was surprised that the windows had not been removed before the Blitz. The reply was that the Benchers did not think them valuable enough to take them out. Dr Ball could not understand that point of view; whether they were 'worth' anything or not, they were beautiful windows and many people thought them so. Apparently Clyde Young, the Middle Temple architect, had recommended their removal but it was now too late. Some of the coloured glass was collected and after the war was set as lozenges into the plain glass of the south windows in the chancel.

Despite the thick dust, the Master held a service,

with the choir unrobed and standing. In his address he told everyone 'not to lay up for themselves treasures on earth.' Stanford's *Te Deum* in B flat concluded the service, and then Dr Ball launched into Bach's *Fantasia* in G. The organ still sounded fine and defiant.

Broken windows in the practice-room were again covered with 'blackout' and dislodged slates to the roof were made good. In February it was surprising to see the effigies being 'protected' with great baulks of timber. Meanwhile Dove Brothers' foreman[3] was bricking up Plowden's and Martin's monuments. The old porter said that many incendiaries had fallen in the Temple one Friday night (14 March), resulting in roof fires in nearby Farrar's Building and Lamb Building. Evidence of this was found on the roof of the Round but there was little damage.

A Templars' Union memorial service took place on 24 March following the death of Sir Walford Davies in Bristol on the 11th, curiously only a few weeks before the destruction to come. With the Benchers approval the Master then arranged morning service to celebrate Easter Day, 13 April. There was a large congregation with Dr Thalben-Ball at the organ and a choir of ten boys and twelve men. Afterwards the Master celebrated Holy communion – the last, had they but known it, in the old church.

The night of Saturday 10 May 1941 was fine and moonlit, with a stiff easterly breeze. The river was at low ebb. A former chorister looked in at the church during the evening and played quietly on the organ to a friend. This truth came out later and rather spoiled the story that the ghost of Father Smith had been heard playing. Then the Templar went off, shutting the door behind him. Before midnight the sirens sounded and almost at once the first bombers were overhead. It was soon evident that it was going to be a 'big' night; in fact it was the heaviest of the Blitz and the last night raid on London of any size until the rocket bombardment in 1944-5. It was the night the House of Commons was burnt out and Westminster Abbey and many other historic buildings were set on fire.

Vivid descriptions of that night in the Temple

108. The Round church on fire, 10-11 May 1941. It shows that the roofs over the chancel were nearly burnt out before the Round caught fire.

are given in two booklets, *The ravages of the war in the Inner Temple* and *Middle Temple Ordeal*, published privately by the two Inns. It is clear that the night was one of great tension and much inevitable confusion. Unfortunately no fire-watching had been organised at the church itself. London was soon ablaze and the raid lasted for five hours. Before long the firemen stationed in the Temple had gone off to fight fires which had already broken out in Fleet Street and elsewhere before the Inns received attention from the skies. *Middle Temple Ordeal* relates how a bomb falling

in the Gardens smashed the water mains and describes how an incendiary lodged on the top of the Temple church in full view of fire-watchers. They were soon to be absorbed in a desperate effort to preserve their own buildings from fires burning closely on all sides. Half an hour later, unchecked, the fire started by this incendiary was out of control and the water pressure was too low to extinguish the blazing roof which soon fell in setting the whole church on fire. The conflagration spread to the fine Master's House, which was destroyed together with the heirlooms of the house. These were Hooker's table and chair, portraits of former Masters and many books presented by the two Inns, all of which were waiting to be placed in safety. One or two local people fought heroically to try to save what they could within the danger area of the burning church but as in 1666 huge fires in London had started tremendous wind eddies and for all their courage and effort they could not stop flying embers catching more and more buildings alight.

A resident of King's Bench Walk, was one of those who dashed into the church to see if there was anything which could be saved before it was too late. Hers was an invidious choice: she came out with the Bidding Prayer, bound in a large folder, which was used in the pulpit. It remains in use in the restored church. It seems that the fire started at the east end of the roof, then spread to the organ chamber and vestries, and from the organ to the pews below. The stone vaulting of the chancel held fast in spite of fire above and below, but the Purbeck marble pillars were grievously split by the heat.[4] The timbers of the conical roof of the Round burnt fiercely like a giant firework and fountains of sparks were thrown in all directions before it caved in onto the monumental effigies below. A remarkable photograph of the Round church roof on fire was taken by a newspaper cameraman (*ill. 108*).[5] It shows that the roofs over the chancel had collapsed before the Round caught fire. The cloisters were not consumed until the early morning, after the 'All Clear' had sounded.

Next day, on Sunday at about noon, two Templars arrived with difficulty and contemplated, almost unbelieving, the terrible prospect of ten hours' destruction. It was to take ten years to mend. The fire was still burning in the centre of the Round, where the piles of timber had unfortunately been placed over the effigies to protect them from blast, thus providing additional fuel for the flames. The heat was terrific and the visitors could not stay long in the church. It was perhaps as well that no water had been available as it would have calcined much of the stone and made the damage even worse. The

pews and choir stalls were reduced to lines of ashes, the words and music still readable on the fragile leaves of what had been psalters and hymn-books. One of the clergy chairs within the altar rails had not caught fire and this was hastily removed, the other one also having been rescued by someone else during the raid. Beyond that, of the vast amount of woodwork in the church,[6] all that remained unconsumed was the great West door, though scorched and slightly charred at the base, the Benchers' two doors at the east end and the door to the triforium stair. Nothing remained of the great medieval triple roofs of the chancel above the vaulting nor of the two roofs of the Round except for two large iron girders remaining suspended from the top of the wall. The Round lay open to the sky (*ill. 109*). Only the small roof over the West porch escaped.

The famous Temple organ was reduced to wood ash and solidifying trickles of molten metal.

109. Desolation on the south side of the Round after the 1941 fire, also the remains of Wren's cloisters before demolition. The bell-tower escaped the fire.

Mr Rothwell, the organ-builder, later retrieved a very small amount of valuable metal, possibly for re-use. Father Smith's pipes were to have been removed that month for safety,[7] but without waiting for agreement, Time decided the matter. Dr Thalben-Ball wrote from Wales shortly afterwards:

> 'The damage to the dear place is quite heart-breaking. That organ can never be replaced, but I hope that something lovely will eventually come in its stead.'

In the centre of the Round the memorial brasses, commemorating those members of the two Inns who fell in the Great War, were buried below the ashes. They were retrieved later but were past preservation.[8] The fine Littleton floor slab and brass[9] near the junction of the Round and chancel fortunately escaped the flames. The practice-room was a scene of desolation; ironic fragments of the choristers' war memorial bronze[10] were salvaged, a few names still discernible, and the remains of the iron frame of the grand piano were recognisable (ill. 110).

There was some excitement upon the discovery of two iron doors now revealed in the floor near the altar and under the former stalls. On opening them a few days later it was found that steps led down beneath the east wall, disused and untrod since 1842, to the seventeenth-century vaults under the Master's garden. The northern Middle Temple vault contained stone recesses, as in a wine cellar, each tablet headed with the name and particulars of the burial within. The southern Inner Temple vault was more macabre, revealing many ornate coffins, skulls and loose bones.

An early visual survey of the state of the ravaged church resulted in a short preliminary report. Copies were sent to the Inns, the Master and the National Buildings Record of whom Walter H. Godfrey was first Director, later to be appointed as architect for the Temple church restoration. He deplored the lack of protection of the church and the stupidity of covering the effigies with timber. Dove Brothers' foreman said that while he was bricking up the Plowden

110. *The Practice-room after the fire, 1941. Compare the photograph of 1904 (ill. 103). The grand piano frame is recognisable. Pictured are Captain A. C. Dewar with choristers. Photograph by David Lewer.*

and Martin monuments before the fire, another firm was bringing the wood into the Round.[11] Protest had been made by Mr Swanson, the Middle Temple surveyor, and also by Clyde Young, the architect, who had wanted to cover the effigies with sand, but to no avail.

One important item escaped destruction. The precious original Charter of 1608, with its ancient chest from beneath the altar, had been sent early in the war to a place of safety in Wales. (The Charter itself is now kept in the Middle Temple strong room.) The safe in the vestry was opened and the church plate was found unharmed but the fate of the registers was in doubt. Fortunately, though charred, they were later expertly restored by the Public Record Office.

The extent to which the building itself had suffered was as yet uncertain. Apart from the organ chamber and vestries, the Purbeck marble appeared to have been damaged the most. However, the marble wall shafts in the Round aisle had not been affected as the fire was roughly confined to the central area within the six main pillars. The triforium roof which had collapsed over the aisle vault, shattered the many monuments consigned there in 1842. The few remaining ones in the chancel escaped the flames, including the bricked up altar tombs of Plowden and Martin, and most importantly, the thirteenth century Purbeck marble effigy of the bishop. Set in its south wall recess, it had merely been covered with hassocks but was comparatively little damaged. But the bust of Hooker on the north wall was broken and did not survive.

Of the nine effigies in the Round only one, de Ros under the south aisle, escaped the fire. In the centre the southern group, including the Marshal family, was less damaged than the northern group. The cross-legged effigy with round helmet, was hardly recognisable. The Purbeck marble coffin lid in the north aisle also suffered. The font survived, and the grotesque heads were untouched, as were the stained glass windows in the north aisle and the rose window over the porch.

It was obvious that immediate protection was urgently necessary, both to cover the vaulting against the weather and to take the weight off the weakened pillars. This was the situation at the end of May.

In June choristers made a start on clearing debris by removing ashes from the altar area and washing it down.[12] One Sunday in July a heavy thunderstorm brought rain pouring through the vaulting where cracks in the stonework were observed. Eventually Dove Brothers started emergency work. The bishop's effigy and remaining monuments were bricked in and temporary roofs were erected over the vaulting and triforium; pillars were shored up and slate courses run to the gables and to the top of the clerestory wall (*ill. 111*). The remains of the cloisters were demolished, part of which crashed into the basement of St Ann's Chapel. This caused general surprise and broke most of the large pavement stones over the chapel.[13] The delightful Lamb

Building, now gutted, was also pulled down, never to be rebuilt. Debris was removed between the buttresses nearby and the small remaining brass[14] remaining in the paving was covered up. Unfortunately it disappeared some time later.

By August all the ash had been removed from the church. Clyde Young said at this time that only first-aid repairs were contemplated. Brickwork was built against the pillars in the Round where parts of the marble had fallen away and the undamaged font and Oliver Goldsmith's tombstone[15] in the north churchyard were bricked

111. Interior of the Temple church in 1941. Temporary brickwork supports the shattered Purbeck marble pillars. The remains of Willement's east windows (1842) are seen. Not a vestige of the seating or organ survived. A chorister surveys the scene. Photograph by David Lewer.

up. Debris over the vaulting was next removed, ready for the temporary roof for which a permit for the timber was awaited as this was in short supply. In the Round the effigies, such as they were, were cleared of ash and bricked up.

Emergency work continued until the end of the year. Timber and sheeting arrived in September and concrete and wood beams were laid, supported by short brick pillars built on the vaulting (*ill. 37*). By October the new low-pitched roof was completed, with gutters north and south, followed by a similar temporary roof to the triforium. The pillars in the chancel remained much as before though two of them, north-east and the second north-west, showed signs of movement. They were supported by somewhat flimsy timber flying shores against the walls.

At the end of November the building was left clear, evidently with no more work intended for the time being. On 28 December carols were sung unofficially in the bare church, although it was decorated with holly and lit with lanterns. It was very cold, yet nearly 100 Templars and friends attended and photographs appeared in the press next day. The Temple spirit had not departed. In the new year, snow was falling in the Round, still open to the sky.

NOTES ON CHAPTER THIRTEEN

[1] The iron railings had been erected at the time of Robert Smirke's restoration in 1828.

[2] The Elizabethan screen was fortunately pieced together and marvellously re-erected after the war.

[3] Dove Brothers Ltd of Islington had been regularly employed at the church during previous Long Vacations.

[4] Purbeck marble was more vulnerable in the fire than Caen stone because of the variation in co-efficient of expansion in its content.

[5] The photograph, taken by H.A. Wallace, appeared in the *Daily Mail*, 29 May 1941.

[6] It will be remembered that the cost of Savage's new stalls and pews in 1842 amounted to almost a quarter of the sum carried out for the restoration.

[7] A few of Father Smith's small organ pipes, formerly in the possession of Mr Rothwell, are now displayed in a case in the practice-room.

[8] The names of members of the two Inns lost in both wars have since been cut in the recesses of the arcade in the Round aisle.

[9] The heraldic brass of Sir Edward Littletons (1664) is illustrated in Mrs Esdaile's *Temple Church Monuments* (Plate XIX). It was removed to the churchyard in 1842 and was in poor condition. On her recommendation it was restored and re-set at the east end of the Round in 1934. It was again restored after the war and now lies between the choirstalls, south side. See P.W. Kerr, *Monumental Brass Society Trans*. Vol. 7, Dec 1934, 5.

[10] Similarly (see n8) the names of the choristers lost in the two wars have since been cut in the buttress in the practice-room.

[11] It was also said that thirty pounds was paid for the carriage of the timber, the remains of an old barn in Rye. An amazing story!

[12] With the Benchers' permission a stone tablet was erected in the triforium recording the thirteen years of meetings here every Sunday morning by choristers, Temple friends and relatives. They were nicknamed the 'Temple Tygers'. The wording on the tablet was suggested by Capt. Alfred Dewar: '*Haud immemores vel in ruinis Templi Templarii 1941-1954*' ('Templars ever mindful of Temple even in ruins'.) Four notebooks recording the Sunday meetings have been useful in writing these final chapters.

[13] 'Ignorance and stupidity is only too often evident', commented Alfred Dewar.

[14] The small brass of Thomas Nash 1648 of the Inner Temple is listed in Mrs Esdaile's *Temple Church Monuments* (176) and also in the *Trans. of the Monumental Brass Society*. It was originally in the south aisle of the church. 'It appears that the memorial was removed in 1842 to its present position, on the pavement within the railings between the fourth and fifth buttresses on the south side of the nave' (i.e. chancel).

[15] 'Here lies Oliver Goldsmith, 1728-74'. Mrs Esdaile adds 'Modern raised gravestone, poor in design and said to be inaccurate in fact.' Walford Davies's joke was to tell the boys 'Here lies Oliver Goldsmith.' The gravestone was made *c.1860*, his burial only known to have been somewhere in the churchyard. The stone was moved to another position after the war (*ill. 64*). In the triforium there was a monument, originally in the chancel: 'This tablet recording that Oliver Goldsmith died in the Temple on 4 April 1774 and was buried in the adjoining churchyard was erected by the Benchers of the Honble. Society of the Inner Temple A.D. 1837. Sir Frederick Pollock Treasr.' Again, Mrs Esdaile comments 'very poor'.

CHAPTER FOURTEEN

Resurgence

The air raid which did so much damage to the Temple church on the night of 10-11 May 1941 was not the last, but the worst was over. In March 1944 a canister of incendiaries was dropped over the Temple area and the tower of St Dunstan-in-the-West caught fire as did the roof of Middle Temple Hall, but both were saved. A burnt-out incendiary was found in the timber-less triforium. Earlier, in October 1942, a loose barrage balloon had drifted towards the church where it became entangled with the eastern gables causing two of the stone crosses to crash into the Master's garden.

Reconstruction of the Temple church would have to wait until after the war was over, but meanwhile measures had to be taken to safeguard the structure. Several proposals were put forward for temporary repairs to enable services to be held there once more, but the Benchers reluctantly decided against this as long as bombing might re-occur. Meanwhile the first of quarterly Temple services was held in St Dunstan's Fleet Street, with the kind assistance of the Rector, Dr A.J. Macdonald.

Nevertheless, in 1942 a joint Reconstruction Committee was set up by the two Inns. Its discussions included the site and design for a new Master's House. Dr Thalben-Ball was, as usual, looking ahead. He had drawn up a specification for a new organ and was pressing for an extra bay where the organ chamber could be rebuilt.

In 1943 scaffolding arrived and at last the Round was closed in, with a concrete roof over the clerestory. It was also divided off from the chancel with a block partition, and the windows

were weather-proofed with substitute glass, though some of the stained-glass windows had survived. In the following summer a length of carpet appeared and was laid from the west door. Chairs, a small pulpit and a simple altar table were installed and even the heating pipes were made to work again. Final touches enhanced the altar with a grey curtain, a seemly frontal and a bowl of flowers. On 3 June 1944 (three days before the invasion of Europe) the daughter of a Middle Temple Bencher was married in the Round. A newspaper report was headed 'Church rebuilt for bride', but it was in fact temporarily repaired so that Temple services could 'come home again'.[1] On 11 June the first public service since Easter Day 1941 was held in the church with a great number of Benchers present. There was a choir of seven gentlemen with Dr Thalben-Ball at the piano.

On the following Sunday, despite the advent of flying-bombs that week, a recital of music was arranged in the Round. It was a beautiful summer's day and although there was an 'alert' for most of the afternoon, the thuds of destruction were distant. The Carter String Trio played Boyce and Beethoven, and the programme included the first performance of Thalben-Ball's unaccompanied motet 'And I saw a new heaven'. The Round's acoustics still sounded perfect.

Services continued to be held monthly in the Round, but in March 1945, when the heating system failed, they took place once more at St Dunstan's. The authorities were also concerned about the safety of the building, small fragments of loose stonework having fallen to the floor on more than one occasion. It was therefore reluctantly decided to discontinue services there until the church should be restored. But the determination that it should 'rise from the ashes' was strong among the Benchers, Master, Organist, Choir and congregation alike.

In 1944, brick piers were built on either side of each damaged pillar in the chancel to take the weight of the vaulting, with a reinforced concrete cradle placed just above the springers. In the future it would be possible to remove the pillars and replace them with new Purbeck marble. In addition, a timber truss was constructed under one of the main arches where there had been some signs of movement in the vaulting. By 1945 extensive operations were going on in the Round. A large steel framework was erected on massive concrete foundations to take the weight of the upper walls (about 900 tons) and the main arcade was bricked in over the beams so that it would be possible to remove the damaged columns in readiness for their replacement.

It was hoped that restorations in the precincts were shortly to begin. The architects appointed for this work were Hubert Worthington, who would design the new Inner Temple Hall, and Edward Maufe, who would design the new Middle Temple Library and Cloisters. Clyde Young had died meanwhile. Worthington was asked to supervise the work of making the Church safe but he was anxious not to be responsible for its restoration, as he was not an antiquary. Subsequently on 17 December 1946 the Choir Committee made the wise appointment of Walter Godfrey FSA, FRIBA, for this task.

Walter Hindes Godfrey (1881-1961), antiquarian, archaeologist, historian and architect, was born in London. His interest in antiquities led him to be elected to the Committee for the Survey of London for whom he wrote four volumes on historic buildings in the metropolitan area. He was responsible with Patrick Geddes for the re-siting of the ancient Crosby Hall from Bishopsgate to Chelsea and in 1940 he was appointed as director of the National Buildings Record, formed to record historic buildings which might be damaged during the war. Its task was considered so important that it continued after the war

112. *Walter Hindes Godfrey and his son Emil Godfrey, of Carden & Godfrey, the architects for the restoration of the Temple church. A photograph taken at Chelsea Old Church on the completion of their earlier restoration.*

as the National Monuments Record. He was the author of many books on historic English architecture. As well as the Temple church, his restoration work included Herstmonceaux Castle and the old parish church of Chelsea.

It had been suggested that a temporary chapel could be constructed within the centre aisle of the chancel while the Round was being restored. But this would have hampered work and it was decided that the work to the chancel would proceed first.

Walter Godfrey began by assessing the damage done by the fire. He summarised the problem that faced him in a broadcast he made for the BBC in January 1961 shortly before his death.

'The conical roof of the round with its load, fell in a burning mass into the centre and burnt through the sleepers which covered the effigies, meant for their protection.

The three great roofs of the choir were burnt and the seats and internal furnishings produced such heat that they split the hard Purbeck of the piers and shafts and the modern Caen stone facing of the walls, but left almost untouched the soft clunch ribs and chalk panels of the vaulting.

'The Smith organ was burnt and destroyed the chamber which had been built for it in the form of a transept one hundred years ago.

'The explanation of why the Purbeck marble columns suffered so much more badly than the clunch and chalk vaulting is that clunch and chalk have a much lower co-efficient of expansion compared to marble and are able to absorb the heat without cracking.'

Godfrey went on to quote Jeremiah Wells. Writing in 1667, after the Great Fire of London when the Temple was faced with a similar task, Wells said:

'Now in despight of the devouring flame
Which has done more than boldest traitors durst
She shall as much outvye her former fame
As the last Temple did exceed the first.
Hither shall best artificers be sent
Their pious zeal improving of their skill
Such to the building of the Temple went
Whom the Almighty did with knowledge fill.'

Godfrey was faced with a severely damaged building, originally built in 1185 and 1240, which had, like many buildings of this kind, undergone a series of major repairs and alterations over the centuries. In particular, very little of the original remained after the 'scrapings' of the nineteenth century. The philosophy of how to proceed with the replacement had to be established. Gone was the heavy handed doctrine of the ecclesiologists of the previous century. Legislation was beginning to be passed to protect historic buildings but this had more to do with unscrupulous owners who placed no value on ancient buildings. This was a very different problem. There could not have been a better architect in charge - someone who had a lifelong interest and knowledge in historic buildings. It had to be accepted that, with so much physical damage and structural instability, it was not possible to follow the best of William Morris's beliefs enshrined in the principles of the Society of the Protection of Ancient Buildings (SPAB). Although conservation of as much of the original fabric as possible was the ideal, it was inevitable that some of it would need to be replaced. This was particularly so as it was decided to restore the church to a state where it could continue in its fullest sense as the church of the two Societies.

Modern practice follows the general principle that an historic building should be conserved 'as found' as any building of some age will reflect the way it has been used and altered and this should be respected. If parts of a building are irreparably damaged, then it is accepted that slavish replacement of what was there before does not need to be followed – especially if it was particularly incongruous. In addition it was accepted that, in the case of the Temple church, the fire gave the opportunity of solving some of the problems that had plagued the church for so many years.

Once it was agreed that some restoration work was necessary the architect then had to decide which historical period should be followed. Godfrey approached this problem in a sensitive but pragmatic way. When writing to the Royal Fine Arts Commission, seeking their views on his proposals for replacing the burnt out roofs of the Round, he set out his ideas under three headings: (a) Historical; (b) Aesthetic; (c) Practical use. He felt 'historically' it was a matter of what could be established as authentic about the appearance of the church at any particular point in time as against speculative ideas of what it might have been or should have been. He considered that this might be of a period later than the original building but this needed to be balanced with how much of the building fabric was left of a particular period. For the Temple church, in descending order, this was likely to be the work of Savage and Sydney Smirke in 1842, Robert Smirke in 1826-8, St Aubyn in 1862, Wren in 1686 and then what was left of the original church as built in 1185 and 1240. In his Communication to the Society of Antiquaries in

1953 on 'Recent Discoveries at the Temple London' he mentioned the particular importance of:

> 'the original plottings made by Frederick Nash in 1818 which were drawn by him and published in a fine series of plates in *Vetusta Monumenta* in 1835. This is a most important record, especially in view of the scarcity of early graphic records of the Temple which is so severe a handicap in reconstructing its past.'

In addition to this, casts and measurements were made and photographs from the National Buildings Record were used, as well as early measured drawings such as those of B.E.T. Langford of 1872.

In summary, Godfrey was sceptical of the conjectural conical roof of the Round of 1862, the decoration to the vaulting and the encaustic tiled floor of 1842. It should be remembered that he was making his decisions before 1958, when the Victorian Society was formed and there would have been some pressure to value the work of this period more highly.

'Aesthetically' Godfrey felt that it was a matter of taking an historical overview of the appearance of the church and choosing a form that was of greatest beauty but at the same time historically authenticated.

In 'practical' terms Godfrey was already beginning to consider an extension to the organ chamber, as recommended by Dr Thalben-Ball, the desirability of a south porch, stone flooring and the arrangement for seating, perhaps on collegiate lines. The latter would answer the pleadings that had been made over the last one hundred years for a totally uninterrupted view and approach from the Round to the altar.

In 1947 it was good to hear that eight leading artists in stained glass were working in competition on designs for a new great east window, which was to be presented by the Worshipful Company of Glaziers and Painters of Glass. In addition the Benchers were anxious to erect as fine an organ as could then be built in England.

A large part of the costs of the repair of the church was to come from the War Damage Commission. In 1949 Dove Brothers of Islington began the building work, with an experienced foreman in Arthur Bernard, who was also an enthusiastic photographer. The firm had also carried out the restoration of the damaged Middle Temple Hall, which the Queen had reopened on 6 July 1944.

In the contract documents, Godfrey made the nature of the work very clear to the builder.

> 'It must be clearly understood that the work to be carried out is a preservation and restoration only. Every endeavour is to be made to keep the original portions of the building in position. Pulling down any part of the original work or the insertion of new work in old must not be undertaken except on the definite instructions of the Architect and in cases where safety of the building absolutely demands such treatment. The new work will be designed in all cases to be in harmony with the old work and no attempt should be made to give it an appearance other than of modern origin.'

It can be seen how different this approach was to that of the previous century when restoration meant the wholesale removal of large parts of the existing fabric of the church.

An early decision needed to be made about obtaining a large amount of Purbeck marble, as nearly all of that type of stone had to be replaced. It was found that W.J. Haysom of the St Aldhelm's Head Quarry in Dorset was the only person who could find and work the marble to the necessary standard. Kenneth Carpmael KC, Bencher and Master of the House in the Middle Temple, was asked by the Inns to oversee the work in the church. Together with Walter Godfrey, his son Emil, Col. Dove, his agent and the foreman, he visited the quarry in Purbeck. They were more than satisfied, but there was a problem in that it was a small quarry with limited machinery. Here the builders came to the rescue and installed extra plant. Even so, the project needed more marble quickly as well as additional masons in the church, of whom there was still a shortage. Eventually Walter Haysom and his men produced most of the finished marble, but another firm was brought in to assist progress. Their masons were used to working with granite but not so well with marble. However all was put right, and the material began to arrive in London from Purbeck, though by lorry and not by sea as it did in the twelfth century.

Another problem for the architect was the inclination of the pillars or piers in the chancel. It was not the result of the fire; the tilt had always been observed before the war. Walter Godfrey explained why they were not being rebuilt vertically:

> 'It is not uncommon in medieval buildings to find that the walls and the piers have settled unequally, causing them to lean to some degree out of upright. Where this has occurred in the whole building, and especially where a triple vault such as that in the Chancel of the Temple Church has accommodated itself to the original movement, it is generally safer not to alter it. The piers could of course have been built vertically beneath the old points of support, thus altering their position, but it was thought better to utilise the old foundations which had taken the weight throughout the centuries.'

The south-east pillar, already split, was taken out first, without mishap in the vaulting. Plaster casts and detailed measurements had been made of the bases, drums and caps. The new Purbeck

113. Purbeck marble quarry, West Lynch, Corfe Castle, 1950. The pit had constantly to be pumped clear of ground water. Photograph by David Lewer.

base and drums duly arrived, followed shortly by the finely wrought stone cap. One Sunday, before it was inserted, four Templars climbed the ladder, signed their names on it and sang Purcell's *Rejoice in the Lord*.

The September 1950 number of *The Templar* described the arrival of consignments of Purbeck marble.

> 'It is of a lovely blue-grey colour, beautifully moulded by hand, each stone being carefully worked in a small hut at Mr W.J. Haysom's St Aldhelm's Head Quarry. The new marble comes from a field at West Lynch, Corfe Castle, about a mile from the old quarry at Woodyhyde which was reopened in 1840 for the Victorian restoration.[2] Nearly enough has been quarried to complete the eight pillars in the Chancel; the Round will be restored later. The first load of marble arrived by lorry direct from Purbeck at the beginning of March, and the foundation stone was laid by the two Treasurers at a private ceremony on the 27th. In August the marblers had a trip to London to see the results of their labours; they were much impressed but were unanimous in voting London 'too much of a rush.'

Meanwhile good progress was being made elsewhere in the chancel in the rebuilding of the north-east buttresses, walls and window openings which had been so badly damaged when the adjacent vestries were on fire. The former organ chamber was demolished to window-sill level, buttresses underpinned and the basement excavated to form a new boiler room. The rebuilding extended westwards to cover the triple lancet windows in that bay. These would remain as openings for the increased sound of the larger organ. The external finish of the chamber, was to be in Kentish ragstone to match the surviving stone of the adjacent Round.

Ketton stone was selected for the replacement external walling where required on the main walls of the chancel. A large part of the exterior had been refaced with Bath stone in the last century. By choosing Ketton stone it provided visual coherence as well as a stone that could

*114. Stonemasons engaged in restoring the south wall of the chancel. Renewal of a vaulting stone is also shown.
Photograph by Arthur Bernard.*

better resist the polluting atmosphere of London.

Farmington stone was chosen for the internal replacement work. The reason stated by the architect was that:

> 'The original stone used in the church was Caen stone and it was now proposed to use Farmington Stone on account of its matching the present quality of texture of the walls.'

Both these types of stone met the criteria of SPAB in that although they blend well with the stone that remained, they were sufficiently different to be able to be distinguished as new work.

The tessellated floor tiles were replaced throughout the church with plain Purbeck Portland flag stones. The tiles had been little damaged and were relaid in the triforium.

A most happy piece of news was that the Inns had accepted, on Dr Thalben-Ball's recommendation, the gift of a splendid organ from Lord Glentanar. He had been up to Aboyne in Feb-

ruary 1950 to play it and reported back that:

> 'The organ, a four-manual 'vintage' Harrison instrument built in 1928 is probably better than anything that could be obtained new at the present time, and in many respects equals, and in a few surpasses, the old Temple organ. It will be transported from Glen Tanar, Aberdeenshire, to London as soon as the new organ chamber has been built for it.'

It rivalled the specification of the previous organ in other ways, having eighty-four speaking stops including three of 32ft and more than 3,000 pipes.

Attention was now turned to the provision of heating by gas and hot air and the necessary ducts. The discovery of the earlier chancel and the basement 'treasury' has been described previously. Much interest was raised in this matter and the considerable excavation approved by the Benchers and by the War Damage Commission delayed progress. However, the work-men were not so pleased with the task of sifting the many skulls and bones dug up together with disintegrated coffins. The former were reinterred in a newly constructed brick vault at the east end of the south aisle and Master Carpmael watched the new slab being placed over it by the foremen. It is now covered by the new stone flooring and stalls. Another discovery below the floor was a seventeenth-century pot which Arthur Bernard photographed in situ.

Much excitement occurred when the actual tomb of the famous jurist and scholar John Selden was discovered at the western end of the excavation several feet below the level of the chancel floor. Later, as part of the restoration work, a glass plate was set into the floor so that the black marble top to this with the inscription *Hic inhumatur corpus Johannis Seldeni* can be seen. It is as sharp as when it was first made. Mrs Esdaile, in her *Temple Church Monuments*, had been much exercised as to its provenance and this new exposure was a satisfactory conclusion to the matter. It is fairly certain that the original black marble inscribed slab that was at floor level now lies in the north churchyard outside the practice-room, where it was removed to that position in 1842. Any inscription or coat of arms has long since worn away. The wall monument to Selden was removed to the triforium in 1842. The account of the funeral by Aubrey was found to be accurate, and the side of the stone tomb may be seen in the basement. Rowland Jewkes lies also in a stone coffin next to his friend Selden.

It had been decided to proceed with a new south porch. After the blocking up of the door in the south of the Round in the nineteenth century, the only entrance into the church was via the West door. The architect proposed that by introducing a second entrance to the church a number of problems could be answered. It would be the general day-to-day entrance to the church, meaning that the West door with its ancient carvings would be more protected as it would only be used for ceremonial occasions. It would also provide a second means of escape should there be a fire in the church. There was

a further practical problem in that, after the war damage, the Round had been blocked off from the chancel. It had been decided to proceed with the restoration of the chancel first and to open this as soon as it was finished. In the event it took another five years before the Round was restored and rededicated. With this in mind a new entrance was required, at least on a temporary basis into the chancel. The argument which finally decided that the new entrance should be permanent was that, by including a staircase in the porch itself, access could be provided down to the newly discovered undercroft and to the remains of the crypt of St Ann's Chapel.

There was more excitement when the first of the new Purbeck marble pillars or piers was completed and the temporary brick piers supporting the weight of the vaulting were removed. This was described by Walter Godfrey in his BBC broadcast:

> 'When the first of the new Purbeck piers had been built we came to the transference of the load of the vaulting on to it. This was an interesting moment, when with twenty men each at a jack or folding wedge, the centerings and struts holding the arches were loosened at one whistle blow from the fore-man. There was quite a gallery of observers on the scaffold and none of us heard a crack or even a creak in the structure as it settled on its new support.'

The last of the eight new pillars was completed by 1952 and the brick piers removed. Good progress was made in replacing the Purbeck marble window and wall shafts, proceeding steadily from the east end. It was reported that:

> 'Mr Haysom has worked some most complicated mouldings in the hard material, particularly for the responds at the entrance to the Round and also for the new moulded arch which Mr Godfrey has redesigned in marble, over the recess in the south wall containing the bishop's effigy. It has been possible to repair its slight damage without moving it. In

renewing the stonework on which it rests, a cavity was revealed in which could be seen the ancient Purbeck coffin containing the skeleton of the ecclesiastic represented by the effigy.'[3]

During further excavations in the church for the new heating ducts, more bones and skulls, some in brick vaults, were exposed and were removed to the Inner Temple vault under the Master's garden. According to the registers, some 2000 burials took place in the church during the seventeenth and eighteenth centuries as well as others in earlier times.

The chancel was now a mass of scaffolding for work on the vaulting (*ill. 115*). The south-east bay had to be reconstructed because the ribs had fractured and slipped. As a result of the fire the familiar ceiling painting of 1842 began to disappear as soon as touched before cleaning. It

115. Restoration of the chancel, 1952, with a forest of scaffolding and new Purbeck marble columns.

was agreed that the highly-coloured decorations by Willement would not be repeated, leaving the building to express its own beauty. Nevertheless some enrichment was desirable, and this was to be provided by two fine contrasting elements, the new coloured east windows and the return of the Wren reredos from its banishment to the Bowes Museum in 1842. The latter was sold back to the Temple for £900. The possible return of the reredos had been the subject of debate for a considerable number of years. By now the climate of opinion had changed, and it was acceptable that contrasting elements could exist side by side as a reflection of the rich history of the church. Details of the Great East window were given by the architect in *The Templar*:

> 'It is in three lights, has some 15,000 pieces of glass and weighs a ton. It is made in sections carried on heavy bronze glazing-bars, themselves weighing several hundredweights. The subjects, though small, are clear, and each piece of glass is surrounded by lead, making up first and foremost a mosaic of colour.'

Carl Edwards, the designer, provided this description:

> 'In the centre light, Christ as the Supreme Judge is depicted at the top, supported by adoring angels. Below, Christ is seen with the money-lenders from the Temple. There follows then the arms of the donors of the window, the Worshipful Company of Glaziers and Painters of Glass, and at the bottom of this light the three vows compulsory to the Order of Templars are symbolised by three figures, a Knight Templar for Obedience, a Virgin and tamed unicorn for Chastity and a Franciscan Monk for Poverty. In the Medallion at the top of the left-hand light can be seen David kneeling in front of Solomon and Ezekiel. The cross of the Templars on a shield follows, and below that the City with St Paul's above the flames symbolises the destruction wrought in the Blitz. Below the arms of the Middle Temple the subject recalls that the Temple was a treasury in medieval times. The top of the right-

hand light pictures St Andrew, the patron saint of Artists and Glaziers, with a Knight Templar and St Augustine whose Rule the Templars followed. Under a shield showing the Cross of Jerusalem, a picture of the Temple Church balances the Blitz medallion opposite, and finally, below the arms of the Inner Temple, is a medallion containing two Templars on one horse.'

When the reredos was re-erected at the east end, questions were asked as to why the new east window was obstructed by the screen. Mr Godfrey replied:

'The centre part of Wren's reredos was higher than the sill of the window and it could not be lowered. Mr Carl Edwards knew of this, and although he preferred to carry his work down to the sill, he arranged that nothing of value would be hidden. I think it will be found that this intrusion of the pediment of the reredos will help to integrate and harmonise the whole effect. It must be remembered that the treatment of the east end of the church is yet to be completed by further stained glass in all the lights of the end windows of the north and south aisles. This breadth of colour and wide treatment may neutralise the present effect of incongruity between two elements, both fine in themselves, which compete for the focal centre of interest – the coloured window, rich and mysterious and medieval in spirit, and the carved screen, ponderous, classical and secular in feeling.'

In order that the historic aumbries in the east wall would not become totally inaccessible again, once the Wren reredos was fixed in position, the two central panels of the reredos were hinged to provide access to them.

The dark oak Wren screen was matched with a new altar rail, designed by Godfrey, which replaced the stone enclosure. The large Communion table was hinged to accommodate the ancient chest containing the Charter. It did return to its traditional place but recently it was removed to the triforium and the Charter is in safer keeping in the strong room at the Middle Temple.

The north aisle Middle Temple stained glass window was installed in 1954 and the Inner Temple in the south aisle in 1957 (both again designed by Carl Edwards).

With the completion of the remaining windows and stone flooring, the appearance of the chancel on a first visit was breath-taking. The contrast with the pre-war, stall-packed building was startling, as it was now spacious and simple (*ill. 116*). But seating was still necessary. Godfrey stated:

'The stalls will all face inwards towards a wide central aisle. They will echo the design of the altar furnishings but the oak is left in its natural colour. The seating is kept low and will not rake up to the walls as formerly. The lighting consists of chandeliers suspended from the bosses and each containing a large number of lamps in grey metal shades arranged in circles at varying heights, with central gilt spheres. The organ loft is in the same position as formerly but the gallery is rather higher than before and is stepped out in oak panelling. The organ case is yet to be completed; in the adjoining window opening to the west, tall metal pipes stand just behind the lancets, with pleasing appearance.'

With a central aisle between the seating (*back endpaper*) the view from the Round to the altar was finally free of any visual interruption (*ill. 94*).

It took six months to install the organ and it was indeed a gracious gift. Nevertheless the total cost, including its journey from Scotland, was in the region of £10,000.

Rededication of the chancel, planned for 16 November 1953, had to be postponed as there was still too much unfinished. The ceremony took place eventually on 23 March 1954, officiated by the Archbishop of Canterbury in the presence of Her Majesty, Queen Elizabeth the Queen Mother. She was escorted to her seat on the north side, she being a Bencher of the Middle Temple. Captain A.C. Dewar sat in the stall of the Lord Chancellor (who was unable to attend).

The Order of Service included music by four

116. *Restoration of the chancel, 1954, before installation of furnishing, except for the Altar and Wren reredos, returned from the Bowes Museum. Only the east window had been completed. Photograph by Arthur Bernard.*

Temple organists, John Stanley (1734-86), E.J. Hopkins (1843-98), H. Walford Davies (1898-1923) and G. Thalben-Ball (from 1919) who contributed the first performance of his new anthem '*Comfort ye my people*'. As there were as yet no new Temple choristers, the Westminster Abbey choirboys, with the ready asistance of the organist Sir William McKie, formed the choir together with the Temple gentlemen. The new organ was voted a more than worthy successor to Father Smith's. Dr Thalben-Ball said:

'We owe Lord Glentanar inexpressible thankfulness for his gift of the magnificent organ which contributed to the grandeur of the occasion.'

The Archbishop, Dr Fisher, in his address, said that at the first dedication of the Temple Church nearly eight centuries ago there were associated in our national life the Christian Church of England, the Christian monarchy, and an order of chivalry; that triple association was still present today.

After the service the Archbishop, Dr Macdonald (Acting Master of the Temple), the Reader, choristers, Dr Thalben-Ball, Lord Glentanar and Master Kenneth Carpmael signed their names in Calvert's book in which are also recorded the names of those who took part in the re-opening service on 20 November 1842.

It was pleasing to know that Harold Anson, Master of the Temple (1935-1954) whose death

117. Harold Anson, Master of the Temple.

occurred on 31 March at the age of 86, lived on in spite of his long illness until a few days after the Rededication of the Temple Church. He heard of it with great thankfulness. He never saw the new building, which it virtually was, and perhaps he would have preferred to remember the church as in the great days before the last war, when he did so much for the Temple and for the Choir and made so many friends among Benchers and choristers alike. In his book of recollections and reflections, characteristically entitled *Looking Forward*, the Master wrote in the chapter on the Temple:

'I was told when I came here in May 1935, what a formidable congregation, and what a host of difficult adjustments I must expect to encounter. I can only say, with the most loyal and friendly co-operation of the Reader at the Temple, the Treasurers and Masters of the Bench, the organist, choir, and the surveyors, I have never had so happy a post, or one which gives great opportunities to anyone who is ready to take account both of its limitations and its openings. Anyone who holds this office must always remember that "the two

learned and honourable societies of this house" (as we call them in our bidding prayer) are composed of men who are not all Anglicans... Yet where else in the world will you find an ancient and honourable profession providing for, and delighting in, the worship of God, with all the added dignity of architecture and music and song?... There have been many wiser and more eloquent Masters of the Temple, but none who loved it better than I do, or took more joy in serving it.'

It is fitting that this chapter should end with an appreciation of the architect and builder for the restoration. Shortly before the rededication of the chancel in December 1953, Lord Goddard, the Lord Chief Justice, and the Treasurer of the Middle Temple, wrote to Walter Godfrey:

'The extent and depth of the destruction which had taken place posed a problem deep and complex in its character, involving not only structural but historical and aesthetic considerations. Your imagination and initiative have been aptly implemented by the work of the master builders Colonel W. N. Dove and his firm, Messrs Dove Brothers, who happily still find it possible to run a group of craftsmen of the old school side by side with the most modern methods of large scale building.... we feel that this is a fitting moment for expressing to you and your son and his partner Andrew Carden, who have assisted you in your work, our appreciation of what you have done, and are still doing.'

NOTES TO CHAPTER FOURTEEN

[1] 'My blood so red, For thee was shed, Come home again, Come home again!' set by Walford Davies in his *Requiem* and often sung on Good Friday.
[2] During the first post-war Temple Camp held near Swanage in 1956, the choristers were able to visit the Quarry and to see the blocks of Purbeck marble being transformed into columns, caps and bases for the restoration of the Round Church.
[3] The coffin first opened in 1811 by Master Jekyll and described by him in his *Facts and Observations on the Temple Church*.

CHAPTER FIFTEEN

The End of an Era

Once work to the chancel was well under way, attention was turned to the restoration of the Round which had undergone dramatic changes to its appearance over the centuries. The question was to which period or form should it be restored. Mention was made in the previous chapter of Godfrey's approach to this problem, as set out in a letter to the Royal Fine Art Commission in 1955. In summary, Godfrey said:

'The steep lead-covered roofs which were added to the Round Church by Mr St Aubyn and his colleagues in their restoration of 1862-3 were destroyed by fire in the air-raid which damaged the church. I have advised the Societies of the Inner and Middle Temple not to reproduce these roofs but to revert to what in my opinion is the more beautiful and dignified form which obtained before the restoration and of which there is ample pictorial evidence, the best view being that of Thomas Malton (1792).' (*ill. 66*)

From an 'historical' point of view Godfrey felt that, from the evidence available, the pre-1862 form of the upper roof, with its shallow pitch hidden behind a battlemented parapet, best represented a continuous tradition from the twelfth century and was most characteristic of the military order for which it was built. This view is confirmed by the beautiful existing Templars' churches at Thomar (Portugal) and Segovia (Spain), although only the corbel table (below the battlements) is preserved at the latter.

'Aesthetically' Godfrey felt that the previous steep lead roofs represented an ecclesiastical taste that is less favoured today whether for historical or for aesthetic grounds. They also dwarfed the proportions of the rest of the Round and visually isolated it from the magnificent chancel to the east. The effortless transition from the Round to the chancel inside the church gave support to this argument. Godfrey felt that the greater beauty of the earlier form shown in the Malton painting (less the classical 'trimmings') could be seen from views of Thomar and Segovia.

In 'practical' terms he said that the former sloping roof to the triforium, springing as it did from the bottom of the former parapet, severely restricted the headroom. The new form would have a height of some eight feet, giving plenty of room within. Maintenance too would be easier if the steep conical roof to the top of the Round was not renewed.

He proposed to replace the upper ceiling in timber as there was no historical evidence that it was ever built in stone, even though there were stone springers.

A current view might take issue with some aspects of Godfrey's reasoning. There is a counter argument that the battlements were not part of the original structure. It could equally have consisted of a corbel table and solid parapet. The battlement could have been a decorative addition from the Tudor period, when that type of ornament was introduced to churches built before the Reformation.

By 1956 all the major rebuilding schemes in the Temple were either completed or were well under way. Queen Elizabeth II, crowned in 1953, had laid the foundation stone of the new Inner

Temple Hall in 1952, which was occupied for the first time on 4 October 1955. It was reported in the Press that, up to 31 December total payments by the War Damage Commission included £634,000 to the Inner Temple, £147,000 to the Middle Temple and £140,000 for the Temple church.

Restoration of the Round continued but was suspended for some time while the new roofs over the chancel were completed. The 1941 temporary roof had given good service but was now removed after an enormous canopy had been contrived on a mass of scaffolding surrounding the chancel. The eastern gables had been rebuilt earlier and the new triple roofs were constructed above the vaulting. The architects decided to use a series of steel beams spanning the main walls and ensuring minimum pressure on the stone vaults and columns. The new steep slated roofs, appearing much as before the war, were supported by strong steel and timber members with heavy lead valleys. The scaffolding was removed in 1956.

Meanwhile, Walter Haysom at St Aldhelm's Head continued steadily with fashioning the remaining Purbeck marble for the Round. Plaster casts had been made of the pre-war caps and bases, and these were being faithfully repeated. As well as the six quadruple pillars in the main arcade, there were forty different marble shafts surrounding the triforium to be newly carved. The stone arrived in London in several consignments and the re-erection of the main piers began. Finally, the temporary steel supports were removed and the new marble columns bore the upper walls once more. The spandrels between the arches and the drum above were refaced in Beer stone.

The Templar reported at Christmas 1957 that

'in the Round, the fixing of the complicated stonework in the triforium is practically complete and the outer roof over the clerestory is being constructed. The concrete slab which formed a cover during the war is being incorporated in the new work. There will be battlements to the upper roof which is of a flat pitch and the aisle roof over the triforium will be finished with a plain parapet.'

Steady progress was made with the restoration of the Round during the latter part of 1958, and nearly everything was completed by the appointed day. The floor was paved with plain Purbeck Portland flagstones, as in the chancel, and the Victorian encaustic tiles of 1842 were relaid with others recovered from the chancel in the triforium which was now much loftier than before. The 'grotesque' carved heads, which had escaped damage, were cleaned and conserved.

Four of eight stained-glass windows in the Round of 1842, presented by the antiquary Charles Winston, were repaired and re-inserted alternately with plain glass windows (*ill. 120*). The upper windows in the clerestory were clear-glazed and the vault was constructed of unpainted timber, rising undisguised from the stone springers. The ribs finally united in a wooden boss over 3ft in diameter. Neil Macfadyen, who made the boss, tells us that in 1954 he was a junior assistant with the architects. (Later he became a partner in charge of the Temple church work.) Walter Godfrey, knowing of his assistant's skill with wood, suggested he might carve the boss in his garden at home. It took most of the summer and the task was difficult as the wood was laminated in West African agba. Finally it was fixed in position and coloured in red and gilt, making a fitting termination to the rotunda ceiling (*ill. 118*).

118. The ceiling boss at the apex of the rotunda, carved by Neil Macfadyen.

David Lewer in *The Templar* of January 1959 reported:

'The grey Purbeck marble beautifully carved, contrasts well with the white stone walling, and is not so mechanically executed as the nineteenth-century work it has replaced. The light fittings, which are circlets suspended from the aisle vault, are a simpler version of those in the chancel. The great west door with its giant key, survives, and little has been done to the stonework of the Norman doorway, no doubt wisely, apart from blowing off the dust. The porch itself and the walls of the aisle have been washed down, to advantage. The exterior of the Round has been restored generally to its former appearance in the eighteenth century; the battlements at the top, with the tall weather-vane and gilt sphere are more pleasing than the old pepperpot cone, but the lower parapet wall to the triforium sometimes seems a little heavy. Nobody really knows what form the roofs originally took, but it seems probable that both over the aisle and clerestory they were pitched without parapets, although not as steeply as St Aubyn made in 1862. However, visually the present restoration is more attractive. The interior of the church at last presents one splendid whole, and it was with the deepest feeling that we sang on the day "I was glad when they said unto me, we will go into the House of the Lord."'

Thus the decisions of Walter Godfrey had been well received, except for the rather heavy lower parapet to the Round which perhaps would have been more elegant if made not so deep (*ill. 92*).

On Friday 7 November 1958 at 12 noon the Round church was re-dedicated by the Archbishop of Canterbury in the presence of the Queen, Prince Philip and Queen Elizabeth the Queen Mother. The other clergy taking part in the service were the Master, the Reader and Dr Macdonald (both former Acting-Masters) together with Dr Carpenter (formerly Master). As it was the Inner Temple's year of administration

119. Re-dedication of the Round church, 7 November 1958. Presentation to the Queen in the cloisters.
L-R: Harold Haysom, Walter Haysom (stonemasons), Fred --- (ganger), A. Sheldon (stonemason), Bill Watson (foreman carpenter), Arthur Bernard (general foreman), and members of the contractors, Dove Brothers Ltd.
On the right of the Queen, Lord Reading, Treasurer of the Middle Temple.

of the church, the Treasurer, Sir Patrick Spens, received the royal party at the west porch. During the singing of Psalm 84 (*O how amiable are thy dwellings*), the procession moved down the church and the royal party was conducted to their seats near the choir, the Queen and Prince Philip on the Inner Temple side and the Queen Mother on the Middle. The church was packed with a distinguished congregation of Benchers, barristers and legal eminences including the Lord Chancellor and the Lord Chief Justice. After the service the Queen then inspected the Charter which, for the occasion, was displayed on a table in the Round church. The architects, the contractors, masons, the general foreman and principal members of the building staff were then presented to her in the cloisters (*ill. 119*). Others, including Dr Thalben-Ball, met the Queen and the Prince at luncheon in the Inner Temple Hall.

Following the death of Canon Anson just after the reopening of the chancel in 1954, it was learned that Canon J.E. Firth was to be the new Master of the Temple. He and his wife moved into the newly-built Master's House in 1955.

Chaplain of Winchester College for 23 years, he was dearly-loved there and not less so at the Temple.

> 'With his great intellectual range, infectious humour, and at times dazzling expository powers, he had an intuitive sense of the mysterious, individual identity of his pupils that usually made them his friends for life. As a friend he was incomparable.'[1]

At the age of 57 and having been at the Temple for only a short time, his sudden death in September 1957 was a sad blow to Benchers and choir alike. He was sorely missed. A fine silver altar cross was presented to the church by Mrs Firth. Two silver flower vases had been given earlier by the Anson family and two silver candlesticks in memory of Master Lilley by his wife. These were all innovations, remembering the empty low-church appearance of the altar when seen before the War.

Dr Macdonald, Rector of St Dunstan-in-the-West and formerly Deputy Master of the Temple before Canon Firth's appointment, died suddenly in 1959. He was remembered both as a great scholar and as an excellent after-dinner speaker. At a dinner given in his honour, together with Dr Thalben-Ball and the Choir, he caused much amusement when he remarked in his speech that 'You must watch your step in the Temple.'

Firth was succeeded at the Temple by Canon T.R. Milford, who was therefore Master on the occasion of the re-dedication of the Round in 1958. He had been Vicar of St Mary's, Oxford and Chancellor of Lincoln. Another formidable theologian, he was well known as a supporter of Oxfam and more so, as a witness for the defence of *Lady Chatterley's Lover* at the notorious trial.

Restoration and embellishment had still to be carried out in the church. Harold Haysom, another brother of this gifted family, spent many hours in repairing the fire-damaged effigies in the Round, under the expert direction of the British Museum (*ills 120-122*). Here, it is interesting to compare Haysom's method to that of Richardson in the 1840s. Richardson's approach,

120. Harold Haysom repairing the damaged effigies.

as set out in Chapter Eight, was to 'restore' the effigies so that it was 'hardly longer possible for even a critical eye to distinguish the old from the restored parts.' He published how he did this work so that 'future antiquarians will have no reason to complain of any want of good faith'. The approach now was a matter of 'conserving' what was there by fixing together fractured parts with minimal replacement, then washing without the use of fine abrasives and applying liquid wax as a finish.

The four effigies on the north side were so badly burnt in 1941 that perhaps they might have mercifully been abandoned or consigned to the triforium or perhaps replaced by replicas, as some were made in the nineteenth century and are in the Victoria & Albert Museum. Ironically the de Ros effigy in the south aisle, which escaped the flames, was not there in medieval times. Haysom also pieced together the few wall monuments which had been rescued from the triforium. They were then restored and coloured by Charles Lewis and were erected in the chancel during 1962-64. There are two on the east wall; one to Sir George Wylde (d.1689) which was, according to Mrs Esdaile,[2] among the best of

122. *The repaired effigy of William Marshal.*
Photograph by Sydney W. Newbery.

121. *The effigy of William Marshal, first Earl of*
Pembroke (d.1219), after the fire of 1941.

William Stanton's minor works in London, and one to Thomas Lake (d.1711) which, as Master Squibb pointed out, displays the coat of augmentation granted to Sir Edward Lake in commemoration of the sixteen wounds which he received at the Battle of Edgehill in 1642.

On the north side is a simple monument to Samuel Prime (1701-1777). A second monument is an impressive – perhaps overbearing – memorial to Sir John Williams, surmounted by a gilt eagle with outspread wings. It was the work of Charles Stoakes and the lettering is particularly good. Sir John was buried, 'near the Saints' bell, on the 26 March 1669.' On the south wall is a finely-proportioned monument to Sir John Witham, Bt. of the Inner Temple (d.1689) (*ill. 76*)

and is signed by Thomas Cartwright who was an assistant of the distinguished sculptor William Stanton of Holborn.[3] The inscribed tablet is flanked by two columns, with a shield of arms on the cornice and a skull and cherubs heads below.

Also on the south wall are the remains of the three tablets to Sir William Morton, Justice of the King's Bench (d.1672), his wife Anne and their son, John Morton of the Inner Temple (d.1668). In an English inscription, Lady Anne is described as:

> 'A lady orthodox and exemplary for piety, charity, humility, chastity, constancy and patient sufferings with her husband for ye Truth in times of persecution and rebellion – in brief one of ye most virtuous among women and worthy of pious and eternal memory.'

167

Mrs Esdaile, who made her great inventory of the Temple church monuments in 1933, strongly recommended the restoration of this and other monuments and their bringing down into the church. As mentioned before, the only two which were moved down then were the Plowden and Martin altar tombs.[4] These had been bricked up early in the war and were thus undamaged. The Morton monument remained in pieces on the floor of the triforium, and it seems that only the inscribed tablets and the coat of arms were salvaged. The monument was the work of Ned or Edward Mitchell, Master of the Masons' Company.

On the west wall, above the tomb of John Selden seen through the glass plate let into the stone floor, is the Petyt monument by Edward Stanton (1707).

> 'On Friday last died Mr William Petyt, in ye 71st year of his age: being one of ye oldest Benchers of ye Inner Temple, and an Eminent Antiquary.'

Only the tablet survives, the setting, discovered elsewhere in the triforium by Mrs Esdaile, was lost in the fire. However, a drawing of the whole monument appears in Plate XI in her book.

One other important monument, which was rescued by Mrs Esdaile, and had survived the fire, is the fine example of a heraldic brass which bears a coat and mantling and has 28 shields. It is the memorial of Edward, eldest son of Sir Thomas Littleton, and of the Inner Temple, Gent. He was 'buried in the Long Walke, June 17, 1664.' This floor slab was banished from the church in 1842 and found a place outside, between two buttresses on the south side, where it suffered somewhat from the weather. In March 1934 it was brought inside again and relaid at the entrance to the chancel from the Round, fortunately escaping the flames in 1941. At the restoration of the church it was transferred to the Inner Temple side of the chancel, in front of the choir stalls. Mrs Esdaile remarked that its exclusion from the church in 1842 'would be inexplicable did we not remember the mutilation of Anne Littleton's monument, the ejection of Selden's, and breaking up of Coke's in this the very home of English Law.' Her disgust at the operations by Smirke and the other Victorians was understandably strong.

At the Remembrance Day service on 14 November 1965, new memorial tablets were dedicated and a Requiem was sung in the Round church. The inscribed stone panels were placed in the wall arcades and commemorate those members of the Inns who lost their lives in the First World War, the original floor brasses being past repair after the fire. More recently, a polished stone was installed in the centre of the floor of the Round in memory of those who died in the Second World War.

Walter Hindes Godfrey, the architect for the restoration of the Temple church, died in 1961. His wise care of the fabric and knowledge of its history had produced a wonderful rebirth of the building (*ills 92-94*). A memorial service was held in the church on 4 December, attended by a great many people. His son Emil then took over the remaining work until his untimely death in a car accident and, sadly, another memorial service took place in the church on 13 October 1982.

> 'By his many friends he will be remembered as a man of quiet charm, with a nice sense of humour and a deep uncomplicated Christian faith. He will be sorely missed.'[4]

The new organ case (ill. 123) was not installed until 1966. It resembles the seventeenth-century case, which disappeared in 1842, and displays the Royal Arms and the emblems of the two Societies, all finished in colour and gilt. The embellishment was by Charles Lewis who also made the reclining angels with their trumpets at the summit beneath the stone arch. He also cut and coloured the lettering on the new buttress in the practice-room in memory of the 23 Temple choristers who lost their lives in the last two wars.

The organ case was completed just before another Royal visit on 21 December 1966, when the Queen and the Duke of Edinburgh attended a service of Thanksgiving, Prayers and Carols and the Amity Dinner of the two Societies in the Inner Temple Hall.

123. The new organ case, with Royal Arms and emblems of the Inner and Middle Temples. Photograph by Robert Dark.

The Benchers have always been vigilant lest they or the Master should appear to give allegiance to the Bishop of London; when in 1846 the Master and Reader were summoned to attend a visitation of the Bishop, the Benchers allowed them to go only under protest and later sent a letter to the Consistory Registrar in support of their action. In 1843, when the Ecclesiastical Courts Bill was about to be introduced into Parliament, which would have had the effect of placing the Temple church under the jurisdiction of the Bishop of London, it was resolved by the Benchers of the Inner Temple 'that the antient jurisdiction and privileges of this Society whatever they may be should not be allowed to be altered or infringed', and pressure was brought to bear for the addition of a clause exempting

the Chapels of the Inns of Court and other private chapels from the provisions of the Bill so that they should 'respectively be subject to the same jurisdiction and institutions as heretofore and none other'.

In 1898 a Report by Sir Alfred Marten on the Temple church as a Royal Peculiar, in relation to legislation and proceedings in Parliament between the years 1874-98, was received by the Inner Temple. In 1874 the church had been recognised as a Royal Peculiar in the discussion on the Bill for the Public Worship Regulation Act. In the Commons a clause was inserted bringing the Temple church within its operation of the measure, but this clause was rejected by the Lords 'because the Temple Church is a Royal Peculiar, and therefore the clause would be inapplicable.' The Commons did not insist on the clause, and it did not form part of the Act. In 1893 a clause was inserted in the Church Patronage Bill to the effect that 'Nothing in this Act shall apply to any of H.M. Chapels Royal, or any Royal Peculiar, or any Chapel belonging to Her Majesty in right of Her Duchy of Lancaster.' Finally, in 1898 under the Benefices Act, it was enacted that the expression 'Benefice' does not extend to any Royal Peculiar, thus excluding the Temple church from the scope of the Act.[5]

In 1968 Canon T.R. Milford became 'The Retired Master', as the head chorister described him. His successor was the Very Reverend Robert Milburn, former Dean of Worcester. For the next dozen years there was a particularly happy period with these three genial experts at the Temple (*ill. 124*). They were the erudite and homely Master – not forgetting his wife's festive parties in the Master's garden, the ideally musical Reader, the Rev. W.D. Kennedy-Bell, who had been at the Temple since 1955, and the brilliant Organist and Choirmaster, Dr Thalben-Ball, who had been there much longer, since 1919.

The choir flourished and the organ poured forth its glorious sound, but by 1975 it was showing signs of mechanical age and was completely rebuilt that year. Many of the pipes were parked in the Round while the repairs were carried out, and a large Allen digital organ took

124. In the Master's garden, c.1975: Robert Milburn, Master of the Temple, Dr George Thalben-Ball, Organist, The Reader, the Rev. Preb. W.D. Kenny-Bell. Photograph by Chris Rutter.

by the two Inns in honour of Sir George at which many Benchers, Dr John Birch, the new Organist, and the Gentlemen of the Choir were present. Sir George in his speech recalled many events in his life at the Temple. His investiture by the Queen took place at Buckingham Palace on 8 February. These events culminated in a Commemorative Concert in the Temple church, followed by a Reception and Buffet in the Middle Temple Hall, attended by well over 400 people.

Other changes occurred at this time. The Master, Robert Milburn, retired in 1980 and was succeeded by Canon Joseph Robinson, formerly Treasurer of Canterbury Cathedral and previously for a time on the staff at St Paul's choir school. In 1979 the Benchers inaugurated the Temple Music Trust, under distinguished patrons, to ensure the continuation of the choir and in particular to maintain the rising cost of the choristers' fees at the City of London School.

Time seemed to move quickly towards the occasion when the Round church would be celebrating its eight hundredth anniversary in 1985. In the year before, as part of the preparation for the celebrations, it was decided to carry out cleaning and conservation work to the West doorway (*ill. 125*). This work was entrusted to Carden & Godfrey, the same firm which restored the church. Sadly Walter and Emil Godfrey had both died and the work was carried out under the direction of Neil Macfadyen. When he inspected the doorway in 1983 he found it in a sorry state. He reported that:

> 'Soot deposits on the stone, combined with traditional treatments of hot oil or wax and limewash, had resulted in an impervious skin of calcium sulphate with a build-up of moisture and chemical salts beneath. Where this skin had burst more rapid decay had set in, causing deep pitting and the loss of much fine carved work. The contrast in appearance between the black encrusted areas and the white freshly decaying parts produced a leprous appearance, making it difficult to appreciate the overall design, let alone the beauty and originality of the embellishments.'

its place for some months. Successful as it was, they were pleased to see the traditional Harrison & Harrison instrument put back in good order. They hoped it would remain for many years.

A few years later, the organist was also showing signs of age and, at the end of 1981, Dr Thalben-Ball retired as Organist Emeritus after more than sixty years at the Temple. In the *Daily Telegraph* of 31 December 1981, 'Peterborough' wrote:

> 'There were emotional scenes in the Temple Church on Sunday when George Thalben-Ball made his final appearance at Matins, with the congregation rising and cheering him at the end of his voluntary.'

The occasion was quite spontaneous and he graciously bowed his acknowledgement. In the New Year's Honours List everyone was delighted to hear of his knighthood. A dinner was held

Macfadyen in this description, summed up the problem of conservation involving new types of materials or coatings in that it is difficult to know the long term effect of this work. Further to carrying out various tests on the stonework of the doorway it was first cleaned using the finest air brush technique, then hardened using a chemical treatment that still allowed the stonework to breath. In the best SPAB tradition no repairs or replacements of the carvings were carried out, other than repointing open mortar joints.

The conservation work provided the opportunity to carry out investigations on the authenticity of the present doorway to see if any light could be thrown on the conflicting views held by various architects and historians over a considerable period of time. The starting point was in 1842 when Sydney Smirke and Decimus Burton reported on the West door that:

> 'On removing the plaster and colouring that filled up the enriched archivolts, which are surprisingly perforated and sunk, we find that those carved stones are so perished as to be for the most part incapable of receiving preparations and that they ought to be entirely new.'

What work was actually carried out is not known. The last detailed look at this puzzling problem was in an article by George Zarnecki in 1975.[6] The quotation from this article in Chapter Twelve shows that even an expert like W.D. Caröe changed his mind over time about whether the doorway was in fact original. Zarnecki concluded that most of the door was original and that only the most decayed stones had been replaced in 1842. In the process of cleaning the stonework Macfadyen noted that there were no traces of colouring from paintwork on the surface of the stone. In 1855 Decimus Burton donated some architectural fragments to the Architectural Museum which were later transferred to the Victoria & Albert Museum. Four carved stones in this collection are similar to the carved work in the West doorway. Macfadyen carried out a detailed inspection of these and, from subtle

125. The West doorway prior to conservation work.

differences in the details of the carving, came to the conclusion that two of them came from the innermost arch. The two V&A stones had traces of colour on them and this led him to believe that the whole of this arch was rebuilt as part of the 1842 work. The other two stones are similar to ones in the outermost arch. However, unlike the two from the inner arch, there was not any change in construction and Macfadyen could not come to any clear conclusions about whether this part of the doorway is original or replacement work. No overall conclusion could be reached other than, as a result of cleaning, it was clear that the whole of the stonework was of Caen stone – the original type of stone used – with one or two minor exceptions. Even this is not conclusive in itself, as Victorian replacement Caen stone was generally inferior to that of earlier times so that it would have decayed more rapidly and was likely to look in a similar condition to much earlier stonework. There we must leave this puzzling subject.

On Sunday 10 February 1985, the anniversary day of the consecration, Lord Coggan was the preacher at the morning service. The presence of the Queen was arranged for Wednesday 26 June, when a Service of Thanksgiving took place. The Duke of Edinburgh also attended. Before the service the Queen again inspected the Royal Charter. John Birch was at the organ and the choir included a number of Old Choristers. At the conclusion of the service Sir George Thalben-Ball and Ernest Lough were presented to the Queen and Prince in the Round church.

Did the Queen come too soon? The question arose as to whether the New Year operated from 25 March as early as the twelfth century; if so, the Round church celebrations might well have been due for February 1986. However, as similar events took place at the Temple in 1885, the question remained purely academic.[7]

It was the end of an era but also a new beginning for this fine building where knights, clerics, lawyers, musicians and many other worshippers have dwelt for a while. Architecture has not been forgotten, with the memory of the great work achieved by Walter Godfrey, his son Emil and their colleagues, and the many dedicated stonemasons and carpenters who made the ancient Temple church flourish again. When Walter Godfrey was about to embark on the post-war restoration, writing about all the alterations that had been made to the church over the centuries, he said that:

'behind the restorers' veneer there is sufficient of the old fabric remaining to make one feel there is still a life to be prolonged and much that is significant to be preserved.'

The overall effect is a church which is one of the most beautiful and perfect specimens of early Gothic architecture (*ills 92-94*). No matter what indignities it has suffered over eight centuries, the sublime and inspiring beauty of its interior remains to be marvelled at and enjoyed.

NOTES TO CHAPTER FIFTEEN

[1] *The Times* 1954.

[2] Esdaile, Mrs Arundell, *Temple Church Monuments* (1933). Plate XIII shows the complete Wylde monument. Only the tablet survives in the church.

[3] Esdaile (*op. cit.*). A drawing of the pre-war triforium (*ill. 76*) shows the Witham monument in its position near the staircase entrance.

[4] Both the Plowden (Plate VIII) and Martin (Plate VI) altar tombs are shown when in the triforium in 1933. They have since been repaired and 're-beautified'.

[5] Silsoe, Lord, *The Peculiarities of the Temple*, (The Estate Gazette Ltd, 1972).

[6] Article by George Zarnecki, 1975.

[7] Lewer, David, article in *The Templar* no. 103, 1985.

Chapter Sixteen

The Music Restored

Soon after the re-dedication of the chancel in 1954, the Templars were delighted to hear that Dr Thalben-Ball had been asked by the Benchers to re-establish the full choir with boys once more, after a break of fifteen years. For the rest of the year, monthly services continued to be held with men's voices while the furnishing of the chancel was being completed. On 5 October 1954 the Prime Minister, Sir Winston Churchill, was present at the memorial service for Lord Asquith, a former Prime Minister and pupil of the City of London School. In 1967 the funeral of Lord Attlee, another Prime Minister, took place in the church, as he had been a resident in the Temple.

Sunday morning services were resumed weekly as from 16 January 1955. During the following months Dr Ball held voice trials for prospective choristers as he did in former times, kindly but expertly, and twelve of them who had passed their tests sang for the first time at Sunday service on 30 October 1955 (*ill. 127*). The youngest among them was Ernest Lough's son Robin, who was soon to be a soloist. The first head boy, Robin Fairhurst, who was aged fourteen when he came, was already an experienced singer and was invaluable in helping Dr Ball to develop the new choir. He made a great impression at the Christmas Concert in the Middle Temple Hall when he sang *Where e'er you walk* and Schubert's *The Trout*. The *Christmas Oratorio* was revived and with carols in the Round, as of yore. (*ill. 128*). Several performances of Britten's *Ceremony of Carols* followed, with harp accompaniment, again in the Round, with great effect. A series of choristers sang the fascinating 'Echo' part in

126. A. Capel Dixon conducting in the ruins of the Inner Temple, c.1945. Photograph by Arthur Newman.

Walford Davies' *Noble Numbers,* from the penitential cell. Unforgettable occasions were the annual concerts held in the Inner or Middle Temple Hall in which the Templars' Male Voice Choir also took part. Their founder and leader, Capel Dixon, had sadly died suddenly in 1949. He had conducted many concerts in the ruins of the Inner Temple Hall with the help of former choristers and friends (*ill. 126*). Perhaps the highlight of these concerts was the choristers' singing

173

127. The Temple Choir in the new practice-room with Dr Thalben-Ball, Master Canon Firth and the Reader with the new choristers on 30 October 1955. Ernest Lough (bass) is third from the left at the back, his son Robin is second on the left in front. On Ernest Lough's right is David Lewer, joint author of this book.

of delightful songs on their own, grouped round the grand piano with their choirmaster who, it may be remembered, was an accomplished pianist before he became a foremost organist. Since that first Christmas the new choir had come far under the continued inspiration of Dr Thalben-Ball who in 1959 completed his fortieth year at the Temple. To mark the occasion the Inner Temple invited him to become an Honorary Master of the Bench of that Society.

The choirboys were once again sent to the City of London School where their fees were paid by the two Inns as before. A great advantage of that arrangement was that a boy could still remain in the choir until his voice broke, unlike in most cathedral schools when he would have to leave the choir-school for a new public school.

Furthermore, Dr Ball preferred to accept more mature boys of perhaps ten to eleven years, some remaining in the choir stalls to the age of sixteen or even seventeen, as in Walford's time; nowadays voices usually break much earlier. Dr Ball also preferred to retain suitable former choristers in the second rows of the choir stalls to sing in his way. Most were not professional musicians, but nevertheless the ensemble proved to be of a high order. Several had been singing in the war-time choir at St Dunstan's.

The Temple church had a strong connection with and influence on the BBC, first with Walford Davies and then Thalben-Ball conducting the BBC Singers for the broadcast Morning Service and weekly Epilogue. Thalben-Ball had a great gift in composing short pieces of music appropriate to the subject and this led to the publication by Novello of *Laudate Dominum* containing

128. Carols in the Round, 1961.

many beautiful introits, sung also at the Temple, and his extroit voluntaries, based on well-known tunes. It was at the BBC that Dr Thalben-Ball first met the Rev. W.D. Kennedy-Bell in the Religious Music department. He quickly recommended to the Benchers that Kennedy-Bell be appointed as Reader of the Temple Church, a post then vacant.[1] This was accepted, and in 1955 he became a member of the establishment, remaining in that post for over forty years, and then as Reader Emeritus. *The Templar* no.75 said:

> 'We are very fortunate in having 'K-B' as Reader. He is a musician and takes a keen and critical interest in the choir's singing. His intoning and reading are models for imitation.'

His conducting of the annual Good Friday service, broadcast from the Temple church with Dr Ball, was a moving experience for many a listener. It was repeated during sixteen years. Following the sad and sudden death of 'Budge' Firth, Kennedy-Bell was made Acting-Master until the appointment of Canon Milford.

The new choristers soon settled into the Temple ways. They learnt to play the ancient game of Prisoners' Base[2] again, first introduced by a Canadian boy who was in the choir at the turn of the century. Football, cricket and firework parties were greatly enjoyed in the Inner Temple Gardens and the annual Camp near Swanage, revived in 1956, continued to give much appreciated concerts in the village hall and parish church.

It would be invidious to mention so many excellent singers, all trained by Dr Ball.[3] A new series of LP gramophone records with HMV were made in the church. The first in 1959,

175

consisted of Christmas Carols and was widely appreciated. A repeat of Bach's *Jesu, joy of man's desiring*, with Leon Goossen's oboe obbligato and Dr Ball at the piano, was recorded after some thirty years and once again both musicians took part. Robin and his younger brother Graham sang with their father Ernest Lough who, as a bass, was a member of the Temple Choir once more. Ian le Grice, as head boy, sang memorable duets with Robin Lough. He had a fine voice and in recent years became assistant organist at the Temple church with Dr John Birch, who was appointed in 1982.

Sir George Thalben-Ball celebrated his ninetieth birthday on 18 June 1986 with a Birthday Tribute at St Michael's, Cornhill, arranged by Jonathan Rennert, the Director of Music there and his biographer.[4] Many musicians were present including Thomas Trotter, Thalben-Ball's successor as Organist at Birmingham Town Hall where Sir George had played over 900 lunch-time recitals (he was given a Civic Reception there).

Shortly after, on 18 January 1987, Sir George died peacefully. On 30 April a Service of Thanksgiving was held in the Temple church with many former choristers, Benchers and members of the Bar present and on 26 May, St Paul's Cathedral was almost full for 'Sir George Thalben-Ball – A Celebration.' Several prominent organists took part with John Scott, Sub-Organist, conducting the music with the choirs of St Paul's and the Temple church, The Address was given by Edward Heath, musician and admirer of Thalben-Ball as well as a former Prime Minister. Afterwards, members of the Templars' Union sang Walford Davies's setting of *Soldiers of Christ, Arise* in the Round Church.

Robert Milburn remembered:

> 'A great man in that remarkable succession, Hopkins, Walford Davies and Thalben-Ball, which created the Temple Choir, gave so much to it, and received a striking response of affectionate loyalty.'

It was truly the end of an era.

And now, in the words of John Lydgate (*c.*1370-*c*1451) and sung traditionally on the last Sunday before the Long Vacation:

> Tarry no longer, toward thine heritage
> Haste on thy way and be of right good cheer.
> Go each day onward on thy pilgrimage,
> Think how short time thou shalt abide thee
>   here.
> Thy place is built above the starre's clear;
> None earthly palace wrought in so stately
>   wise.
> Come on my friend, my brother most dear!
> For thee I off'red my blood in sacrifice.
> Tarry no longer!

NOTES TO CHAPTER SIXTEEN

[1] The Rev. A.H.M. Kempe MA succeeded J.F. Clayton MA, MC as Reader in 1940, but resigned in 1955 having been a priest in Sussex during the War and as the Temple Church was out of action. He had been an occasional supernumerary alto in the Temple Choir from 1927.

[2] A proclamation of Edward III forbade children to play the game of Prisoners' Base near the Palace of Westminster. A set of Objects and Rules for playing the game is given in an appendix to *A Spiritual Song* by David Lewer (1961).

[3] Mention must be made of a Temple Choir head boy during the 1960s. Michael James was a gifted musician and his voice lasted beyond his 17th birthday. He became a promising organist, pianist, teacher and conductor and, from being assistant-organist in Wimborne Minster, was about to take up a similar appointment at Rochester Cathedral when cancer struck. He died in 1981 at the age of 30. In his memory the Michael James Trust was established to found scholarships for young organists. *Michael – the story of a young Christian musician* (George Mann Publications, 1997), was written by his mother, Margaret Ann James. It contains interesting chapters on his time at the Temple Church.

[4] Rennert, J., *George Thalben-Bell* (David & Charles, 1979).

Appendices

APPENDIX ONE

Masters of the Order of the Temple in England
(*Magistri Militiae Templi in Anglia*).

Richard de Hastings 1155-1164
Geoffrey Fitzstephen 1180-1185
William de Nunham
Aymeric de St Maur 1200-1218
Alan Martel 1218-1228
Robert de Sanford 1229-1248
Rocelin de Fos 1251-1253
Amadeus 1259-1260

Ambesard 1264
Imbert Peraut 1271
Guy de Foresta 1273-1274
Robert de Turvill 1276-1290
Guy de Foresta 1291-1294
Brian de Jay 1296-1298
William de la More 1298-1312

APPENDIX TWO
Masters of the Temple since the Reformation

WILLIAM ERMESTEDE (was Master in 1540)
RICHARD ALVEY, M.A., B.D. 1560
RICHARD HOOKER, M.A. 1585
NICOLAS BALGUY or BAGLEY, D.D. 1591
THOMAS MASTER, B.D. 1601
PAUL MICKLETHWAITE, D.D. 1628
JOHN LITTLETON, D.D. 1639 (buried in Temple church)
Mastership declared vacant 1644
RICHARD VINES, M.A. 1645
(Appointed by House of Commons but did not take office.)

The following were appointed Ministers or Preachers to the Societies during the Interregnum:
JOHN TOMBES, M.A. 1645
(by view of letters patent from Parliament).
RICHARD JOHNSON, M.A. 1646
RALPH BROWNRIG, M.A., D.D. 1658 (buried in Temple church)
JOHN GAUDEN, M.A., D.D. 1660

After the Restoration
RICHARD BALL, M.A., D.D. 1661 (buried in Temple church).
WILLIAM SHERLOCK, M.A., D.D. 1684
THOMAS SHERLOCK, M.A., D.D. 1704
SAMUEL NICHOLLS, M.A., LL.D. 1753
GREGORY SHARPE, LL.D. 1763
GEORGE WATTS 1771
THOMAS THURLOW 1772
WILLIAM PEARCE, B.D. 1787
THOMAS RENNELL, D.D. 1797
CHRISTOPHER BENSON, M.A. 1826
THOMAS ROBINSON, M.A., D.D. 1845
CHARLES JOHN VAUGHAN, M.A., D.D. 1869
ALFRED AINGER, M.A., LL.D. 1894
(Reader of the Temple church 1866).
HENRY GEORGE WOODS, D.D. 1904
ERNEST WILLIAM BARNES, M.A., D.D., F.R.S. 1915
WILLIAM HENRY DRAPER, M.A. 1920
SPENCER CECIL CARPENTER, M.A., D.D. 1930
HAROLD ANSON, M.A. 1935
ALLAN JOHN MACDONALD MACDONALD, M.A., D.D., F.S.A. 1950
JOHN D'EWES EVELYN FIRTH, M.A. 1954
THEODORE RICHARD MILFORD, M.A. 1958
ROBERT LESLIE POLLINGTON MILBURN, M.A. 1968
JOSEPH ROBINSON, B.D., M.TH., F.K.C. 1980.

APPENDIX THREE
Inventory of the Temple church at the time of the Suppression in 1307-8
(from T.H. Baylis, 'The Temple Church' (1900, App. F.)

Among the contents in the Cellar were 22 silver spoons, cups of maple and silver, tankards, two cross-bows and three coffers.

In the Storehouse there were items of ironwork, lead, tables, spoons and hemp.

In the Kitchen there were pots, pitchers, plates, gridirons, frying-pans, and one 'great brass plate in the furnace'.

In the Stable were two palfreys, one ridden by Brother John de Stoke, Treasurer, and another by the Grand Master, William de la More. There were two horses for Michael, the Preceptor, a horse for a cart and two others for the mill 'and two mills with the apparatus.'

In the Brewery there were seven vats, fifteen casks, nine empty hogsheads, tables and trestles, and irons, and utensils belonging to the oven.

In the Wardrobe of the Grand Master there was a gold buckle, 22 pieces of Birmingham, three bed coverings, hanging, a gown, a pelisse of budge (lamb's fur), a bench cover, a little flask, a cross-bow without bolts. A canvas sack with three supertunics of fur, and a white cloak of Brother William de Scurlage, (of Ewell who died before the trial), a panier, barrels, books, vestment and a wash-basin were also found there. As mentioned previously, the Master was allowed to keep his wardrobe, at least for the present.

In the Chamber of Brother John de Stoke there was a coverlet of scarlet, linen sheets, two veils, a cloak, a tunic with a hood and two pairs of boots, a cap, a little flask, five cushions, cloth, a trunk, a maple cup, an iron fork, an iron and again a wash-basin.

In the Chamber of Brother Thomas de Burton there were two coverlets, four pairs of linen sheets, three towels, a robe of burnet (a woollen cloth) a robe of say for summer wear, three hoods, three pairs of linen cloths, one basin, one wash-basin and a mantel.

In the Chamber of the Prior there was a counterpane 'de Reynes', a trundle-bed, four cushions, and three carpets used at the chapel of the Blessed Mary.

In the Chamber of Brother Richard de Herdewikes there was a coverlet, two pairs of linen sheets, a bread platter, canvas, two corslets, two forms, one pair of boots, a trunk, a sack for garments, one great pouch, two cups of silver with covers, twelve silver spoons, a pair of stools (*statutorum*), one mantel three-fold, a bound casket, a sword, a sealed coffer and a chest, and one sealed coffer with the charters and muniments of the House.

In the Dormitory were a number of coverlets, linen sheets, canvas sheets, two robes, one mantel, two towels, one ewer, wash-basins, a casket, a sack for garments, a trunk of Brother Michael de Baskevile, a sword and an axe from Ireland of Brother William de Hereford, and a sword of Brother Thomas de Staundon.

We now come to the contents found in the Temple Church.

The Great Church contained a silver-gilt chalice, two silver-gilt censers, two silver cruets, two silver ewers, one copper ship (a vessel for incense) with one silver spoon. It also contained an ivory pix with silver cup, a pewter crimatory, a metal and silver cross with banner, one mass book, one silver text in which the gospels for the whole year are written, six pairs of vestments with tunics and dalmatics, one vestment for aestivals, one pair of albs and amice for deacon, two pairs of albs for boys, two offertories, two rochets, one pair of corporals, one towel, one covering upon altar, one frontal before the altar, two choir copes, two candlesticks of Limoges work for Processional Lights, six candlesticks of metal before the great altar, two pairs of organs (i.e. two ranks of pipes), one iron candlestick and two carpets.

In the Choir were five antiphonars, four psalters, two legends (stories, one secular and one of the saints), two bibles, one ordinal, one capitulary, one matyrology, one pastoral, four grails, three tropers, one epistolar, nine processionars, two cushions, chanters' chairs, one book for the organs, one ivory comb.

At St John's altar: one silver gilt chalice, one mass book, one pair of vestments, four *tuellis benedictis* (hallowed towels), one rochet, one towel, one ivory comb, two cruets and one pewter basin.

At St Nicholas' Altar: one silver-gilt chalice, one mass book, one vestment for festivals, one corporal, five consecrated towels, two other small towels, one rochet, one ivory comb, two cruets, one basin of pewter, one small bell.

In the Church of the Blessed Mary: one mass book, seven tropers, one book of Divinity, one book which is called 'Chabeham', two vestments, two towels at the altar, one rochet, one surplice, one chalice, two towels, two cruets, one platter of pewter, one sconce, two 'paxbredes' (a board plated with silver, by which the kiss of peace was given to the faithful). Found in the church without *hostium* (the door of the hall.)

In the Vestry was one silver-gilt chalice, one

mass book, two silver candlesticks, nineteen divers books, 22 banners, eleven chasubles or mass vestments of divers colours, 28 choir copes and four little copes for the choristers, nine albs with apparel, three albs with vestment, one frontal of cloth of gold and canvas (often adorned with jewels or gilding) and canaber, two cloths, one of silk, the other of gold, one ridell (curtain) before the altar, 24 dalmatics and tunicles, eight towels for the altar, seven towels, five surplices, two rochets, an offertory and other small things in a certain coffer, one cross with Mary and John, two silver basins, one silver vessel with a silver censer, one silver ship with one silver spoon, two crystal candleticks with silver feet, one silver-gilt case (*sapsa*) with divers relics, one sword with which the blessed Thomas of Canterbury was killed, as it is said, the price of which they are ignorant. Two crosses with the wood on which Christ was crucified, the price of which they are ignorant, one piece of ivory. The common seal of the Temple, a silver vessel in which is placed the blood of Christ, price of the vessel, one mark. One piece of silver with a paten of a head of a certain Saint. A crystal vessel, with a silver foot and silver cover, with divers relics. One text with the Gospels, with silver-gilt tables, one little pix with divers relics, also a pix with divers phials enclosed with glass, one pix ditto and enclosed with glass, two coffers made of pieces of ivory shut up, under lock, full of divers relics, two silver feet, three ivory pieces for placing therein the body of our Lord, one chalice, one vestment, two mitres, two small coffers of ivory, two tables with ivory images, four texts, one whereof with a precious stone, one pastoral staff called a 'croce', with a silver head, two cedar staves for the chanters, one staff for a cross, two silver crosses, two ivory horns, one sparver (a hanging), one vase of Limoges (work), six chests, eight coffers, one copper horn, one pondere (weight).

APPENDIX FOUR

Report on a survey of the Temple Church, London made in pursuance of the request of the Building Committee appointed by the two Societies for conducting the repairs and restoration of the same by L.N. Cottingham, Architect, October 26th 1840.

Date of Building

If no distinct record of the date of this ancient Structure existed, the styles of the building would clearly point out the periods of its erection to be in the 12th and 13th centuries for notwithstanding the alterations additions and beautifyings it has undergone at various times, it has fortunately so much of the original left as will enable the Architect to trace all its parts and thereby make a complete and most satisfying restoration of the fabric.

The gradual change from the circular to the pointed arch style is curiously exemplified in the round part of the Church which seems to belong as much to one style as to the other; the pointed arches and mouldings so far preponderating as to prepare the way for the full establishment of the early pointed style which followed in the Eastern part of the Church and is the most chaste and perfect specimen of plain light Gothic work in existence.

Previous Repairs

It is deeply to be regretted that in the repairs of 1811 and those of 1826 and 1827 which were much more extensive, greater research was not made to ascertain more correct detail. Works of this kind if correctly maintained, become standards of the Art, but if innovation creep in, as has done in the repairs alluded to, the beauty of the composition is lost and the building as a work of art is worthless.

The works in 1826 and 1827 being a mere external casing of the south side of the Church (with a partial restoration of the columnar dado and ornaments at the back of the stone benches in the Aisle of the round Church or Nave) did not much effect the stone groining or interior roof of the Church which it appears has been in a very shattered state for many years. The repeated operation of 'wash stop and white' had so far concealed the defects from time to time as to allow the crippling settlements of the stone ribs to increase without much appearance on the face of the work till the repairs in 1811 when the extraordinary measure of supporting some of them at the East end of the Church by means of iron rods passing through the stone ribs into timber beams above was adopted. The absurdity of this mode of supporting stone arches needs no comment.

Drainage

The Drains on the north side and east end of the Church were so defective in construction and broken down in many parts as to render them quite useless; and the foul and stagnant matter deposited in them had become exceedingly offensive. It was therefore imperative to reconstruct them in a better plan which has been performed under Mr Savage's direction in the best possible manner.

The whole area of the church appears to have been in a very damp and unwholesome state for a long time past, which has occasioned all the ground joists timber supports and floors of the old pewing to fall into decay, and, thereby make the air of the Church extremely unhealthy.

Inner Roof or Stone Groining

A scaffolding having been erected for the purpose of repairing the defective parts a very little scraping on the surface and raking out the loose joints of the stone ribs brought to light the real condition of the roof which proved to be in a very dilapidated and dangerous state throughout repairing such work is very tedious and difficult but in the present case absolutely necessary.

129. *The interior of the chancel before the commencement of the 1840 restoration work. Only by scraping off the accumulation of whitewash and stopping, removal of monuments, wainscoting and pews was the extent of decay ascertained.*

Timber roof

The roof of the Church is composed of oak and chestnut timber, and is a vast mass of woodwork framed in three Compartments with coupled rafters having no ridge-trees or wind-braces. The whole body of the roof has a leaning over towards the east end of the Church to counteract which oak sills, purlins and braces have been judiciously inserted over the nave and South Aisle and I think it would be advisable to put in similar timbers to secure the roof of the North Aisle. For the size of the Church this is the heaviest timbered roof as I ever met with. It is in a very sound state and has been reslated, with new lead gutters, during the present repairs.

Paving

The removal of the decayed timber work under the pewing has discovered the original line of paving. Retaining this level will give additional height and great value to the appearance of the Church.

Columns

The Purbeck marble columns supporting the groining of the roof are exceedingly light and beautiful; but having been at various times puttied and painted over the defects occasioned by the tooth of time could not be seen until these modern blinds were removed, which being done the joints of the marble and considerable portions of the surface of the small cluster columns were found to be in a very decayed state requiring a great number of new pieces to be inserted. The bases also require lengthening out in the same marble down to the original floor line. The beauty of these columns when restored will well repay the labour.

Stone Seats
The ancient stone seats on the north and south sides of the Church should be restored.

Altar etc.
A stone altar piece and table should be erected in suitable character and the walls ashlared with Caen stone.

The beautiful marble piscina or lavatory on the south side of the altar should be restored.

The small almeries or lockers, for containing the sacred utensils used at the small altars on the north and south side of the High Altar might be preserved and would be useful for books.

Decoration
On washing off the numerous coats of lime white and common colour from the chalk groins several pieces of ancient decoration in various colours were discovered which fully warrant the revival of the beautiful embellishments used in the middle ages on the ceilings of similar buildings.

Exterior
The north side and east end of the Church require attention. Erecting the new organ chamber against the former will greatly add to the strength of the wall the buttresses of which are in a very weak state and the modern 9-inch brick parapet with which it is surmounted is in a dangerous state and will not be safe to leave standing during the winter. The east end has been pasted over with a thin coating of cement which is peeling off in many places. These portions of the Church should be restored; no part of the present detail is correct.

The Round Church or Nave
The six clustered columns of purbeck marble which divide the central area from the aisle were repaired in 1811 with a coating of Roman Cement and slabs of Portland stone were cased round the bases. The remains of this modern patching and pasting have been cleaned off and the venerable mutilated marble once more shewn, but they are in so shattered and decayed a state that new marble columns are indispensable for the safety of the fabric. Fortunately sufficient mouldings are in existence to enable the Architect to make a faithful restoration of these unique pillars.

The twelve columns which surround the aisle and rest on the stone bench to support the groining have very meagre modern bases. These should be restored to their proper character.

The discovery of the original window over the entrance door is a most valuable acquisition towards a perfect restoration.

The lowering of the pavement and the carrying it out so as to include on the same level the lower portion of the columns and bases of the beautiful circular headed doorway will produce a very splendid effect on entering the Church which would be greatly enhanced by removing the chambers over the entrance passage and bringing the window just discovered into its legitimate operation.

The groined ceiling round the circular aisle is in a very loose and shattered state and requires a very careful reparation throughout.

The twelve original apertures in the Triforium or Gallery should be restored as also the marble columns which support the arcade of interlaced Arches. The six clerestory windows which surmount the Arcade should have the modern masonry cut back to its original depth of recess below the windows down to the cornice which supports them.

The modern wooden window frames should be removed and the glass carried back to the original stone window jambs. Great lightness would be effected by this restoration.

The lean-to roof over the Triforium or gallery is of oak and in a very sound state on the south and tolerably so on the north or Middle Temple side.

I have paid very great attention to the finishing of the inner roof of the nave of this circular part of the Church which in an antiquarian as well as architectural point of view, is an object of the most important consideration. The result of my investigation is that the present roof does not carry the original design of the Architect.

1st: Because the six stone springing mouldings tending to the Horse Shoe form of domical groining are not carried through by the wooden spandrils but terminate in a flat ceiling.

2nd: Because the six pointed arches above the clerestory windows could not according to the design and construction have been inserted for any other purpose than that of receiving the plain spandrils of a groined roof.

These important facts being ascertained leave no doubt in my mind as to the course which ought to be pursued - namely that of constructing a chalk groined inner roof according to the original design which may be performed at a very moderate expense and without disturbing any of the exterior masonry. Trinity Chapel and Becket's Crown at Canterbury Cathedral afford beautiful examples of this kind of interior roofing.

The timber roof of the nave of the Circular part of the church is in a very decayed and crippled state so much so that the whole requires to be taken off. If the inner roof be constructed in the manner alluded to the timbers of the new roof above may be lighter than the present. I am of opinion that the present fabric is perfectly capable of carrying the weight of a new chalk groined roof without the slightest risk or hazard. It will rise several feet higher than the present horizontal ceiling and give to the whole composition an air of grandeur and beauty of the highest order.

The staircase turret on the north side of the Church should be restored. It is now merely patched up with brickwork and plaster.

Monuments

The removal of the monumental tablets which had accumulated to such an extent as to destroy the beauty of the building and greatly injure its stability by cutting into the walls and columns regardless of consequences, is a very important improvement. Some place should be provided for their reception: to replace them in the Church after such extensive repair and reparation would destroy the beautiful Architectural effect to produce which so much expense and care will have been disposed. A cloister might be judiciously erected in the Garden at the east end of the Church to contain them.

The Monumental Effigies of the Knights Templars are not well disposed. They would have a much better effect if placed between the main pillars of the Round Church north and south thereby leaving the area of the Nave clear and unencumbered.

From the careful inspection I have ben inabled to make of every part of the Church I am of the opinion that the whole of the repairs now being executed are indispensible for its security and preservation and that delay might have been attended with the most serious consequences particularly as regards the very insecure state of the chalk groining.

Lewis Nockalls Cottingham.
Waterloo Bridge Road, Lambeth

Upon receiving the letter of the Committee of the 22nd of Sept., I find they are pleased to request to be informed 'How far the dilapidated state of the Building, could, or could not, have been known until the work, now in progress, had proceeded so far as it now is.'

To which I beg to answer, that it was utterly impossible to become informed of the state of the building, previous to the cleaning off the superficial matters from the face, nor could the state be fully known, till the progress of the repair developed the parts in successsion.

It is a curious fact that several chalked, groined roofs, which I have had occasion to inspect, of the same period as the Temple Church should have become equally dilapidated about the same time particularly St Saviours Church Southwark, the north transept at Rochester Cathedral – all constructed on the same principle.

Wedging up with tiles and slates and stopping

in the joints, as has been the case at the Temple Church, will prevent their falling for some time, but eventually increases the evil, as such superficial means only tend to throw the arches off their proper bearing and disguise, instead of repair, the defect.

I have no doubt the builders employed at the Church, in 1811, were aware of the insecure state of the inner roofs, though not to the full extent that actually existed, but they were probably not instructed to go into the matter beyond a kind of Churchwardens 'lick and promise' which left the building quite as bad as they found it.

I saw the Church at the commencement of the present repairs, and certainly had no conception that the dilapidations from time and mutilations occasioned by the monuments were of so extensive a nature as they turn out to be.

The scraping of the whitewash, coloring and painting, and the slight coating of plaster, was the only way of ascertaining the fact and the removal of the wainscoting, pews, floors, organ loft and monuments, brought to light great imperfections in the clustered columns, piers and side walls, and I have no hesitation to say that it was impossible for any Architect to get at the real state of the fabric till those means of examination were afforded.

Previous to the repairs of 1826 and 1827 every thing appears to have been done in the most superficial manner, except the braces of the timber roofs.

I am also of opinion that the present repairs, extensive as they certainly must be, could not have been dispensed with much longer, with any degree of safety to the Congregation, and, after thirty years extensive practice in similar works, I feel it my duty to state that your Committee are most fully justified in the steps they are taking as far as regards the absolute necessity of an immediate and extensive repair and restoration.

Lewis Nockalls Cottingham

Selected Bibliography

Addison, C.G., *The Temple Church* (1843)

Baker, J.H., *The Inner Temple: a Brief Historical Description* (1991).

Barber, M.C., *The New Knighthood - a History of the Order of the Temple* (1994).

Baylis, T.H., *The Temple Church and Chapel of St Ann etc. An Historical Record and Guide* (1900, 3rd edn).

Bellot, H.H.L., *The Inner and Middle Temple* (1902).

Billings, R.W., *Architectural Illustrations and Account of the Temple Church, London* (1838).

Britton, J., *The Architectural Antiquities of Great Britain* (1835).

Britton, J. *Account of the Temple Church* (1824).

Burge, W., *The Temple Church: an Account of its Restoration and Repairs* (1843).

Campbell, G.A., *The Knights Templars* (1937).

Clapham, A.W., *English Romanesque Architecture after the Conquest* (1934).

Colles, H.C., *Walford Davies* (1941).

Crook, J.M., 'The Restoration of the Temple Church: Ecclesiology and Recrimination', from *Architectural History*, Vol. 8 (1965).

Crosland, J., *William the Marshal, the Last Great Feudal Baron* (1962).

Curzon, H. de, *La Maison du Temple de Paris* (1888).

Curzon, H. de, *La Regle du Temple* (1886), (trans. M. Melville, 1934).

Dugdale, W., *Origines Juridiciales* (1680, 3rd edn).

Ecclesiologist, The

Esdaile, A., *Temple Church Monuments* (1933).

Essex, W.R.H., Smirke, S., *Illustrations of the Architectural Ornaments etc, of the Temple Church; with an Account of the Recent Restoration by Sydney Smirke* (1845).

Fawcett, J., *The Future of the Past* (1976).

Freeman, A., 'The Organs of the Temple Church', *The Organ* (Oct. 1923).

Fuller, T., *Church History of Britain* (edited 1845) Vol. 5, and *The History of the Worthies of England*, Vol. 1 (1662).

Gentleman's Magazine

Godfrey, W.H., *A History of Architecture in and around London* (1962).

Godfrey, W.H., *Recent Discoveries at the Temple, etc.* (Society of Antiquaries, 1953).

Godwin, G., *A Short Account of the Temple Church, London with Illustrations by R.W. Billings etc.* (1837).

Godwin & Britton, *Churches of London* (1838).

Gooder, E., *Temple Balsall, the Warwickshire Preceptory of the Templars* (1995).

Harrison, S.E., 'The Wren Screen from the Temple Church, London', from *The Collector*, Vol. XI.

Hart, E.A.P., *The Hall of the Inner Temple* (1952).

Herbert, W., *Antiquities of the Inns of Court* (1804).

Hoffbauer, M., *Paris à Travers les Âges, 1875-82*, Vol. 2, The Temple.

Hope, W.H. St John, 'The Round Churches in England' from *Archaeologia* Vol. LXI (1908).

Ingpen, A.E. (ed)., *Master Worsley's Book* (1910).

Inderwick, F.A., and Roberts, R.A., *A Calendar of the Inner Temple Records*, various dates.

Inner Temple General Account Books

Ireland, S., *Picturesque Views of the Inns of Court* (1800).

Jeffery, G., 'The Church of the Holy Sepulchre, Jerusalem', from *RIBA Journal* (1910).

Jekyll, J., *Facts and Observations relating to the Temple and the Monuments contained in it* (1811). (British Library copy)

King, E.J., *The Knights of St John in England* (1924).

Larking & Kemble, *The Knights Hospitallers in England* (1857).

Lees, B.A. (ed), *Records of the Templars in England in the 12th Century* (1935).

Lewer, D.J., *A Spiritual Song, the Story of the Temple Choir and a History of Divine Service in the Temple Church* (1961).

Macfadyen, N., 'Temple Church, London: the Great West Doorway', from *ASCHB Transactions*, Vol. 9 (1984).

Macrory, E., *Notes on the Temple Organ 1859/61*, ed. by M. Muir Mackenzie (1911).

Maitland, William, *The History and Survey of London* (1756).

Melville, M., *La Vie des Templiers, Paris* (1951).

Merriman, Lord, *The Ravages of the War in the Inner Temple* (1946).

Middle Temple, *Middle Temple Ordeal* (1948).

Middle Temple Treasurer's Account Books

Paris, Matthew, *Chronica Majora*, ed. H.R. Luerd (1880).

Pearce, C.W., *The Life and Works of E.J. Hopkins*.

RCHM (Hart), *London*, Vol. IV, *The City* (1929).

Rennert, J., *George Thalben-Ball* (1979).

Richardson, E., *The Monumental Effigies of the Temple Church with an Account of their Restoration* (1843).

Richardson, E., *The Ancient Stone and Leaden Coffins, Encaustic Tiles etc., lately Discovered in the Temple Church* (1845).

Roth, D., 'Norman Survivals in London', from *RIBA Journal* (1935).

Round, J.H., *Geoffrey de Mandeville - a Study of Anarchy* (1892).

Ryan, F., *The House of the Temple* (1930).

Silsoe, Lord, 'The Peculiarities of the Temple', from *The Estates Gazette* (1972).

Simon, E., *The Piebald Standard* (1959).

Williams, E., *Early Holborn and the Legal Quarter of London* (2 vols. 1927).

Williamson, J.B., *The History of the Temple, London* (1924, 3rd edn).

Worley, G., *The Temple Church of the Knights Templars in London* (1907).

Zarnecki, G., 'The West Doorway of the Temple Church in London', from *Studies in Romanesque Sculpture* (1979).

Subscribers

The authors and publishers are grateful to the undermentioned for subscribing in advance to this volume.

HARRY ABBOTT
THE RT HON. LORD ACKNER
HIS HONOUR JUDGE FRANCIS
    AGLIONBY
MR AND MRS JULIAN ALGAR
DIANA ALLEN
GEOFFREY ALBERT ALLEN
ROSINA LYDIA ALLEN
MR ASA ANDERSON
MR LEOPOLD J. ANTELME
COMMANDER GORDON
    ARMSTRONG, RN
MS MARYAM ARMSTRONG-JAMES
MICHAEL ASHE QC
J.W.F. ASPINWALL
PROFESSOR J.H. BAKER
HUGH BAMBRICK
HIS HONOUR MURRAY BAND
STUART BARBER
DAVID BARNARD
TODD D. BARR AND FAMILY
GEORGE BARTLETT, QC
H.H. STEWART BATES
HIS HONOUR JUDGE BATTERBURY
MR AND MRS RANDAL BEATTIE
MISS J. BECKESS
MR CHADWICK BEECHER-MOORE
MRS NAONA BEECHER-MOORE
MR STEPHEN ROBERT BEET
RICHARD ANTHONY BENNETT
    ESQ.
FRANCIS BENNION
SIR CHRISTOPHER BENSON, FRICS
GUY BENTON
MISS JULIET BERNARD
MRS JUNE BERRY
DR JOHN A. BIRCH
MICHAEL BLAIR, QC
ARTHUR BLANEY
TRUMAN BODDEN
LORD BORRIE, QC
IAN BOURNE
MICHAEL BOWSHER
PETER BOYDELL, QC
MR TIMOTHY BRIDEN
J.R. BROMLEY-CHALLENOR
RT HON. SIR STEPHEN BROWN
DR WALTER R. BROWN
HIS HONOUR JUDGE JOHN BURKE,
    QC

RICHARD BURTON ESQ.
BRIAN AND MARIAN CALWELL
CARDEN & GODFREY ARCHITECTS
MR JUSTICE CAZALET
MR GERALD CLARKE
ISABEL, JAMES AND EDWARD
    COBB
SIR COLIN COLE
CHRISTOPHER CRITCHLOW
IVOR W. CLEMENCE
MRS MARGARET E. CLINCH
JUDGE ROGER COOKE
DIANA COTTON
THE HON. MRS COWAN
PAUL CRONIN
IAN GRENVILLE CROSS, QC, SC
L. JOAN CRUMP
ROBERT M. DAVIDSON
E.R. ANDREW DAVIS
JOHN B. DEBY
J.A. DENNISS
JOHN-PAUL DE SOISSONS
ROBIN DE WILDE, QC
K.G.E.R.W. DHARMAWARDENE ESQR
CHARLES H. ('CHUCK') DICKSON,
    JNR
CHARLES H. DICKSON, SNR.
GARRY DOWNES, AM, QC
MR AND MRS K.C. DOWNHAM
LORD DUNBOYNE
JOHN DUNN
MR AND MRS ADAM EDWARDS
MICHAEL EDWARDS, QC
DR H.W. ELDRIDGE
M.J. ELLIS
MR AND MRS DAVID EVANS
MR RICHARD EVANS
ROGER EVANS, MP
HIS HONOUR JUDGE SIMON
    EVANS
ROBIN FAIRHURST
MR MATTHEW JONATHAN
    FARMER
BRUCE FARTHING
MR IAN FERRIER
THE HON. SIR THAYNE FORBES
MR AND MRS MICHAEL G.
    FOWLER
ALEXANDER EMILE FORSTER-
    JONES

DAVID H. FRANCIS
MR I.E. FRASER
MATTHEW GACEK
PETER JAMES-HENRY GADSDEN
THE HON. MR JUSTICE GARLAND
WILLIAM J. GLOVER
MILLICENT GODFREY
MARTIN AND ANN GOODWIN
JOHN C. GRACEY
PROF. COLLEEN GRAFFY
DR J.D. GRAHAM
MR RICHARD C.M. GREEN
THOMAS HENRY GREENSLADE
MR AND MRS MARTIN GRIFFITHS
STEVEN HADLEY
ARTHUR HALES
DUNCAN HAMILTON, ICE
    SCULPTOR
DAVID HANDS, QC
M.R. HARDWICK, QC
DR J.F. HARE
HIS HONOUR JUDGE RICHARD
    HAVERY, QC
MARY HAYSOM
TRELEVEN HAYSOM
L.T. HEMMINGS
R.A. HENDERSON, QC
PAUL HESTER
D.E.M. HEWITT ESQ
RICHARD HODGSON
ANNE HOLDEN
MR J.A.G. HOPKINS
GAYNOR HOUGHTON-JONES
DR ROBERT HOYLE
IAIN HUGHES, QC
JOHN HUGILL
DAVID HUMPHREYS
MRS MERLIN HUTCHINGS
LAURENCE INCE
DONALD JOHNSON-PROCTOR
HIS HONOUR JUDGE J.G. HULL, QC
F.G. AND S. JACOBS
MARGARET AND RAYMOND
    JAMES
MRS L.S. JAMES
DEREK AND SUSAN JOHN
MRS JACQUELINE S. JOHNSTON
MAGGIE JONES
MARGARET JONES
SIR IGOR JUDGE

MR COLIN KANG
MR PHILLIP A.F. KEAR
MR DAVID KELLY
MICHAEL KEMPSTER
THE REV. PREB. W.D. KENNEDY-
BELL
ANITA KENNETT
IAN LANGRISH
MR SIDNEY LANIER
MRS LISE LANIER-BERKELEY
MRS SARA LANIER-CARTER
WILLIAM CHARLES LANIGAN
THE RT HON. SIR JOHN LATEY
NICHOLAS LAVENDER
CAPTAIN ROBERT LAW
YUK CHING CHRISTINE LAW
SIR JOHN LAWS
THE REVEREND HIS HONOUR
CHRISTOPHER LEA
ADVOCATE T.J. LE COCQ
SIR GODFRAY LE QUESNE
MR MARK ANTHONY L'ESTRANGE-
CORBET
ERNEST LOUGH
GRAHAM LOUGH
ROBIN LOUGH
LADY LOWRY, QC
JOHN LUMSDON
CHRISTOPHER AND KAREN
LUNDIE
RAPH LUNZER
MICHAEL JOHN LYNCH ESQ
STUART McCABE
ROXANNA McDONALD
LORD MACKAY OF CLASHFERN
MR AND MRS HAMISH McLEAN
ANGUS MacPHERSON
MRS RODICA MAGER-BARBU
MARC C. MAITLAND
S.J. MAJUMDAR ESQ.
DR MARY MALECKA
WILLIAM ROBERTS MARSHALL, QC
MR DAVID MASSAM
GEORGE MATHERS
RIGHT HON. SIR PATRICK
MAYHEW, QC
THE REVD A.H. MEAD, READER OF
THE TEMPLE
WALTER MENDELSSON
N. PERCY METCALFE
MR ROGER MEYER
VERY REV. R.L.P. MILBURN
MRS JENNIFER MILLER
REVD PROF. DR AND MRS JOHN
WARWICK MONTGOMERY
MR J. MORETON
PHILIP MOSER
TERENCE MOWSCHENSON, QC
MICHAEL G. MURRAY
MASTER MURRAY AND MRS
NIGEL MURRAY

SIMON MURRAY
PROF. THOMAS MURRAY
MUSEUM OF THE ORDER OF ST
JOHN
DR ANTHONY MUSSON
MRS B.A. MYERS
DENNIS NAISH
SIR BRIAN NEILL
CLIVE R. NEWTON
GEOFFREY NICE, QC
LORD NICHOLLS OF BIRKENHEAD
MICHAEL GEORGE NORKETT
FR ROBERT OMBRES
DR AND MRS RICHARD N. OUGH
DENIS G.A. OWEN
JOANNE OXLADE
NICHOLAS PADFIELD, QC
DAVID PAGET, QC
HON. SIR JONATHAN PARKER
M. PARROY
DR MARTIN GRATTON PARRY
B.R. PATERSON-TODD
DAVID PENRY-DAVEY, QC
P.B.C. PEPPER, QC
RT HON. SIR IAN PERCIVAL, QC
MURRAY PICKERING
HIS HONOUR PIGOT, QC
MR G.W. PIGGOTT
DR D. POVEY
JUDGE HENRY POWNALL
MR TIMOTHY PRESTON QC AND
MRS PRESTON
HIS HON. P. STANLEY PRICE, QC
MR NICOLAS ALEXANDER PRIEST
ANTHONY RATCLIFFE
ALASTAIR YATES REDPATH-
STEVENS
HIS HONOUR JUDGE PAYNTER
REECE AND MRS EDWARD
PAYNTER REECE
CLEOTA REED
R.C.D. REES
STEPHEN RENOUF
JONATHAN RICH ESQ
MISS SARAH RICHARDSON
MS ANDRÉE RUSHTON
JEREMY J. RUSSELL
DAVID RYAN
BARRY RYLAND-HOLMES
RICHARD SALTER, QC
COLLEEN SAMUEL
JOAN FUGUET SANS
PETER SAYER
MISS NICOLA L. SAYERS
PATRICK SHEEHAN
SIR KONRAD SCHIEMANN
ROBERT SEABROOK, QC
BARRIE SEAMAN
MARK SEAMAN
MRS ANNE C. SELLON
SIR BARRY SHEEN

NIGEL SHEPHERD
CHRISTOPHER J. SHERLIKER
MISS C.A. SHRIMPTON
DENNIS SMALE
JAMES AND ANNE SMART
GEORGE SMEDLEY
HIS HONOUR JUDGE DAVID
SMITH, QC
DAVID SMITH
EDWIN C. SMITH
MRS NATALIE SMITH
DEBORAH SUSAN SMYTHE
BRYCE SOMERVILLE
RICHARD SOUTHWELL, QC
MRS JEAN STANLEY
MS DEBORAH STENE
RT HON. SIR JOHN STEPHENSON
ROGER P.D. STEWART
MISS M.V. STOKES
EVAN STONE, QC
MISS J.L. STRATFORD
MISS L.E. SULLIVAN, QC
THE LORD TEMPLEMAN
HOWARD THOMAS
THE REVEREND CANON PETER
RHYS THOMAS
A. THOMPSON
JOHN W.A. THORNELY, ESQ
ADRIAN HEBER THORNTON
J.K. TOULMIN CMG, QC
MR JUSTICE TOULSON
HIS HONOUR JUDGE UZIELL-
HAMILTON
ROBERT VENABLES, QC
HARALD VON RAFFAY
MR M.J. WAKEFIELD
SIR JOHN WALSH OF BRANNAGH,
THE DUKE DE RONCERAY
SIMON WALSH
ANTHONY MICHAEL WALTON
ANTHONY D. WARD
THE HON. SIR RONALD
WATERHOUSE
MR ANTHONY WEBB
MALCOLM WEBB
PHILIPPA J.E. WHIPPLE
HIS HONOUR JUDGE WHITE
ANDREW WHITE
MRS R.J.G. WHITELAW
MISS D.E. WICKHAM
MR DAVID E. WICKHAM
DAVID WIDDICOMBE, QC
MRS ANN WILLIG
ALLISON WOLFGARTEN
DR DEREK WRIGHT
LYNDA J. ZADRA-SYMES

INDEX

The figures in **bold type** refer to *illustration* numbers, not page numbers.

ADDISON, Charles C. 27, 30, 45
Agnus Dei, seal 11, **3**
Ainger, Alfred 111, 131, 132, 134, 135, **79**
Albert, Prince 108
Alexander, S.A. 132, 134
Allenby, General 138
Almeric de Montforte 43
Altar and Altar-piece 44, 48,50, 71, 97, 98, 100, 102, 136, 138, 141, 152, 160, 166, **72**, **82**, **107**
Alvey, Dr 57, 58, 60
Angmering Camp 136, 143
Anson, Harold 143, 146, 161-2, 166, **117**
Apollo Club 76
Apse 14, 20, 29, **21**
Archbishop of Canterbury 34, 43, 55, 58, 60, 82, 131, 132n, 143, 160, 161, 165
Archbishop of York 30, 53, 58
Arnold de Torroge 30
Atkinson, Maud Tindal 30, **24**
Aumbries 44, 136, 141, 160, **107**
Aymer de Valence 54
Aymeric de St Maur 30, 33

BALDWIN, King of Jerusalem 9, 30
Ball, Dr Richard 66, 76
Balguy or Bagley, Dr Nicolas 60
Barnes, Dr Ernest William 138
Barrett, stonemason 95, 105
Barthel, Denis 140
Bartylby, John 56
Bastelle 30
BBC 138, 153, 174, 175
Beauséant 10, 11, **2**
Becket, Thomas à 51, **42**
Belfry and Bells 11, 29 30, 68, 73, 87, 136, **8**, **109**, **114**
Benson, Christopher 102, 106, 109, 110, **77**
Bernard, Arthur 155, 158, 165, **119**
Bidding Prayer 60, 148
Birch, Dr John 170, 172
Bishop, effigy of a 33, 37, 48, 150, 158, **26**
Bishop, J.C. 105n21
Blom, Roger 54
Blomfield Sir R. 136
Blore, Edward 98
Blow, Dr 74
Boswell, James 83
Bowes Museum 71, 77, 97
Brick Court 83
British Broadcasting Corporation 138,153, 174, 175
Britton, John 13, 21, 24, 42

Buc, Sir George 48
Buckler, John 41, 86
Budgett, Tom 144
Burford, Sir John 56
Burge, William 107, 108
Burials and Vaults 64, 77, 80, 149, 159
Burnell, stonemason 87, 95, 105
Burton, Decimus 95-97, 103
Butteries 15, **21**
Byfield, John 82

CALVERT, John 107-109
Cambridge, round church 18, 20, 21, 29, 39, **13**, **14**
Camden Society 96, 97
Camp at Angmering and Swanage 136, 143, 175
Candles, candlesticks 63, 64, 65, 66, 82, 94, 128 141, 151, **12**
Canterbury 25, 26, 50
Carden & Godfrey 162, 165, 170
Caröe, W.D. 137, 171
Carols, Christmas 134, 146, 151, 173, **128**
Carpenter, Dr S.C. 141, 143, 165
Carpmael, Kenneth 155, 161
Cassocks and Surplices 135, 137, 144, **104**, **124**, **127**
Cathedral Service 107, 108
Chambers, Sir Thomas 132n5
Chancery Lane 18, 23
Chapel Royal 59, 76 108, 143
Chaplains (priests) 16, 48, 50, 55-57, 61, 129
Charles I, King 64, **68**
Charles II, King 62
Charter, Letters Patent and Chest 62, 127, 129, 130, 149, 165, 172, **49**
Chettle, Henry 130
Choir of the Temple church 50, 56, 57, 59, *Chs.* 9, 11-16 *passim*, **43**, **101**, **104**, **127**, **128**
Choir Committee 109-111, 133, 135, 137, 138, 140
Choir school 110, 130
Choirstalls 109, 111n3, **95**
Choristers, boy 107, 109, 110, 128, 130, 132, *ch.* 12 *passim*, 145, 146, 170, 173-176, **101**, **103**, **104**, **110**, **111**, **127**, **128**
Christ Church, Newgate Street 77
City of London School 111n10, 132, 144, 145, 170, 173, 174
Clapham, H.W. 20, 22
Clarkson, E. 27, 43
Clayton, J.F. 141, 143
Clerk of the Temple church 61, 63, 67, 68, 106, 107, **53**
Clerkenwell, Priory of 18-20, 29, 30, **11**
Cloisters 15, 16, 32, 51, 66, 70, 85, 102, 148, 150, **21**, **34**, **65**, **99**, **109**, **119**
Coffins and graves 29, 35, 37, 48, 98, 126, **28**, **29**, **30**
Colles, H.C. 133
Communion service, plate, table 48, 58, 63, 64, 82, 138, 146, **57**

Consecration of the Round, 1185 9, 30, **24**
Consecration of the Chancel, 1240 47
Cooper, George 108
Corbels 25, 45, 46, 104, 105, **38**, **91**
Cottingham, Lewis 25, 95-96, 98, 101
Council for the Care of Churches 44, 141
Crests **45**
Crook, J. Mordaunt 95
Cross, altar 141, 166
Crown Office Row 90, 145
Crusades 9-11, 20, 32, 49
Cummings, W.H. 107, 108
Custodian, Custos 52, 129, 146

DANDO, J.H.B. 110
Davies, Sir H. Walford 133, 135, 136, 137, 138, 139, 146, **102**, **103**, **104**
Deed of Partition 81
Dedication stone 32, 77, 84, 97, **25**
Devil Tavern 76
Dewar, Alfred C. 143, 151n12, **110**
Dickens, Charles 84, 94
Dixon, A. Capel 135, 136, 143, 144, 173, **103**, **104**, **126**
Dove Brothers Ltd 146, 149, 150, 155, 162, 165, **119**
Draghi, Giovanni Battista 74
Draper, W.H. 139, 141
Dugdale, Sir William 22, 57

ECCLESIOLOGIST, The 96, 97, 103, 123, 125, 127
Edward I, King 43, 48
Edward II, King 48, 50, 52, 54
Edward III, King 54
Edwards, Carl 159, 160
Effigies 33, 35, 37, 38, 77, 97, 98, 135, 148, 150, 151, 166, **26**, **27**, **28**, **32**, **72**, **120**, **121**, **122**
Elizabeth II, the Duke of Edinburgh, and the Queen Mother 160, 165, 168, 172, **119**
Ely, Bishop of 23, 47, **21**
Emmett, William 24, 30, 71, 73, 77
Ermestede, William 56, 57
Esdaile, Mrs Arundell 32, 33, 65, 102, 141, 158, 166, 168
Essex, Earl of 55
Etty 98
Evelyn, John 65
Exeter, Bishop of 23, 55

FARRAR'S BUILDING 23, 146, **21**
Fairhurst, Robin 175, **127**
Faversham, Earl of 70
Fawcett, Jane 104
Fikettesfield, Fikettescroft 23
Fine Office 70, 85
Fires:
    Holy Sepulchre, Jerusalem, 1808 11, 13
    Great Fire of London, 1666 54, 65, **51**
    also in the Temple, 1677, 1678, 1683, 65, 66, 69, 70, 85, 94
Church boiler chamber, 1850 112
Church organ, 1880 128
Church and Master's House gutted, 1941 13, 47, 83, 103, 104, 135, 146-148, 37, **108**
Middle Temple Hall and St Dunstan's Church on fire, 1944, 152
First World War 137
Firth, Canon J.D. 165, 166, 175, **127**
Fleet Street 54, 55, 66, 77, 130, 147
Font 97, 150
Forington, W. 135
Forges 23, 55
Forster & Andrews 128
Fortescue, Sir John 56
Foundlings 80, **61**
France 9, 13, 15, 18, 24, 49, 51, 53, 54, 143, 145
Franck, César 130
Fuller, Thomas 49, 56, 59

GENTLEMEN OF THE CHOIR 57; 19th century 106, 107, 109, 110; 20th century 134-136, 139, 144, 145, 161, 172, 174, **104**, **128**
Geoffrey de Charney 53
Geoffrey de Mandeville 33
Gerard, Brother 19
Germany 39
Gibbons, Grinling 71
Gladstone, William 130
Glaziers' Company 159
Glentanar, Lord 157, 161
Goddard, Lord 162
Godfrey de St Omer 9
Godfrey, W.H. & W.E. 20, 27, 29, 42, 102, 149, 153-165, 168, 170, 172, **112**
Goldsmith Building 143, 145, **96**
Goldsmith, Oliver 83, 150, **64**
Goossens, Leon 111n10, 176
Gothic Revival 76, 86, 92, 94-96, 104
Grey, Sir Edward 137
Grotesques 27, 47, 89, 90, 92, 105, 150, **18**, **68**, **69**, **70**, **80**, **93**

HAKEWILL, Henry 94, **85**
Hales, Robert 55
Handel, G.F. 82, 131, 132n5
Hare Court 69, 86, 98
Harris, Renatus 73-75
Harris, Sir William 144
Harrison, Sydney 71
Harrison & Harrison 157, 170
Hast, Gregory 135
Haysom, W.J. & H. 155, 156, 158, 164, 166, **19**, **119**, **120**
Hear my Prayer (Mendelssohn), 130, 140
Heath, Edward 176
Heating of the church 29, 84, 94, 97, 112, 134, 159

Henry I, King 13
Henry II, King 20, 23, 30, 32-34, **24**
Henry III, King 9, 37, 47, 48, 104, 105
Heraclius, Patriarch of Jerusalem 30, 32 33, 77
Hilbert Blanke, Preceptor of Auvergne 49, 52, 53
HMV 140, 175
Holborn 18, 23, 24
Holy Sepulchre, Church of, Jerusalem 10, 11-13, 20, 29, **4**
Hooker, Richard 58-60, 148, 150, **47, 48**
Hope, St John 20
Hopkins, Dr Edward John, *Chs* 9-11, 101, 133, **78**
Hospital of St John 20, 54
Hugh le Despencer 54
Hugh de Lichfield 56
Hugh de Payens 9, 13, 15
Humm, Henry 130, 131

INNER TEMPLE, Society of 54-56, 63, 64, 66, 70, 75, 81, 85, 87; Hall 15, 51, 73, 94, 131, 153, 163-4, 165, **21, 52**; Library 66, 70, 145; **52**
Inns of Court 15, 56, 64, 65
Inquisition of 1337, 51, 52, 54, 65
Inscription 32, **25**
Inventory of 1307, 44, 50, 51, App. 3
Ireland 18, 34
Ivanhoe (Sir Walter Scott) 18

JACQUES DE MOLAY 49, 52, 53
James I, King 62, 127
James II, King 75
James, Michael 176n3
Jeffery, George 11
Jeffreys, Judge 75
Jekyll, Joseph 37, 84
Jerusalem 9, 10, 20, 29, **1, 4**
Jerusalem (Parry) 138, 140
Jewkes, Richard 158
John, King 29
John de Stoke 30, 49, 51, 52
Johnson, Dr Samuel 83, 130
Jones, Inigo 76
Jones, John 93n4
Jonson, Ben 76

KEDGE, Kenneth 144
Keilway, Robert 56
Kennedy-Bell, W.D. 161, 165, 169, 175, **124, 127**
King's Bench Walk 66, 67, 69, 92, 148, **51, 52**
King's College School 132
Knights Hospitallers 10, 13, 15, 17, 19, 21, 30, 39, 47, 54-6, 62, **10**
Knights Templars 9, 53, 100; Absolution by the Master 17, 52; Classes of 14; Dress of 11, 17, **2, 10**; Homosexuality 49; Preceptories 18, 21; Provinces 13; Rule of the Order 13; Trials of 51, 52

LAKE, Dennys 140
Lamb Building 38n31, 55, 66, 84, 146, 150
Lamb, Charles 89, 90, 93, 131
Lamb & Flag (Middle Temple) 131, **45**
Langham, William 56
Lecturers 59
le Grice, Ian 176
Leland, John 20
Lewis, Charles 166, 168
Lewis, E.H. 130
Lighting of the church 128, 134, 160, 165, **72, 94, 95, 103**
Lincoln, Bishop of 22, 38n19, 43
Lincoln's Inn 23, 64, 110, 130
Lind, Jenny 130
Little Maplestead, round church 20, 21, 29
Littleton brass 149, 151n9, 168, **107**
London, Bishop of 43, 51, 82, 169
London, gates of 52
London, Lord Mayor of 55, 65
Long Vacation 133, 145
Lonsdale, Canon 110, 134
Lough, Ernest and sons 135, **108, 127**
Ludgate 23, 52
Ludlow Castle, round chapel 20

MACDONALD, Dr A.J.M. 132n4, 152, 161, 165, 166
Macfadyen, Neil 164, 170, 171
Mackenzie, Muir 138
Mallett, Ronald 140
Marlborough College 145
Marriages, 47, 70, 76, 131, 132n4, 152, **57**
Marshal, William, Earl of Pembroke, and sons 33-35, 150, **27, 121, 122**
Martin, Richard 63, 73, 146, **50**
Masonic influence 15, 27, 43, 73
Master of the Temple 23, 55-58, 62, 129
Master's House 66, 76, 77, 130, 132, 135, 145, 146, 147, 152, 165, **81, 124**
Maufe, Edward 153
Maule, William 94
Meddings, Tom 144
Mendelssohn 110, 111
Michael de Baskevil 49
Micklethwaite, Dr Paul 64, 109
Middle Temple, Society of 11, 15, 54, 55, 57, 63, 77, 131, 145; Hall 57, 145, 152, 155, 170
Middle Temple Lane 76, 77, 145
Milburn, Robert L.P. 169, 170, **124**
Milford, Canon T.R.M. 166, 169, 175
Monmouth, Duke of 70
Monuments 95, 102, 103, 150, **76, 80**
Morris, William 86, 92, 104
Music 50, 56, 59, 68, 134, **42**

NASH, S.A. 101, 102
New Boswell Court 110, 111n

New Temple, the 19, 20, 23, 26, 29, 30, 47, 48, 51, 54, **21**
Newbolt, Sir Henry 137
Newsom, G.E. 135
Nicholson, Sir Charles 140
North, Roger 77
Northampton, round church 20, 22, 29, **15**, **16**

OLD TEMPLE, the 18-20, 24, 33
Omne datum optimum, Bull of 16, 17n15
Organ 50, 56, 59, 70, 71, 73-76, 94, 98, 112, 148, 155, 157, 161, 168, 169-170, **55**, **59**, **72**, **95**, **105**, **123**
Organists 106, 107, 108, 110, 131
Organ Music Society 143
Outer Temple 23, 55
Oxford Movement 76, 106, 107, 108

PARIS 39, 53
Paris, *le Temple, enclos* and church of 14-17, 24, 29
Paris, Matthew 11, 13, 47
Parkin, Henry 16
Parratt, Sir Walter 133, 138
Parry, Sir Hubert, 137
Parson's Court 55
Peasants' Revolt 55
Pegasus (Inner Temple) 55, 70, 131, **45**
Penitential Cell 30, 51, 173, **44**
Pepys, Samuel 69, 76
Petyt, William 168
Pews/Stalls 71, 101, 102, **58**, **72**, **74**, **75**, **129**
Philip (*le Bel*), King of France 49, 53
Phillips, William 73
Pigott, Francis 76
Pigott, John 76, 82
Piscinas 29, 44, **23**, **36**
Plague 65, 66
Playford, John and Henry 67, 68, 69, **53**
Plowden, Sir Edmund 57-58, 73, 146, **46**
Polgrean, Alan 144
Pollock, Sir Frederick 38n31
Popes, 'Popery' 13, 33, 54, 56, 58, 130
Porch 14, 27 63, 69, 84, 123, 124, 126, 137, 155, 158, **6**, **8**, **21**, **28**, **32**, **54**, **85**, **86**, **88**, **89**, **92**
Practice-room 112, 127, 130, 139, 146, 149, 168, **103**, **110**, **127**
Preceptories 14, 18, 21
Prisoners' Base 175
Psalms 110, 131, 139, 143
Pulpit 64, 71, 77, 109, 152, **56**, **58**, **129**, **back endpapers**
Pump Court 51, 69, 70, 145
Purbeck, Isle of, and Quarries 156, **19**, **113**
Purbeck marble 24, 25, 33, 37, 43-45, 48, 84, 89, 97, 136, 148, **111**, **115**
Purcell, Henry 69, 74, 107

RAILINGS 77, **67**, **72**, **80**, **85**
Ralph de Barton 30, 49, 52, 145

Raymond du Puy 19
Red Cross 22, 38n49
Registers, church 149
Rennell, Thomas 106
Rennert, Jonathan 176
Reredos (Wren) 160, **57**, **94**, **116**, **129**
Richardson, Edward 11, 35, 46, 90, 98, 100, 104
Robert de Sanford 47
Robert de Sautre 50
Robinson, Canon Joseph 170
Robinson, Dr Thomas 110, 129
Robinson, Sir Thomas 70
Robson, T.J.F. 112
Ros family effigy 33, 150, **27**
Roth, Daniel 20
Rothwell, Frederick 136
Round, J.H. 19
Round churches 14, 19-22, 163, **4**, **5**, **6**, **9**, **11**, **12**, **13**, **14**, **15**, **17**, **21**, **24**, **28**
Rounthwaite, William 73
Royal Arms 70, 71, 100, 168, **123**
Royal Courts of Justice 111n11
Royal Peculiar 59, 62, 129, 169
Rowlatt, W.H. 110
Rynd, R.F. 143

ST ANDREW'S, Holborn 18, 75
St Ann's Chapel 39, 41-43, 50, 70, 81, 84-86, 93, 150, **21**, **34**, **35**, **81**, **82**
St Aubyn, J.P. 21, 87, 121-128, 165
St Clement Danes 23
St Dunstan-in-the-West 23, 55, 132n, 152
St John of Jerusalem, Clerkenwell 19, 54-57, 61
St Paul's Cathedral 53, 59, 65, 71, 75, 107, 110, 132, 137
St Thomas à Becket Chapel 50, 54, **21**
Saladin 9, 13, 30
Salvin, Anthony 21
Sanders, Henry 110
Sandys, George 11
Savage, James 94, 95, 96, 103, 105
Schreider, Chistopher 82
Schulze, Edmund 136
Scotland 13, 18
Scott, Sir George Gilbert 126
Scott, John 176
Screen (Wren) 45, 70, 71, 98, **55**, **58**, **59**
Seals (Templars) 11, 21, **3**
Second World War 77, 145, **108**, **109**, **110**, **111**
Sergeant's Inn 64
Selden, John 64, 158
Shaw, Martin 137
Sherlock, Dr Thomas 64, 82
Sherlock, Dr William 64
Shops 61, 63, 68, 69
Shuttleworth, Obadiah 82
Simon, Edith 33

Smirke, Sir Robert 85-89, 92-94, 98, 103
Smirke, Sir Sydney 25, 86, 96, 97, 98, 100, 102, 103
Smith, Father 73, 76, 82, 136 146
Society for the Protection of Ancient Buildings (SPAB)
   86, 103, 104
Spens, Sir Patrick 165
Staffs of the Societies 131, **95**
Standish, Rev. John 77
Stanley, John 82, 83, **63**
Stationers' Company's School 130, 132
Stevens, R.J.S. 93n6
Stone and types of 18, 24-27, 33, 43, 44, 84, 87, 89, 97,
   122-124, 137, 154, 156, 157
Stow, John 18, 61
Strype, John 25, 60
Surveyors 85, 136, 137, 149

TANFIELD COURT 55, 66
Templar magazine 136, 137, 145, 156, 164, 165
Templars' Male Voice Choir 143, 173
Templars' Quartet 136
Templars' Union 136, 137, 146
Temple Bar 23, 54
Temple Bruer, round church 20, 29
Temple Choir **104**, **127**, **128**; establishment of 1842
   107, 109, 135, 136; re-establishment 1954 160
Temple Music Trust 170
Temple Stairs/Bridge/Pier 26, 43, 77
Terry, Ellen 135
Teutonic Knights 10
Thalben-Ball Sir George, *Chs* 12-16, **124**, **127**
Thames, river 22, 23, 26, 48, 77, 146, **51**
Thomas, Lewis 110
Tiles, encaustic floor 46, 101, **39**, **72**, **73**
Transitional architecture 9, 21, 24, 26, 29, **17**
Travers, Walter 58-60
Treasury 30, 42-44, 48, 51, **21**
Trotter, Thomas 176
Troyes, Council of 1129 13
Turle, James 107

VAUGHAN, Charles J. 129-132, **100**
Vestries 44, 81, **103**
Victoria, Queen 131-133
Victoria Embankment 132
Vienne, Council of, 1313 53
Viollet-le-Duc 15

WALTER, Prior of Clerkenwell 19
Walter le Bacheler 30, 51, 52, **44**
Warne, George 106, 107
Webb, Sir Aston 140
Wedding March 110
Wellington, Duke of 110
Wesley, S.S. 130
West door, 1842 148, **20**, **71**
West doorway, Norman 23, 27, 84, 98, 126, 137, **71**, **125**
Westminster Abbey 26, 43, 44, 47, 48, 59, 62, 101, 104,
   108, 137, 146, 161
Whitefriars 23, 66
Willement, Thomas 98, 100, 101, 146
William de Langeford 54
William de la More 49, 51, 53
William Plantagenet 48
Williamson, J. Bruce 16, 77, 135, 141
Windows 146, 150, **83**, **90**, **107**
Winston, Charles 164
Witham, Sir John 103, **76**
Woods, Rev. H.G. 32, 135
Wolverhampton 75
Works, Ministry of 44, 141
Worthington, Hubert 153
Wren, Sir Christopher 70, 71, 73, 75-77, 84, 97

YORK, Duke of 66
Young, Alan 144
Young, Clyde 146, 149, 150, 153
Young, Thomas 110

ZARNECKI, George 171

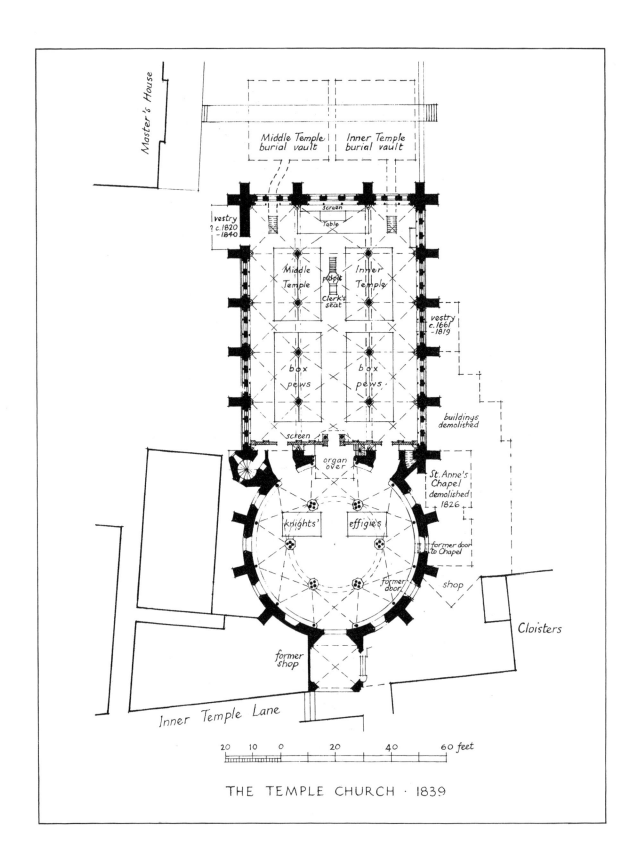

Master's House

Middle Temple
burial vault

Inner Temple
burial vault

screen

Table

vestry
? c.1820
-1840

Middle
Temple

Inner
Temple

pulpit

Clerk's
seat

vestry
c.1661
-1819

box
pews

box
pews

buildings
demolished

screen

organ
over

St. Anne's
Chapel
demolished
1826

knights'

effigies

former door
to Chapel

former
door

shop

Cloisters

former
shop

Inner Temple Lane

20 10 0   20   40   60 feet

THE TEMPLE CHURCH · 1839